Men Who Played The Game

Men Who Played The Game

Sportsmen who gave their life in the Great War

Mike Rees

Seren is the book imprint of
Poetry Wales Press Ltd
57 Nolton Street, Bridgend, Wales
CF31 3AE
www.serenbooks.com
Facebook:
Twitter:

ISBN 978-1-78172-286-2
Ebook 978-1-78172-287-9
Mobi 978-1-78172-288-6

A CIP record for this title is available from the British library.

The publisher acknowledges the financial assistance of the Welsh Books Council.

Printed in Baskerville by Pulsio, Paris, France

Contents

List of Illustrations

Introduction

August 4th 1914, another sunny day in a glorious English summer. Benny Green wrote in the *Wisden Anthology 1900-1940* that during the previous afternoon Jack Hobbs, 'The Master', scored his second double century of the season while playing for Surrey against Nottinghamshire at the Oval watched by 15,000 Bank Holiday spectators. Meanwhile 150 miles away at Derby the home county were being bowled out twice in a day by a rather average Essex attack. At Lord's, even then the home of cricket, England's most promising schoolboy batsman, John Howell, was making an undefeated 78 for the Rest against Lord's Schools. As Osbert Sitwell memorably phrased it, "The world was a ripe peach and we were eating it." Cricket was experiencing its first 'Golden Age', the national sport of Great Britain and its global empire. Indeed Hobbs was in the process of making a substantial contribution to Surrey's seventh county championship with 2,499 runs making him England's highest run scorer for the second year running. Not that Surrey lacked challengers. The holders, Kent, could still rely on slow left arm bowler Colin Blythe to lead their defence. In 1914, Blythe was the highest wicket taker in the country for the fourth time in his illustrious career with 159 victims, one more than the highest total in the previous year achieved by Yorkshire all-rounder Major Booth. Also on August 4th, Leicestershire were playing Northamptonshire. Their batsmen A.T. Sharp had been dismissed for 2 in the first innings and the report in *Wisden* suggested that he was 'preoccupied'. This is quite possible as the second innings scorecard read 'A T Sharp – absent – 0'. Sharp had packed his bags on the night of 4th August and returned to his regiment. It was not really a typical English summer's day at all. War had been declared and the world had slid into a conflict that would have unforeseen consequences for Europe in particular. By 1918, Hobbs had seen action in the newly formed Royal Flying Corps while Blythe, Booth and Howell were all dead, killed on the battlefields of France and Flanders.

The scale of the conflict could not have been predicted that

August. Nobody could have predicted that 6,000,000 men from the British Isles would serve and that 12% would be killed. A smaller proportion killed than in either France or Germany and a similar percentage to that lost in the longer Napoleonic Wars, but enough to give rise to the idea of 'the lost generation'. Of serving men aged 20-24 in 1914, 30.58% were killed, while the figure for boys aged 13-19 who died in service was 28.15%. The catastrophe affected all classes of society. Those serving soldiers, who had left the safety of academic study at Oxford or Cambridge, many of whom were junior officers, had a twenty per cent chance of being killed. The Prime Minister, Herbert Asquith, and the Leader of the Opposition, Andrew Bonar Law, both suffered personal tragedy during the conflict. Asquith lost his multi-talented son Raymond on the Somme, while two of Law's sons perished. On Sunday evenings in the school chapels of prestigious public schools up and down the country, headmasters would read the latest list of ex-pupils killed in the conflict The loss was not confined to the upper classes. In the rural and industrial towns and villages keen young men joined up in their thousands, often forming their own local battalions. In some cases 80% of the soldiers in these battalions would be wiped out in a single battle.

It wasn't just the loss of life which defined this tragedy. The physical nature of the injuries suffered by the soldiers was life changing for many. The mental scars suffered by soldiers, more difficult to measure, left many families to cope with unforeseen difficulties. Men physically unscathed had witnessed sights and images unimaginable during the summer of 1914. The sight of hideously wounded comrades, shorn of limbs surrounded by the stench of decomposition, fleas and rats left men lost in mind and unable to communicate. The continued presence of the dead throughout the war affected both mind and attitude. The lack of movement by the armies meant that men would be living with the dead for months at a time. Following a bombardment, buried men could reappear causing great distress to their former friends and colleagues. The eerie unfamiliarity of the world that soldiers now inhabited is illustrated better than anyone by the paintings of Paul Nash, while poets such as Siegfried Sassoon talked of 'the hell where youth and laughter go'. It should be remembered that some paintings, for example those of Henry Tonks, were considered too disturbing to be shown to the general public for fear of lowering morale or even fuelling opposition to the war. The Western Front quickly became what J.M. Winter described as the "extraterrestrial landscape of destruction produced by artillery fire, barbed wire and mud." As chaplains braved the dangers of the trenches in order to give comfort and solace to the wounded and dying, and surgeons risked their lives performing operations of almost unimaginable horror and complexity, it became clear that this was not a war that would be 'over by Christmas'. The emergence of casualty clearing stations, mobile hospitals stationed a few kilometres behind the lines, out of range of all but the heaviest artillery, saw surgical teams working in relays. They identified and retained the 10% of casualties that needed immediate surgery or who could not be moved, while others were sent to base hospitals, usually by train.

In order to fight this war nations had to mobilise as never before. The power of the European states ensured that the war would be fought on a scale previously unheard of. As soldiers were killed, more were sent to replace them. Killing a few thousand more made little difference. The nature of the war changed with the emergence of tanks to replace cavalry and the use of poison gas (first used at Ypres on 22nd April 1915) and, later, aerial combat. By 1915 the advantage in warfare had shifted in favour of the defensive. Once a nation is committed to war then somebody has to pay a levy in blood, in this case people from all walks of life including those innocent cricketers enjoying the beautiful English summer of 1914. It has led us to look back in awe at the experience of the soldiers, unable to contemplate their suffering. Martin Middlebrook, the First World War historian, challenges the idea that the soldiers who died were somehow different from previous and subsequent generations,

> The soldiers of 1916 were not supermen; they did not belong to a special generation. They were merely ordinary Britons, who believed that they had to fight to save their country. It turned out that theirs was to be an unlucky and ill-used generation

He might well be right but, as we mark the centenary of this cataclysmic war, public interest shows no sign of abating. The absence of any surviving serving soldier has made no difference.

The growth of interest in family history, and the unease over recent conflicts in Iraq and Afghanistan, has added a new dimension to the debate. The First World War is as relevant as ever it was.

Why embark on a study completely devoted to the loss of sportsmen in this conflict? Even among the general population most soldiers came back and not every home was affected. Most people did not lose an immediate family member and it follows that the number of sportsmen killed in the war was relatively small in number. With no TV or social media and no access to twenty-four hour news being broadcast by clubs' TV stations, sportsmen were not as instantly recognisable as they are today. Yet they were a significant group. Indeed the government at the time recognised their worth as propaganda material for recruitment purposes. Sportsmen became a very important tool in passively encouraging the civilian population to support the war effort. As significant a figure as General Haig came to recognise the importance of every platoon possessing a football! The idea that shooting, hunting and outdoor sport was a perfect preparation for soldiers was a long accepted wisdom. As Benny Green says

> The idea that team games and the ritual slaughter of animals was a kind of fortuitous preparation for the Greatest Game of all was ridiculous but had existed since ancient times.

Moreover, loyalty to one's group was an essential characteristic of any soldier, and team players, it was thought, possessed this in abundance. So from the historian's point of view sportsmen do form a significant group. Sport was important and becoming increasingly more so as these men captured the public imagination with their regularly reported deeds. They were the Rooneys, Murrays, Pietersens and O'Driscolls of their day. But they were also 'men of the people' from ordinary families with ordinary lives who used public transport and local pubs, sharing their lives with the communities in which they lived in a way that is unimaginable for most of the stars of today. Their loss is no more tragic than the loss of the other millions of the slaughtered, but in our sports obsessed age, the age of a London Olympics, Champions League football, Ashes success, Grand Slams and Lions tours, what better way is there to illuminate the memory of those who died than by studying the lives of the sports stars who made the ultimate sacrifice. At the very least, we can reclaim their names for history.

The Growth of Organised Sport 1870-1914

The leading sportsmen of the day did not attract the same amount of attention in 1914 that exists today. Reporting and coverage of sport was very different from the twenty-four hour coverage that we now experience. Newspapers printed reports but the quality press in particular gave less than full coverage of sporting events. The front page of *The Times* was filled with advertisements, with sport generally taking up less than a page situated somewhere towards the back of the paper (but not the back page). Football in particular was barely reported. Only the scores (and not the scorers) were given unless the match was a full international between two of the home nations or the FA Cup Final. The quality press gave more coverage to the Amateur Cup Final than to Saturday First Division games. When the final matches were played in the season 1906/7 and Newcastle United clinched the league title, *The Times* covered events in one paragraph. That same season the Rugby County Championship between Devon and Durham had as much coverage as Sheffield Wednesday's 2-1 victory over Everton in the FA Cup Final, both events recorded in brief reports that dealt with the essential details with the minimum amount of analysis.

Cricket and Rugby Union, the sports of the wealthier classes, fared better. Here details were given of the County Championship (Rugby and Cricket), Test matches, Rugby internationals and the progress of Oxford and Cambridge Universities, as well as the leading public schools, Eton and Harrow. Local newspapers were much fuller in their football coverage, especially where local teams were involved.

Nevertheless it would be misleading to assume that the most successful sportsmen did not demand attention. Indeed from the 1870s, with the possible exception of prime ministers William Gladstone and Benjamin Disraeli, the most recognisable figure in Victorian England was the father of English cricket, W.G. Grace. Just as no social history of Britain telling the story of the 1960s can be taken seriously without addressing the influence of The Beatles, no nineteenth century study should avoid discussing the importance of W.G. Grace. He dominated English sport in a way that nobody since has come near. Stories of how he once replaced the bails when bowled before curtly telling the bowler that "it must have been the wind" are probably apocryphal, but add to the legend. As Grace reminded the bowler when replacing the bails, and whilst simultaneously pointing at the crowd, "they have come to see me bat not you bowl." There has only ever been one 'W.G..'

Despite the inconsistencies of the press coverage, the rise of organised games in late Victorian and Edwardian Britain was nothing less than a sporting revolution. This was largely the result of some very significant social changes. These included the shortening of working hours, thereby creating more leisure time; mass literacy following the provision of compulsory education; the development of national and municipal transport services; and the success of the working class in forging a collective identity which allowed working people to assert themselves in politics, industry and, finally, sport.

Of particular significance was the increase in leisure time. This had been developing within the upper classes since before the 1870s, but the working class now had their first experience of 'leisure'. Legislation first passed in the 1870s led to a shorter working week of around 55 hours. Saturday afternoons were now free and four Bank Holidays were created. This gave greater opportunities to play and watch organised sport and the sports loving public were finally getting a varied selection. The media was quick to embrace the opportunities. *The Times* cut its price from 7d to 3d with a subsequent rise in daily circulation to 70,000 by 1870. Other newspapers saw an even more dramatic rise – the *Standard* to 130,000 and the *Telegraph* to 150,000. All these papers reported sporting events.

Improvements in public transport were also significant and helped in the development of organised sport. The growth of the railways was particularly important, linking towns and villages in a way that had never happened before. County cricket grounds were linked by ease of access to the railways and travelling to 'away' football grounds now became possible. As old pastimes such as cockfighting, bear baiting and even the grotesque spectator sport of public executions died out, other more acceptable pastimes took their place. Spectators took it all very seriously with some sports such as golf, tennis and riding demanding the correct fashionable clothing to be on display. In the 1890s the London Underground railway opened and by 1896 a car no longer needed a man with a red flag to walk in front of it.

The result of these changes was the development of organised competitive sport. Cricket led the way and soon established itself as the national sport, both domestically and internationally. The county system emerged in a rather prolonged and messy way. Four private county clubs – Sussex, Nottinghamshire, Surrey and Kent – existed by 1860 and by 1888 this number had increased to sixteen. There was, however, no official championship, only an unofficial acknowledgement of a 'champion county.' In 1890 the title became official although only eight counties took part. This increased to the full sixteen by 1914 with Glamorgan joining in 1921 and Durham in 1991, thereby making up the current eighteen first class counties. Test matches were soon an integral part of the cricket calendar with regular matches against Australia, the first taking place in 1877. South Africa joined the fold during the 1890s and the modern format began to take shape. The game was evolving quickly. It is worth remembering that even as late as 1876, batsmen were still unfamiliar with overarm bowling and for many years certain county matches were considered to be more important than a test match.

By the turn of the century, cricket was enjoying a burst of popularity and was the most popular sport in England. Indeed the 'Golden Age' of cricket is generally thought to run from the mid 1890s until the First World War. It was a glamorous era with Grace leading a group of English players who excite cricket followers even today. Ranji, Fry, Jessop, MacLaren, Rhodes, Hirst, Jackson, Peel, Briggs, Lohmann and Richardson are names which adorn the pages of *Wisden*. Hobbs followed soon after, while in Australia, Trumper was the main man. It is still said today that no cricketer has ever been more loved than Victor Trumper. The crowds poured into the newly established grounds to see their heroes, making full use of improvements in public transport and shorter working hours. The third class carriages, affordable by most of the population, pulled into the stations near the county grounds full of expectant spectators. In 1900 people were twice as likely to watch cricket than football, helped by the comparable cost, 6d a day, of the two sports. By 1903 the MCC boasted 5,000 members with crowds of 30,000 attending some matches. Indeed, the two highest attendances for a three day match in England ever recorded date from the early years of the twentieth century. In 1904 a total of 79,000 watched the three days of the 'Roses' match at Leeds, while two years later 80,000 attended the fixture between Surrey and Yorkshire at the Oval. For the largest and most popular grounds of the major counties, annual attendances were regularly in excess of 200,000. Spectators were considered to be important, the life blood of the game. In an echo of W.G. Grace quoted earlier, George Plumptre in his book *The Golden Age of Cricket*, quotes Bob Thomas, a leading umpire of the time, when Gilbert Jessop was clearly stumped but given not out. Jessop was the most dashing batsman of his generation and a real crowd puller. Thomas explained his decision to the fielders:

> "Sixpenny crowd – Saturday gate – can't disappoint 'em – near thing, near thing – but not near enough for the occasion."

Although the success of cricket in this 'Golden Age' was enjoyed by all those taking part, there was a great divide in the players, between the amateurs and professionals. The pay for the working class professionals was generally poor and needed to be supplemented by winter work, while the amateurs, usually lawyers, senior civil servants or other 'men of means', pocketed generous expenses. Moreover they used separate dressing rooms, entered the playing field through different gates, and ate their meals separately. Scorecards highlighted the difference. The names of the amateurs were always preceded by a title and the team captain was always an amateur even if he wasn't worthy of his place in the team. This distinction continued for many years. As late as the 1920s the controversial Surrey captain Percy Fender was reprimanded by Lord Harris for leading his team, amateurs and professionals, onto the field together and it wasn't until 1952 that a professional cricketer, Len Hutton, captained England. In 1907 *The Times* referred to the three great fixtures of the coming summer as being Oxford University v Cambridge University; Gentlemen v Players; and Eton v Harrow. Nevertheless cricket had never been healthier, commanding full press coverage. This was highlighted in 1904 when 'Plum' Warner's team regained the Ashes 'Down Under', while the British

Lions success in the same country was barely mentioned.

Despite the early popularity of cricket it was inevitable that eventually football would become the national game. Social change ensured that, just as in the first three decades of the twentieth century the Labour Party would supplant the Liberal Party as the main opposition to the Conservative Party, football, the game of the 'working man', would become the country's most popular sport. However, this was not clear from the outset. The Football Association was formed in the Freemasons Tavern in London on 26th October 1863 though this was not exactly earth-shattering news. The occasion warranted only thirty-five lines in *The Times* the following day. Nevertheless they got to work quickly. A common set of rules was established, for example the size of the goals, which had varied from the whole width of the pitch to twelve foot wide, now became a standard size. In 1882 the English, Welsh, Scottish and Irish football associations met and formed the International Football Association Board, only thirty two years before the start of The First World War. As early as 16th October 1871, it was agreed to hold the FA Challenge Cup competition. Fifteen clubs entered including Queens Park, Scotland's oldest club, although they did not play a game until the semi-final. They drew 0-0 with The Wanderers, but pulled out of the replay due to lack of funds. The Wanderers went on to defeat the Royal Engineers 1-0 in the final watched by a crowd of 2,000 people who paid one shilling each for the privilege. Professionalism was only legalised in 1885 following a special meeting of the FA. This led to the formation of the Football League in 1888. It was agreed that, as there were only twenty-two free Saturdays, there was room for only twelve clubs. No clubs from the south of England saw fit to join, and the first winners of this new league in season 1888/9 were Preston North End, 'The Old Invincibles,' who won the championship without losing a match and the cup without conceding a goal.

The game was spreading rapidly, and in 1892 the Second Division was formed followed by the Southern League in 1894. By 1900, football was established in almost every conurbation in the land with teams emerging from churches and chapels, as well as from works teams set up in the industrial towns and cities. Clubs were now supported with a passion, and the game was being talked about the length of the country. Professionalism tended to be largely prevalent in the north but the game was also popular in the south where teams had some success in the FA Cup with Southampton runners up in 1900 and 1902 and Tottenham Hotspur winning in 1901, the only non-league side ever to do so. This cup final was the first to be filmed, with 110,000 squeezing into Crystal Palace, the attendance undoubtedly helped by the presence of a London based team. Following a 2-2 draw with Sheffield United, only 20,000 attended the replay at Burnden Park, Bolton.

Players were now becoming household names. The best known was Steve Bloomer of Derby County, the leading goal scorer in the English League five times in eight seasons. The scorer of 28 goals in his 23 England appearances, Bloomer had an interesting war. Coming to the end of his illustrious career in 1914, he had taken up a coaching job in Berlin. On the outbreak of war, Bloomer was interned where he spent the war organising football matches and setting up an association which even had its own league. In 1905 another star player, Alf Common, became the first £1,000 footballer when he moved the short distance from Sunderland to Middlesbrough.

The increase in the popularity of football had financial implications. By 1905, the income of The Football League topped £17,000 for the year (it had been under £5 in the first year), while nearly three hundred clubs were now entering the FA Cup with total attendances of one and a half million. It was not only attendances at cup finals that were breaking records: total attendances in the football league in its first year were 600,000, rising to 5,000,000 by 1905. In 1914, attendances in Division 1 alone exceeded 9,000,000 supporters. The cost of watching these new heroes was affordable for the majority. Costing 6d a game, the equivalent of £1.50 today, supporters could attend the majority of games, nearly all played at 3.00pm on a Saturday afternoon. As for the players, the professionals based mainly in the North and Midlands, earned £4.00 a week, but increasingly were able to supplement their income by selling anything from cigarettes to lotions. The sum of £4.00 a week was double the wage of a skilled tradesman in 1900, although it should be remembered that the players were paid less in the summer months. In England, the number of professional players continued to increase in the years leading up to the outbreak of war. In April 1909, when the prolific Tottenham centre forward Vivian Woodward withdrew from the team, the England XI consisted entirely of professionals. Only Scotland, where the game tried to hang on to its middle class roots, held out against professionalism. Here illegal payments were often made with the Scottish FA turning a blind eye.

By 1914, football had overtaken cricket as the number one spectator sport in the country. Not everybody, however, was happy with this new state of affairs. In September 1906 *The Times*, rather pompously, talked of September being the month when cricketers spent their time playing in country houses while footballers plied their trade earning their £208 a year. The only football, they argued, was league football and this did not count as it was played by "the indentured coolies in the employ of the League Clubs." Clearly, for some, football still had a way to go before it attained respectability. The cause was helped, however, in 1914, when King George V became the first reigning monarch to attend an FA Cup Final. Following advice from his advisors who told him that the monarchy was losing touch with the people, King George presented the cup to Burnley centre half and captain Tommy Boyle after a 1-0 victory over Liverpool at Crystal Palace. In front of over 72,000 supporters, football had received its royal seal of approval and, on the eve of war, the nation could appear as one.

Rugby Football too made great strides in the latter years of the Victorian era. Although it is highly unlikely that William Webb Ellis, a pupil at Rugby School, ever did 'pick up the ball and run' in 1823, the game did gain in popularity. Indeed, by the time that the legend took hold in 1876, Webb Ellis had already been dead for four years and there is no evidence to substantiate the story. As a dayboy, and therefore an 'inferior' pupil, Webb Ellis would more likely have been disciplined for such an indiscretion rather than be hailed as a great innovator.

The Rugby Football Union, reacting to the formation of the Football Association eight years earlier, came into existence in 1871 and the other home countries followed suit over the next ten years. The historian Gareth Williams, in his perceptive and fascinating book *1905 And All That*, states that "The chief characteristic of the growth of organised sport in the late nineteenth century was its diffusion from the middle class downward." It was, says Williams, "the middle class who created, modified and standardized the new model football games of soccer and rugby." The result was the spreading of organised sport into the British Empire. Rugby Football spread to Australia, Canada, New Zealand and South Africa, taking hold in the latter two countries in particular. The International Rugby Football Board came into being in 1886.

By the early years of the twentieth century, touring sides were a regular feature of the rugby calendar. New Zealand toured in 1905 (as we shall discover), South Africa in 1906 and Australia in 1908. The first official rugby international had taken place at Raeburn Place Edinburgh on 23rd March 1871, when Scotland defeated England only for the result to be reversed at the Kennington Oval a year later. In 1877, the numbers allowed in each team was reduced from twenty to fifteen: nine forwards, two half-backs, two three-quarters and two full backs.

Although the growth of sport was a development which was well received by all classes in society, Williams also points out that there existed a rift between middle class exponents of 'sport for sports sake' and working class practitioners more concerned with material rewards. This began to deepen in the 1880s. The professional and working class were making their presence felt. The Rugby County Championship, established in 1888/9, was won by Yorkshire in seven of its first eight years, while another county in the heart of industrial England, Lancashire, won it in the other year. When England defeated Wales in 1892, eleven of the winning team were 'northerners'. The result was the formation of the Northern Union in 1895. Rugby League was born. Shorn of their 'northern stars', England now had to rely more heavily on the southern based, ex-public school boys working in the professions. Sixty-five percent of those who represented England at rugby between 1902 and 1911 were from social classes one and two. In Ireland it was almost impossible to play unless you were in a profession or been to the right school. Scotland had the least number of working men playing the game. In 1901, every member of the Scotland XV who played against Wales had received a public school education. Scotland refused to play Wales in both 1897 and 1898 following 'The Gould Affair.' Welsh star Arthur 'Monkey' Gould had been given a testimonial and presented with the deeds of his house following his magnificent service to Newport and Wales. This greatly offended the Scottish Rugby Union, still trying to cling to the ideals of the amateur game.

Wales, however, was different. Here the game was socially 'inclusive' while elsewhere in the United Kingdom it was 'exclusive'. Gareth Williams once again, (in conjunction with Dai Smith in *Fields of Praise*, the official history of Welsh rugby), explains the significance of sport to the working class. For the working class, they argue, "a mass participation sport… supplied the social and cultural needs displaced by industrialisation." They talk of the working class forging its identity resulting in the growth of sport, both as participants and spectators, among this group. The evidence is clear to see. The South Wales Rugby Challenge Cup was first introduced in season 1877/78 and was won by Newport who defeated Swansea in the final. The following year they won again, this time defeating Cardiff. From 1880 the competition was arranged in such a way as to ensure an East v West final. The benefits of this were confirmed when a crowd of 6,000 watched the 1883 final once again between Newport and Swansea. The game continued to grow in Wales. In 1891 the *South Wales Daily News* expressed this clearly:

> Football in South Wales has steadily gained in favour during the last few years, until it has now become the one great pastime of the people. For one club that existed ten years ago, there are now twenty, and that the influence the game has exercised on the youth of the country has been all for the good cannot be gainsaid, occasionally denunciating utterances from the pulpit notwithstanding.

Newport's first game against Cardiff in December 1876 had attracted 200 spectators but, by 1879, 5,000 watched them entertain leading English club Blackheath. In 1881/2, Cardiff had an average gate of 3,000-4,000, while by the end of the decade 10,000 were attending international matches in Wales. Top English opposition fuelled the interest in club rugby with Newport and Cardiff leading the way. The method of communicating these events to supporters unable to attend a game was in its infancy however. On one occasion in the 1890s, Tommy Vile, a future Wales and British Lions scrum half, took two homing pigeons to a Newport game. At half time, and then again at full time, a bird was dispatched carrying the score to Tommy's brother James who had been unable to arrange time off work. One can only imagine what song Max Boyce might have created out of this piece of ingenuity.

Not that everybody approved of the way in which the game in Wales was becoming more democratic. When Wales defeated New Zealand in 1905 to confirm the nation's place as a major rugby power, the English critic, E.H.D. Sewell, stated in the *National Review* that "Wales were met when the New Zealand team was at its weakest.... Wales have set about strengthening her forwards by the introduction of a 'miner' element into the pack, a move undoubtedly good from a Welsh point of view but of questionable good to the game as a whole." David Parry-Jones tells us, in his biography of Gwyn Nicholls, that the English born Welsh captain responded through the *Western Mail* saying that "In Wales the miner and the dock-worker have as great a chance of playing for their country as the man from a university. Rugby in Wales is democratic, all depends on a man's ability."

Far away from events in the rugby cauldron that was South Wales, developments of a more international nature were taking place. In 1896, in Athens, the first modern Olympic Games were held. The revival of this ancient theatre of sport was the brainchild of Pierre de Coubertin whose vision was based on the ideology of Thomas Arnold and *Tom Brown's Schooldays*. This vision was the recognition of the importance of games in the making of young men, the idea of sport treated with honour. To begin with progress was slow. In 1896 only thirteen countries – eleven European countries supported by the USA and Chile – took part. Great Britain sent 6 competitors who joined the other 305 athletes involved. In Paris four years later, those numbers had increased with 22 countries and 1,319 competitors taking part. However, these games were a disaster with poor organisation and a shortage of suitable officials. Some of the competitors, even winners, did not know that they were taking part in an Olympics. The games of 1904 in St Louis were even worse. At the last minute President Theodore Roosevelt had requested that the Games be moved from the chosen city of Chicago to St Louis in order to fit in with the World Trade Fair. The result was that only 12 countries and 617 athletes took part. The USA contributed 85% of the competitors and won 84% of the medals. Coubertin didn't even attend. An interim Games was held in Athens in 1906, but it suffered due to a lack of events, matters made even worse when Rome pulled out of staging the 1908 Olympics. London, as it was to do in 1948 following the Second World War, stepped into the breach.

The 1908 Olympic Games was a turning point. With 22 countries and 2035 athletes, it was an important stepping stone. In 1912 at Stockholm, with Australia and New Zealand competing as one country and Finland competing under the flag of Tsar Nicholas II, 28 countries and 3,889 athletes took part. By the onset of the Great War the glamour of the Olympics, particularly in athletics and swimming, was established. Sports fans everywhere keenly awaited the 1916 games scheduled for Berlin.

By the eve of war it is clear that organised sport had come to be part of the fabric of people's everyday lives. As bare-knuckle fighting died out to be replaced by boxing with gloves or 'muffles', and archery, golf and polo became popular leisure activities for those who could afford it, participation rates increased rapidly. Golf was particularly popular in Scotland as long ago as1860 when the first British Open was held in Prestwick, and polo made its introduction in 1869. Tennis had developed from real tennis (played by Henry VIII) and badminton, although it took time to become popular. The first All England Tennis Championship took place in 1877, but there were only 22 entrants and one of those didn't turn up. Spencer Gore became the first champion watched by 200 spectators, 30 of whom had seats, and paid 1/- per head. The final, however, had to be postponed over the weekend as it clashed with the Eton v Harrow cricket fixture. Horseracing, meanwhile, had been popular since the sixteenth century and many of the sports rules and regulations had been established in Great Britain by the nineteenth century. However, with improved transport, increased newspaper publicity and the growth of on-course betting, by 1900 horseracing was nearly a national obsession, the 'Sport of Kings' as well as a pastime enjoyed by the working class.

Organised competitive sport had come a long way by 1914, expanding rapidly across all classes. Although emerging from a moral code defined by the middle classes and setting out to develop character and morality, to be played for its own sake rather than for reward, it had become much more than this. There was now organised sporting involvement expanding rapidly across all classes. It was true that, while the different classes played their sport separately and public school athleticism still dominated, the male working class influence had increased. Commercialisation was now a factor as the number of professionals increased. Sport had become a matter of national concern. As war was declared however, it remained to be seen how a sports mad country and its governing bodies would react to the demands that were about to be placed upon it.

'This is not the time to play games'
The Reaction of Sport to the Outbreak of War

The events leading to the outbreak of war in 1914 are well known enough but it is worth reminding ourselves of the sequence of events. Archduke Franz Ferdinand, Crown Prince of the Austro-Hungarian Empire, and his wife Sophia, chose to visit Sarajevo in Bosnia on 28th June. Bosnia was, at this time, an imperial province but had only been incorporated in the Empire since 1908. Previously it had been part of the Turkish Ottoman Empire. Most of the inhabitants of Sarajevo were Serbs who felt more affinity with the neighbouring kingdom of Serbia. On the 28th June a handful of students, members of a fanatical Serbian nationalist organisation called the Black Hand, tried to assassinate the royal couple. They failed with their first attempt but the second attempt, carried out by Gavrilo Princip, an eighteen-year-old student, succeeded.

Events moved quickly. Following consultation with their German allies on the 5th and then the 6th July, Austria-Hungary presented Serbia with a set of political demands which effectively took the form of an ultimatum deliberately designed in a way that Serbia would reject. The ultimatum was dispatched on 23rd July and was immediately seen by Russia as a challenge to the status quo in the Balkans. Russia now mobilized and the quarrel quickly developed into a Russo-German dispute. The network of alliances, which had been forming during the preceding years, now ensured that the dispute would escalate. A war between Russia and Germany would lead to the intervention of Russia's ally, France. A German attack on France based on the 1905 Schlieffen Plan meant the German army passing through neutral Belgium. The sovereignty of Belgium had been guaranteed by all the major powers, including Britain, as long ago as 1839. A threat to 'little Belgium' was bound to result in British involvement. The dye was cast. On 28th July Austria-Hungary declared war on Serbia and four days later both Germany and France began to mobilise. On the 3rd August Germany declared war on France and a day later, following the German invasion of Belgium, Britain entered the fray.

In 1914, Britain appeared to be at the height of its powers with an empire covering a fifth of the world's surface. The Empire controlled a vast network of trade and communication and possessed a supremely powerful navy. Although some of its industrial structure was beginning to lag behind that of Germany and the USA, its position in international trade was unchallenged. The City of London was the world's greatest money market and placed a huge volume of investments abroad, particularly in the USA and the Empire. The German entry into Belgium changed everything. War was not seen as imminent in Britain in 1914. After all, alliances had been formed with France and Russia in 1904 and 1907 respectively, and relations with Germany were better than they had been for some time. Even after the demise of Franz Ferdinand, Sir Edward Grey, the British Foreign Secretary, believed that the dispute could still be settled by an international conference in London. Nevertheless, by 29th August the Germans had forced the British and French to retreat at Mons, Le Cateau and Charleroi. Although the German advance was halted along the River Marne between 5th and 10th September the result was the digging of the first trenches five days later. World War One was born, a war which was to impoverish Britain and mark the beginning of its decline into a second rank power.

The first question which faced governments all over Europe was how to get as many men as possible into uniform and into the field. The immediate reaction in Britain was impressive, and there was enthusiasm coupled with a belief that it was time 'to teach the Kaiser a lesson'. Indeed, there was something of an 'August rush' when it came to enlistment. The lack of preparation didn't discourage potential soldiers. Many British recruits had to train with umbrellas instead of guns, which were in short supply in the early months of the war. Volunteering was made easier as most believed in 1914 that military service would be a brief interlude in their lives. The glamour of uniform, the prospect of steady pay, an escape from a life of monotony, all played a part in the enthusiasm to see action. There was also loyalty to community, nation and Empire (in that order), a sense of duty. Duty was a key factor throughout Europe, duty coupled with a sense of adventure.

However, not all men rushed to join the fray. Britain was not yet 'the nation at arms'. While there was a broad consensus of support for the war, those prepared to act and not just cheer were more likely to come from the better off in society. These families were more likely to have a tradition of military service or, at least completed some military training in school or university. Moreover, nearly all the better off shared in the culture of empire. The highest rates of enlistment were among middle class men employed in finance, commerce and the professions. However, between 1914 and the introduction of conscription in 1916, only 40% of those working in these jobs volunteered. For the working class the figure was lower. These men worried who would support their families when they were away and whether they would have jobs to return to when they got back, a not unreasonable concern as things turned out. Some were told not to go. Early on it was realised that railwaymen and miners would have a crucial role to play at home, particularly in the production of energy and the transportation of munitions. By the time of conscription, only 28% of industrial workers had volunteered. The higher up the social scale, the more likely it was that a man would volunteer, although because the British male population was in the main manual labourers, the British army was still preponderantly working class.

When war was declared on the 4th August 1914, the Government moved quickly. The War Minister, Lord Kitchener began a recruiting campaign almost immediately. By 7th August the War Office was encouraging men aged between 19 and 30 to join and soon approximately 33,000 were committing themselves to the cause every day. Three weeks later the age was increased to 35 and by the middle of September 500,000 had joined one or other of the armed forces. One challenge for the authorities in raising volunteer armies was to discover who could stand up to the rigours of military life and who was physically unfit. To have unfit men at the Front would lead to problems. The pressure on fit young men whose lives revolved around sport was therefore not long in coming. On 28th August Lord Roberts, the distinguished Field Marshal, recipient of the Victoria Cross and veteran of wars from the 1857 Indian Rebellion to the Boer War, made his feelings clear when addressing those men who had joined the 'Stockbrokers Battalion', a 1,600 strong battalion made up of mainly business men based in the City of London:

> How very different is your action to that of the men who can still go on with their cricket and football, as if the very existence of the country were not at stake! This is not the time to play games, wholesome as they are in times of piping peace. We are engaged in a life and death struggle.

The Dean of Lincoln, T.C. Fry, was not far behind him when he suggested that all professional contracts for sportsmen should be cancelled, football coupons stopped and nobody under the age of forty be allowed to attend matches. Religious leaders were to the fore when it came to encouraging men, particularly sportsmen, to join. The Revd. W. Youard of St. Swithuns Church, East Grinstead addressed his congregation on August 30th with the words:

> I would say to every able-bodied young man in East Grinstead to offer yourself without delay in the service of your country. The Welsh Rugby Union Committee has passed a resolution declaring it the duty of all football players to join immediately. Blackheath Rugby Football Club has cancelled all its matches for the same reason. That is the right spirit. I hope it will be imitated by our own clubs. Go straight to the recruiting officer and offer yourself. That is the plain duty of every able-bodied young man today.

At first the Football Association were unmoved by these reactions. This should not surprise us as the War Office had left it to the FA to decide whether or not football should continue. Their rather vague advice was that it "would depreciate anything being done which does not appear to be called for in the present situation." At a meeting of the FA held on August 31st, it was agreed that to suspend football would be 'mischievous'. Meanwhile, the Football League advised clubs to fulfil all engagements at the same time as allowing every young man to do what they could to respond to the country's call. The Football League recommended that clubs should provide military training for all players and that miniature rifle ranges should be provided for them.

Football authorities made donations to the National Relief Fund and The Prince of Wales Fund. However this was not enough for some. Right wing politicians such as the future Home Secretary William Joyson-Hicks responded by contrasting professional football with their amateur counterparts. During August 1914 sixteen players from Dulwich Wood F.C. set the example and enlisted for service. Amateur leagues and all fixtures were cancelled with immediate effect. Frederick N. Charrington of the brewing family was also very critical of footballers and their supporters over their reluctance to join the war. Indeed Charrington, who was also noted as something of an East London philanthropist, used the tactic of trying to shame players and officials through public denouncement of their behaviour. His aim was to ensure that all professional football in Britain was suspended. At half time in a game at Fulham on September 5th, Charrington made a speech in which he reprimanded the astonished spectators for attending the game. He was escorted from the ground.

Many people involved in football felt the criticism to be unjust. In the early months of the war many people still felt that hostilities would be over by Christmas so clubs were reluctant to release players who were on a one year contract. They wanted football to carry on as normal. After all, Rugby League and horseracing were in a similar position and had taken the same stance as football. Cricket was in a different position as the bulk of the season was already over when the hostilities began and few doubted that the war would have finished by the time cricket took centre stage again. Doubts concerning the likely duration of the war were not confined to Britain. When the it began, the question was asked everywhere whether Germany still had the right to stage the Olympic Games, scheduled for Berlin in 1916. The Germans saw no need to give them up. They had been preparing since early 1913 and Kaiser Wilhelm had already opened the stadium. Days before the war started, the German government had sent a team to the USA in order to bring back the latest ideas from the universities and military academies, ideas that would help in ensuring the success of the games. The German Government didn't foresee any problems and well into 1916 they remained convinced that the games would still go ahead. At one stage the Imperial Board even went as far as to select a team before the futility of their planning became clear.

As the numbers of dead and wounded began to mount, so feelings began to harden and, by October, Kitchener was calling for more to join in order to replace those already lost. The original specifications of a thirty-five inch chest and height of five feet six inches were now relaxed and Kitchener did his best to embarrass those still on the sidelines. He argued in a letter published in *The Times* on November 7th

> A man may be doing his duty in other fields than the Front but there is no excuse for diverting from the front thousands of athletes in order to feast the eyes of inactive spectators, who are either unfit to fight or else unfit to be fought for.... Every club who employs a professional football player is bribing a needed recruit to refrain from enlistment and every spectator who pays his gate money is contributing so much towards a German victory.

Kitchener saw those playing and watching football as part of a national scandal. He was not alone. Lord Robert Baden Powell, the founder of the Scout movement, saved his wrath for the supporters. In 1909, he had described them as:

> pale, narrow-chested, hunched-backed, miserable specimens, smoking endless cigarettes, numbers of them betting, all of them learning to be hysterical as they groan or cheer in panic unison with their neighbours – the worst sound of all being the hysterical scream of laughter that greets any little trip or fall of a player.

Newspapers joined in repeating that men who did not join up were contributing to a German victory. Indeed, there was evidence that the German newspapers did exploit the lack of total commitment from British footballers. The German newspaper *Frankfurter Zeitung* told its readers that "young Britons prefer to exercise their long limbs on the football ground, rather than expose them to any sort of risk in the service of their country." The *Morning Chronicle* and *The Times* were especially critical of the FA and the latter ran adverts for "petticoats for footballers." It was not long before religious leaders were reported as having rejoined the fray. On December 2nd, the *Stratford Express* reported a sermon given by the Bishop of Chelmsford at Bethnal Green. According to the newspaper

> The Bishop, in an address on Duty, spoke of the magnificent response that had been made to the call to duty from the

> King. All must play their part. They must not let their brothers go to the front and themselves remain indifferent. He felt that the cry against professional football at the present time was right. He could not understand men who had any feeling, any respect for their country, men in the prime of life, taking large salaries at a time like this for kicking a ball about. It seemed to him something incongruous and unworthy.

Others were not so much critical of the footballers but of the men who managed them. In an attitude very different from many of the war poets in later years, Robert Bridges, the Poet Laureate, wrote the following, once again published in *The Times*:

> The amateur Rugby footballers set them a good example for they not only discontinued their play, but volunteered a full complement of fighters; and thus acted as the true sportsmen that they are. As for professional football, the sight-seeing crowds are not, I hope, as much to blame as they appear to be; I take it that they are ignorantly misled by the small body of men who cater for them; but surely it is impossible that those few managers should be so unintelligent or unpatriotic as to be beyond the reach of an appeal to reason.... It is high time that our footballers let the world see what they are really made of and that they do not deserve the execration that is falling upon them.

Eventually, the pressure on the FA and Football League began to tell. An agreement was reached between the War Office and the FA that football matches could be used for the recruitment of soldiers. The clubs were told by the FA that they could release players for active service if they were unmarried. The FA agreed to continue matches "where, by so doing they could assist, and did not hinder the authorities in recruiting." Prominent men made pro recruitment speeches during the half time intervals and, at the end of the game, a military band would lead the volunteers in a march to the recruiting station. Despite this rather dramatic show, recruitment at football matches had little success. On 23rd November *The Times* reported only one new recruit at an Arsenal game while, at Chelsea, even a speech by the MP Colonel Charles Burn had no effect. On this occasion, no men were recruited at all.

When the idea of a 'Footballers Battalion' was discussed and a meeting held on December 15th attended by over five hundred footballers, only thirty-five enlisted and ten of these were from Clapton Orient. However, with the war continuing through Christmas and into the New Year and the national situation becoming more serious by the week, there was only one outcome. When Everton secured their second league title and Sheffield United defeated Chelsea 3-0 in the Khaki Cup Final at the end of the 1914/15 season, professional football in England, in its established form, stopped. Although regional leagues were formed, the players were no longer paid and there were no medals or trophies. Scottish football carried on and the league ran throughout the war with Celtic dominant, but even here footballers, paid a maximum of £2 a week, could not make a full time living from the game and had to work in war related industries as well.

Not everybody, however, agreed with the decision to suspend league and cup football in England. It was often pointed out that of the 5,000 professional footballers playing in 1914, 2,000 had joined up by the end of November. Moreover, it was calculated later that of the first 600 to enlist, 500 were killed and these figures do not include the 100,000 amateur footballers who had been recruited. On November 28th, the Honourable Secretary of Hertfordshire FA wrote to *The Times* and pointed out that football had contributed more men and money to the war effort than all the other sports put together. Some felt that newspapers such as *The Times* were picking on working class sport. The Manchester based *Athletic News* went further and saw it as an example of class war:

> The whole agitation is nothing less than an attempt by the ruling classes to stop the recreation on one day in the week of the masses.... What do they care for the poor man's sport? The poor are giving their lives for this country in thousands. In many cases they have nothing else.... These should, according to a small clique of virulent snobs, be deprived of the one distraction that they have had for over thirty years.

The *Socialist Pioneer* argued that, by stopping professional football, the country had effectively introduced a compulsion to enlist. But there was to be no turning back, and, by the time of the passing of the Military Service Act in January 1916, the debate within football circles was well and truly over.

The change in the position of the FA is illustrated by the story of Jimmy Hogan, an English footballer of Irish descent who had spent his playing career with Fulham, Burnley and Bolton. Following his retirement in 1913, he turned to coaching and had success across Europe including Austria, Hungary, Switzerland and Germany. He coached the Austrian national team to the Olympic final in 1936, as well as experiencing success with a number of clubs. Hogan's methods, based on his emphasis on ball control rather than purely physical fitness achieved by constant running around the training ground, proved to be very influential, particularly in Hungary. The great Hungarian team of the 1950s owed something to the influence of Jimmy Hogan and his influence was still felt as late as the 1960s. Long before the success of Bobby Robson and Terry Venables on the European club scene, Jimmy Hogan was blazing a trail. How was this seen back home? Frederick Wall, the secretary of the FA, described him as a traitor because he had stayed in Europe for the duration of the war. The FA, Government and the Press were now singing from the same hymn sheet.

There had been no such divisions within the world of Rugby Union. Nine days after war was declared, the Rugby Union made a country-wide appeal to its members and all national, county and club games were immediately cancelled. The Welsh Rugby Union followed this lead and called upon players to enlist from the start. Dai Smith and Gareth Williams in *Fields Of Praise* quote the WRU:

> Considering that our players… the very pick of men eligible for service in the Army, and considering that Welshmen have the reputation for not being wanting either in patriotism or pluck, we feel we shall not appeal in vain…

The WRU go on to show their confidence in their players being able to make a difference:

> If only every man in every First XV in Wales were to enlist, what a magnificent body there would be at the service of

> our country, and even then there would still be plenty of players left to enable the game to be played as usual....
>
> We therefore appeal with confidence to all Welsh rugby footballers, players untrammelled by imperative domesticities, not to allow any selfish reason to prevent them from answering the urgent call of their King and Country.

A recruitment poster published in autumn 1914 emphasised the example of rugby footballers:

> Rugby Union footballers are doing their duty. Over 90% have enlisted. British athletes! Will you follow this glorious example?

By the time that J. Ackerman Smith, the Honourable Secretary of the Scottish Rugby Union, had issued a notice in September 1914 asking that rugby should no longer be played, he was too late: the players had already gone. Although a Barbarian XV did play a Wales XV in April 1915, this game was played with the purpose of recruiting more men for the Welsh Guards.

For the cricket authorities, decisions over participation were somewhat easier. The season was nearly over and it was clear that Surrey could not be caught in the race for the county championship. The last game was Sussex v Yorkshire at Hove on September 2nd and the championship was brought to a premature end with two games to go. Many cricketers joined up willingly, encouraged by influential figures such as W.G. Grace. The editor of *Wisden*, S.H. Pardon, had thought of preparing a list of cricketers who had joined the Army and publishing it in the 1915 edition of *Wisden*. He decided against this as "the number is so great that I could not be at all sure of accuracy.... Any accidental omission might have involved protest and correction." It was clear to Pardon by 1915 that this war was not a six month adventure but a "long, savage, obscene slaughter." However not all cricketers joined quickly. Jack Hobbs was heavily criticised by some when he went to play in the Bradford League each weekend. Frank Woolley, another of England's premier batsmen, did likewise. Hobbs did eventually become involved in munitions work and later joined the newly formed Flying Corps but never quite removed the suggestion that he had received preferential treatment and experienced an 'easy war'. The counter argument was that to lose Hobbs in the conflict would have been a huge blow to British morale, such was his status in 1914. Nevertheless the vast majority of English cricketers did what was expected of them. 'Plum' Warner, the England captain, went straight from Lord's where Middlesex were playing their final match, to report to his commanding officer. With this rather abrupt action can be seen the end of cricket's 'Golden Age'.

The pattern was set. Among the approximate 4,000,000 men that had fought in the British Army by 1918 were a sizeable minority of the finest sportsmen in the British Empire. This book focusses on those sportsmen who played either in order to earn a living or were fortunate enough to satisfy a desire to play regularly while retaining their amateur status. It will not include a detailed study of talented sportsmen such as Noel Chavasse. Chavasse devoted most of his time to his work as a surgeon but still found the time to run, with his twin brother Christopher, in the 400 metres at the 1908 London Olympics. He also played lacrosse for Oxford in the varsity match and was a free scoring wing when playing rugby for his college. A sportsman of undoubted talent, he is, of course, best remembered for being one of only three men to win the VC and Bar, the only one to win both in the same war, the second being an award given posthumously following his death at Passchendaele.

Noel Chavasse stands as one of the best examples of what was lost in the Great War, a gentleman proud to do his duty, to serve King and Country and to do all that he could to help his fellow soldiers. It is with full-time sportsmen that this book is concerned. Sir Arthur Conan Doyle advised British sportsmen

> If the cricketer had a straight eye let him look along the barrel of a rifle. If a footballer had strength of limb let him serve and march in the field of battle.

It was time for a generation to put aside sport and to embark on war. When the Earl of Derby presented the FA Cup to Sheffield United after defeating Chelsea 3-0 in The Khaki Cup Final of 1915, he reminded everybody that "It is now the duty of everyone to join with each other and play a sterner game for England." How stern that game would be he could never have foreseen.

'Sound o'wind, strong of limb, eager for the fray Every soul for the goal Hearts! Hearts! Hearts lead the way'

Despite their perceived reluctance to commit to the cause in the early months of the war, footballers were joining up. Difficulties over contracts meant that when the 17th Service (Football) Battalion of the Middlesex Regiment was formed on 12th December 1914, only amateurs like the England and Tottenham centre forward Vivian Woodward and the former Bradford and Leeds international Evelyn Lintott were able to join. This battalion was formed as part of a 'pals battalion' which had at its core a group of footballers. By the time the battalion took part in the Battle of the Somme in 1916 it contained many professional players but in the early days obtaining their release was a difficult task.

The first club in England to respond was Clapton Orient, now known as Leyton Orient, the second oldest club in London, led by their captain Fred Parker. Forty players and staff followed him including the two leading goal scorers, William Jonas and Richard McFadden. William Jonas was a particularly popular player with a large female following. By 1914, he was receiving up to fifty letters a week from his female admirers and, so great a problem did this become, that he placed a statement in the match programme asking for this to stop in case it upset his wife. Quick and skilful, with good passing ability, this twenty-six year old Geordie from Blyth, Northumberland, was one of the most versatile players at the club and scored twenty-one goals in seventy league appearances for the team. McFadden, a childhood friend of Jonas, who had left Lanarkshire in Scotland as a boy to live in Blyth, was a striker with the impressive record of scoring sixty-six league goals in one hundred and thirty seven appearances. The two boys had begun their careers together at Blyth before ending up at Clapton Orient.

Jonas, along with teammate George Scott, was killed on the Somme. Trapped in a trench on 27th July, McFadden recorded his friend's demise.

> Willie turned to me and said, 'Goodbye Mac, best of luck, special love to my sweetheart Mary Jane and best regards to the lads at Orient.' Before I could reply to him he was up and over. No sooner had he jumped out of the trench, my best friend of nearly twenty years was killed before my eyes. Words cannot express my feelings at this time.

Although McFadden was to win a Military Medal on the Somme, he died of wounds inflicted during this action on 23rd October 1916. A hero in civilian life after saving a young boy from drowning and by rescuing a man from a burning building, McFadden's death was felt throughout the football community.

Although Clapton Orient led the way in England in their willingness to serve in the 'Footballers Battalion', they were not the first club to show this commitment. Whilst clubs in England were waiting for a decision to be made regarding the possible postponement of competitive football, in Scotland players from Heart of Midlothian, Edinburgh's foremost club, were already in the action. Two of their players, George Sinclair and Neil Moreland who were army reservists, had already joined up.

The history of Heart of Midlothian FC was already a very proud one. They had been formed in 1874 and in 1890 they were founder members of the Scottish Football League. Even without Sinclair and Moreland, the Hearts squad assembled by manager John McCartney for 1914/15 was one of the strongest in its history. They started the season with eight wins in succession including the defeat of defending champions Glasgow Celtic in the opening game of the season, eleven days after Britain had declared war. A new stand had been opened to seat up to 4,000 supporters at a substantial cost of £12,780.00 and a healthy, optimistic crowd of 18,500 watched the Celtic game. By late November 1914, when the pressure was mounting on footballers to join the action on the Western Front, Hearts had only lost one game and they comfortably led the league table with their attractive football. By the time another player, Jimmy Speedie, had decided to volunteer, Hearts seemed certain to win the Scottish League.

Mirroring events south of the border, the football authorities in Scotland were feeling the pressure to show commitment to the war effort. The chairman of Airdrie, Thomas Forsyth thought that "playing football while our men are fighting is repugnant." He was not alone. A motion was placed before the Scottish Football Association to postpone the season and, although it was defeated at the ballot box, the SFA decided to wait and take the advice of the War Office. It was at this point that Sir George McCrae, a keen Hearts supporter, enters the story. A hatter by profession now working in local government, McCrae had been the Member of Parliament for East Edinburgh. He decided to approach the War Office with a request to be given permission to raise a local Edinburgh battalion for service. Once this permission was obtained McCrae informed the Press that he would raise 'McCrae's Battalion' in seven days. Given that some players were earning up to £4 a week playing football and that a private soldier was paid between 1/- and 2/- a day, one might expect a slow rather limited response. However, within six days thirteen more Hearts players and 600 supporters, all "men of an excellent type" according to the local press, had joined a battalion which now totalled 1,350 officers and men. The ground and the recruiting office at Haymarket became a hub of activity as men rushed to become one of 'McCrae's Own', part of Kitchener's new army, the 16th (Service) Battalion (2nd Edinburgh) The Royal Scots. The Hearts minute book recorded that "the lead established by these gallant youths reverberated through the length of the land." The good name of football was on the way to being restored. Meanwhile, sixteen Hearts players were on their way to war to be trained, many for the Somme Offensive.

The loss of these talented footballers did not have an immediate effect as players were still available from time to time. Indeed, the club went on a twenty match unbeaten run between October 1914 and February 1915 which put them in control of the race for the title. The players could carry out their initial basic military training and receive their inoculations while remaining with Hearts. The greatest impact of the players in volunteering for the Army was on the communities around them. Other clubs, including Falkirk, Hibernian and Raith Rovers reported a surge in volunteers and five Raith Rovers players together with a further six from Falkirk joined 'McCrae's Own' soon after the Hearts players. The Hearts club themselves continued to support the war effort in other ways such as supplying relief parcels to service men and women. However such total commitment was bound to take its toll. As players flair and energy began to fade following intense military training the fitness coach, James Duckworth, suffered a nervous breakdown. Two ten hour nocturnal marches on the eve of important matches took their toll on the players, some of whom began to lose form. Vital points were dropped, with a 4-3 defeat to Glasgow Rangers proving to be particularly significant. In the final three games of this emotionally difficult season, Hearts drew with Aberdeen and lost to Morton and St Mirren. After leading the table for thirty-five of the thirty-seven weeks the title was lost. Celtic were champions by a four point margin. The Scottish media had no doubt that the early commitment of the Hearts team to the war effort had cost them the title. The energy expended on the necessary military training had taken its toll and the loss of form in the last third of the season was seen as a direct consequence. The media were quick to contrast the willingness of Hearts players to volunteer with the efforts of their illustrious Glasgow neighbours, Celtic and Rangers. As far as the Scottish press were concerned there was only one champion club.

What of events in France? In January 1916, the battalion arrived in France as part of the 34th Division heading for the Somme, but not all the Hearts players were with them. Jimmy Speedie had already been lost. The twenty-one year old inside left and part time insurance clerk had been among the first to volunteer. He had responded to an appeal made at half time during a game against Falkirk. Speedie, who unlike his teammates had joined the 7th Battalion of the Queen's Own Cameron Highlanders, saw action early on. He took part in the first big push at Loos on 25th September 1915 when his regiment swept on to Hill 70. Speedie, however was killed in the fighting, the first Hearts casualty of the war. His body was never found. In a story that was to be repeated all too often in the next four years, Speedie also lost a brother John, a Second Lieutenant, killed at Arras.

The story of Tom Gracie is equally distressing. Gracie, a meat salesman, had joined the 16th Royal Scots with his teammates in the autumn of 1914. An established player at both Everton and Liverpool, Gracie had been good enough to gain representative honours in 1915 when he played for the Scottish League against the Irish League. Bought by Hearts for the bargain sum of £400 in May 1914 from Liverpool, the club had been rewarded with 28 goals in his first season, a club record and made Tom Gracie the joint highest scorer in the league. Gracie had felt unappreciated in England after failing to hold down a regular place in Liverpool's starting line up and, although he had been a reserve for the full Scottish team in 1911, felt that his career had stalled. The move back to Scotland changed all that and, on the surface at least, Gracie's future seemed bright. However underneath all was not what it seemed. Gracie, as a high profile footballer with Scotland's leading team, had been a particular target for those leading the campaign to have professional football in Britain banned. The intensity of the debate was having its effect and Gracie, by now a volunteer, told the media that he "felt rather ashamed of not joining in". On the evening of Friday 4th December 1914, McCrae asked Gracie to speak at a recruitment meeting in Oddfellows Hall, Edinburgh. Gracie explained his reasons for volunteering saying that he felt it was "high time that I stepped forward" and that "if you had no encumbrances it was your duty to offer your services". The following day McCrae ensured that any volunteer from the meeting was allowed free entry to Hearts home game that afternoon.

Although Gracie had now volunteered, the criticism had left its mark. More worrying still was the diagnosis of leukaemia that Gracie had received in March 1915, something that he shared only with his manager. Against medical advice, Gracie continued to play throughout the spring until the end of the season, making a contribution and still scoring goals. However the twenty-six year old Corporal Gracie did not make it to France. In the autumn of 1915 he was taken ill in Leeds following his training at Ripon and died of leukaemia in Glasgow on 23rd October 1915, the only Hearts player to have a known grave. This capped a dreadful year for the Gracie family as Tom's brother John and brother-in-law Tommy had already been lost in battle, at Loos and Gallipoli respectively.

Those Hearts players stationed in France were to play a very significant role in the events of the summer of 1916. In December 1915, it had been agreed between the Allies agreed that the Somme offensive would take place over a twenty-five mile front both north and south of the River Somme. With the Battle of Verdun occupying many of the French divisions from February 1916, the bulk of the responsibility now fell on Kitchener's largely untried volunteer army. The 15th and 16th battalions of the Royal Scots were given the task of attacking the village of Contalmaison, a very challenging task as it involved driving up 'Sausage Valley' overcoming barbed wire and a sophisticated trench system in the face of machine guns and trench mortars. On the somewhat hazy morning of July 1st, the Hearts players of the 16th Battalion prepared to join the battle in the second wave of attack. As the mist was lifting and the sky became clearer, McCrae's Own would have been aware of the detonation of the large mines around them. Indeed Lochnager Crater was just to their left, the largest crater ever created in warfare which displaced 300,000 tons of earth, a crater of which it is said that the largest piece of body found after the explosion that created it was a foot in a boot.

The outcome is well known: the worst day in the history of the British Army. The first day alone saw 57,470 British casualties, 19,240 of whom were killed. There were successes for the British at Montauban and Mametz but the overall picture was one of disaster. Failures at Gommecourt, Serre, Beaumont Hamel, Thiepval and la Boisselle contributed to the heavy casualties. The second day, with 30,000 casualties, wasn't much better.

The 15th Royal Scots had led the way and took severe losses totalling 637 casualties. The Hearts players in the 16th Battalion had managed to cross No Man's Land with relatively light losses but about 8.45am they were starting to lose contact. This is where the damage was done as there were 1,000 casualties according to Harris and Whippy. On July 1st three of that entertaining, free scoring Hearts team met their death. Sergeant Duncan Currie, a full back and former hairdresser from a renowned footballing family, just short of his 24th birthday, courageously led his men over the top accompanied by Private Henry Wattie, a twenty-three year old inside forward expected to achieve great things and Private Ernest Edgar Ellis, a boot operator from Norwich who had only signed for Hearts in August 1914. All three perished, their bodies never to be identified. Henry Wattie was a particular loss to Scottish football. He was seen as the replacement for the great Bobby Walker, an established Scottish international who was acknowledged to be one of the best players in the world at his peak. Wattie had made a sensational debut for Hearts, scoring both goals in a 2-1 win against the powerful Rangers at Ibrox, and was tipped to be the player who could become the focal point of future Hearts teams. He was seen to fall by Annan Ness, one of the teams half backs, as he advanced against a hail of bullets only minutes after 'going over the top'. Ellis had married only days before leaving for France and had recently become a father to a daughter he was destined never to see. The last Hearts player to die on the Somme was Lance Corporal James Boyd, the brother of Hearts goalkeeper Archie Boyd. Jimmy, an underground worker in the shale mines, had signed for Hearts in August 1914, just after the outbreak of war. He died on a relatively 'quiet' day on the Somme, 3rd August, but his loss was none the less tragic for that. Following an injury, Jimmy had been moved to a field hospital which was then hit by artillery fire. He was twenty-one years old. His body was never recovered.

By the end of the Battle of the Somme, it was reported that the 16th Battalion of the Royal Scots had suffered 80% casualties. Those left at home could only try to imagine the horrors being experienced by the Hearts players. John McCartney, the manager, received regular correspondence from his players. The letters, each one faithfully transcribed by McCartney, give an indication of the closeness of this team in battle. Alfie Briggs was a regular correspondent and wrote to McCartney to tell him of the loss of Jimmy Todd, the Raith Rovers winger, who was the first footballer in 'McCrae's Own' to be killed. Annan Ness gave McCartney a full account of the first day on the Somme and reported the deaths of Currie and Ellis as well as the probable fate of the missing Wattie. Ness also told of the injuries suffered by Paddy Crossan. McCartney, who had been very supportive of his players decision to join the fray, had already, the previous year, encouraged people to raise money so that footballs could be sent to the front to enable soldiers to find some recreation, the 'Footballs for Soldiers Fund'. What he must have felt on receiving Ness's letter we can only try to imagine. An army that had taken a year to create had been destroyed in one battle and the team that McCartney had been patiently building since 1910 ripped apart. The sacrifices were recognised in the football world and beyond. So great was the impact that the Hearts players had made on the Somme that the club received many letters of sympathy and support, one even from the King of the Belgians.

The losses suffered by Hearts were not confined to the Somme battlefield. Sergeant John Allan enlisted in the 9th Battalion, Royal Scots, the only Royal Scots battalion to wear kilts. They were part of the 51st Highland Division, 'the Shock Troops' of the British

Army. Allan became involved in the fighting at Arras, in what was seen as very much an 'infantryman's battle'. The early stages of the battle went well and 13,000 Germans were taken prisoner but the fighting soon became a real struggle. Allan was sent on a patrol to reconnoitre a wood but was caught in the crossfire and died on 22nd April 1917, the last of the Hearts players to be killed.

It should be remembered that, although the first to make the commitment, Hearts were not the only Scottish football club to suffer severe losses. Their great rivals in the 1914/15 title race, Celtic, lost a total of seven past or present players. The best known of these was also killed at Arras. Peter Johnstone, from Collessie in Fife, was a versatile defender or midfield player who is now remembered as a 'Celtic Great'. When he joined Celtic in 1908, they were in the middle of a period of domination that would see the club capture six league titles in a row between 1905 and 1910. Playing at inside left and then at left half, Johnstone didn't establish himself as a regular until 1911/12 when he won his first cup winners medal and, in 1912, he finally cemented his place in the team at centre half. Playing in this position, Johnstone was to win three league titles and another Scottish Cup as well as winning the hearts of the Celtic fans. This part time miner, part time footballer impressed everybody with his courage and 'never say die' attitude. The poet, John Conway, had written in 1913,

> A loyal servant you have been
> Long may you wear the hoops of green
> Your well knit face of old be seen on our own Paradise.
> No warmer Celtic heart than thine
> Long may your star ascendant shine
> Full sure when Celtic made you sign
> They booked a prize.

In March 1916 Johnstone, eager for some action, signed up to the 14th Battalion of the Argyll and Sutherland Highlanders. Frustrated at not getting to the frontline, he transferred to the 6th Battalion Seaforth Highlanders in May 1917 but sometime on 15th/16th May he was killed, along with 68 others, attempting to capture a chemical works. On 6th June it was confirmed that Peter Johnstone had indeed been killed at Arras. This twenty-eight year old veteran of 223 Celtic matches left a wife and two children, his body never found.

But it is the story of Hearts, and in particular its connection with the Somme, that has provided Scottish football with its clearest link to the Great War. The extent of the losses suffered by the British Army on the Somme is imprinted on the memories of everyone with an interest in their country's history. There are 153,040 British graves on the Somme, 53,409 of which are graves of 'soldiers known unto God.' Another 53,564 bodies still lie lost in the now beautiful countryside around the Somme, giving a total of 206,604 British dead, among them four of that exciting Hearts team. One look at the Thiepval Memorial with its 73,357 missing is enough to confirm the extent of the tragedy.

Some Hearts players survived this catastrophe. Bob Mercer was a powerful centre half and captain who hadn't been able to leave for France with his teammates due to a lengthy knee injury. When he was passed fit, along with midfield schemer Harry Graham, this influential player, sometimes called 'the mastermind of modern soccer', left to join his teammates. Mercer was greatly missed during the war and supporters looked forward to his return. However the returning player was a very different creature to the powerful influence pre-1914. The effects of being gassed had left Mercer with a weakened heart, so much so that Hearts refused to play him. Eventually he moved to Dunfermline for two seasons with little success. On 23rd April 1926, while playing in a friendly fixture at Selkirk, Bob Mercer collapsed and died ten minutes into the game, another victim of the Great War. He was 37 years of age.

The story of Paddy Crossan has a similar outcome. Crossan, a native of Addiewell, a mining village in West Lothian, was a powerful robust defender, usually as an exceptionally quick full back who had won sprinting competitions racing against professional sprinters, often under an assumed name. He was also one of the characters of the team. A handsome man, whose nickname in the Hearts dressing room was 'The Handsomest Man in the World', it was said that although Crossan could pass a ball, he found it impossible to pass a mirror. It was reported that the relatively high number of female supporters attending Hearts matches was largely due to him. His teammates didn't appear to object as Paddy Crossan was good for morale and a popular soldier. Unfortunately he was badly injured after being buried alive when a shell exploded. It took him three days to crawl back to the British lines through No Man's Land. On recovering, Crossan later returned to the front only to be gassed as well as suffer another serious injury, this time in the leg. Crossan was told that amputation was the only answer. He pleaded with the surgeon, stressing that as a footballer amputation was not an option. The leg was saved following an operation carried out by a German prisoner of war and, on his return to Scotland, Crossan resumed his career. He played for three more years, eventually retiring to open a pub, 'Paddy's Bar', in Rose Street, Edinburgh. However the effects of poison gas had a dramatic effect on his health, finally destroying his lungs and killing him in 1933. Paddy Crossan, the fastest and handsomest man in Scotland, was 39 years old. 'Paddy's Bar' survived under his name until the 1990s.

Although they didn't have such a dramatic death, the list of Hearts survivors and their wounds only serves to confirm the sacrifices that were made. Corporal Alfie Briggs suffered a broken leg, a broken foot and a badly injured arm. Although he recovered from his wounds, Alfie Briggs never played football again and became prone to bouts of depression. He died in 1950 still with two machine gun bullets in his back. The other regular letter-writer, Lieutenant Annan Ness, was wounded twice after initially refusing a commission in order to remain with his teammates. Annan Ness, a reserve team player, was not the most talented footballer in the regiment but had proved to be the most respected of soldiers. Sergeant Neil Moreland was wounded three times and Pte Jock Wilson twice, although Wilson did return to play for Hearts. Pte J. Hazeldean, Pte E.M. McGuire and Pte J. Martin were discharged as 'invalids', such was the severity of their injuries, while Pte Robert Preston and Pte Willie Wilson also suffered significant wounds, although Wilson played until 1923. Lieutenant Jimmy Low was wounded twice and the Hearts directors refused to reinstate him after the war. Low signed instead for Newcastle and played in their FA Cup winning team of 1924. He lived until 1960.

The effects of war were felt by everybody at the club, some with distressing consequences. Fitness coach James Duckworth had already suffered a nervous breakdown and he died in 1920, worn out by the physical exhaustion of the intense training and nocturnal expeditions that he had undertaken in support of his players before they left for France. His assistant, Alex Lyon, had already died in similar circumstances five years earlier. The founder of 'McCrae's Own' Battalion, Lieutenant Colonel George McCrae DSO was, by November 1916, suffering with ill health and exhaustion. The events of the Somme had nearly destroyed him. He was declared unfit for further service and returned home. Popular with his men, McCrae found it increasingly difficult to risk further casualties after July 1st. On his return, McCrae did all that he could to help the survivors and the families of those who had died. He stood in three general elections as a Liberal, winning Falkirk and Stirling in 1923 only to lose it a year later. As late as 1928, the memories his 'boys' still haunted him. From his fireside he wrote to D.M. Sutherland, a veteran of the 16th Battalion,

> In the flames I see the faces of my boys. So young and full of promise. The sorrow and the pride are overwhelming. Sorrow at the loss and pride in the manner of their dying. They never flinched. Faced by a veritable storm of shot and shell, they marched towards the guns beside their friends. In remembering them, we must acknowledge our debt and find some way to justify our own lives so that when we meet our comrades in that better place we are able to say with a brave heart that we did not let them down.

He died five weeks later aged 68.

Hearts had to carry on. Inevitably following such losses, performances began to dip. The successful days of 1914/15 could not be reproduced and in 1922 Hearts only just avoided relegation, finishing 19th, only two points above the drop. But their reputation and the affection in which the club was held had never been higher, their crowds being the highest in Scotland throughout the 1920s.

A memorial to those players lost paid for through public subscriptions was unveiled by the Secretary of State for Scotland, Robert Munro, on 9th April 1922 at Haymarket. In front of 35,000 people close to where most of the players had enlisted, Munro addressed the crowd and spoke of the players' great example and willingness to serve from the very earliest days of the war. The *Edinburgh Evening*

News reported that "some of those lads fell in the Battle of the Somme. They fell in the morning of their days with the dew of health upon their brows." Even today players, supporters, officials and relations of the players gather for a short service on Armistice Day; a service attended since 2010 by representatives of Raith Rovers, Falkirk and Dunfermline as well as regular attendees, rivals Hibernian. In the rebuilt village of Contalmaison, on the Somme, can be found a memorial to McCrae's Own Battalion and the men who fell there. It was finally erected in 2005, over 85 years after the original plans for a memorial were abandoned for lack of funds. As recently as 2013 the 'Tynecastle Bronze Memorial' was unveiled on the wall of the main stand at Hearts ground. We can now be confident that the sacrifices made by that exciting Scottish team of 1914/15 will never be forgotten. In case we do, there is always the Hearts song to remind us.

When the Empire is in danger, and we hear our county's call
The Mother-land may count on us to leave the leather ball.
We've hacked our way in many a fray, we've passed and gone for goal
But a bigger field awaits us, and we were keen to join the roll.

Chorus:

So its right wing, left wing, frontline and goal;
Half back, full back, every living soul;
Sound o'wind, strong of limb, eager for the fray,
Every soul for the goal Hearts! Hearts! Hearts lead the way.

We thank the Lord Almighty He has made us strong and fit,
Our muscles are like iron and we don't know when we're hit
We take a lot of mauling, we can give as good as we get,
And we wish to show the Germans we are not decadent yet.

Chorus:

So its right wing, left wing, frontline and goal;
Half back, full back, every living soul;
Sound o'wind, strong of limb, eager for the fray,
Every soul for the goal Hearts! Hearts! Hearts lead the way.

Grandstand, pavilion, friend or foe, we bid you adieu,
We know your thoughts are with us when we go to fight for you.
You've seen us win, you've seen us lose, but now we join the fray
Where brute and bully must go down and honour win the day.

Chorus:

So its right wing, left wing, frontline and goal;
Half back, full back, every living soul;
Sound o'wind, strong of limb, eager for the fray,
Every soul for the goal Hearts! Hearts! Hearts lead the way."

Leigh Roose – 'The Prince of Goalkeepers'

Researching the stories of sportsmen who gave their lives in the Great War, it becomes clear that they share a common characteristic, their bravery. What is more variable is the success that these men achieved in their sporting lives. Some became household names, known and revered throughout the country, while others had to settle for less distinguished careers, known only to those keen supporters of their particular team. That Leigh Richmond Roose belongs to the first group is beyond dispute. In 1905, when the *Daily Mail* selected an imaginary World XI to play a hypothetical fixture against another planet, Leigh Roose was the undisputed choice to keep goal. Not only was Roose a naturally talented keeper combining his talent with almost reckless bravery, but such was his effectiveness that new rules had to be devised in order to accommodate him.

Leigh Roose was born in Holt, a small medieval market town near Wrexham in the north east corner of Wales, on 26th November 1877. This area towards the end of the century, would see the rise of Billy Meredith, possibly the greatest player of his generation. In later years it would also witness the development of such household names as Ian Rush, Mark Hughes and Michael Owen. Roose could bear comparison with any of them. He was the fourth son born to Richmond Leigh Roose, a Presbyterian minister, and his wife Eliza. His childhood, although comfortable, was not without tragedy. When he was four years old his mother died of cancer and his father was left to bring up five lively sons. The boys were brought up in a middle class environment where the domestic servant carried out most of the many chores associated with bringing up a young family while the Revd. Roose entertained visitors such as H.G. Wells, a teacher at nearby Holt Academy.

Young Leigh showed an interest in football from the outset but, unusually, was attracted to the position of goalkeeper. Unlike most young boys, Leigh was more interested in saving shots rather than scoring goals. Perhaps this position appealed to his rather eccentric nature. As a well built young boy he was able to cope with the physical aspects of the position and didn't allow the lack of protection given to goalkeepers to bother him unduly. Such was his physique that if Leigh had been born in the South Wales valleys then it is quite possible that he would have been lining up for Wales against the 1905 All Blacks rather than keeping clean sheets against England.

Academic work was not sacrificed in the pursuit of success on the football field and in 1895 Leigh enrolled to study Bacteriology at the University of Wales College, Aberystwyth. The choice was a good one. Aberystwyth had a good sporting reputation and Leigh soon became the star of its football team. Socially too, Aberystwyth satisfied his needs and Leigh became the life and soul of many student parties taking place around the town. It was not all plain sailing and he was deeply affected by the loss of his older brother Edward, who died of hypothermia after watching Leigh play in the rain against Liverpool University. But despite this his days at 'Aber' were happy and he gained his degree in 1899. Indeed he was in no rush to leave and stayed on another year in order to play for Aberystwyth Town. It is from here that Leigh was called up by Wales to play against Ireland on 24th February 1900, a match which Wales won 2-0. During the game he knocked an Irish player unconscious when barging him into touch, explaining after the game was over, "If a forward has to be met and charged down, do not hesitate to charge with all your might." Leigh had made his mark, a point made clearer when his performance was compared with his predecessors. In the previous Welsh match against Scotland, Fred Griffiths had conceded five. There remained, however, a desire to follow a medical career and to continue his football on a purely amateur basis. In the autumn of 1900 Leigh left the comfort of life in Aberystwyth for London, taking a job as an assistant at Kings College Hospital. Yet success on the international stage meant that the professional clubs would soon pursue his signature. Following three more international matches in the spring of 1901, he could hold out no longer so that summer Leigh signed for Stoke.

At first sight Stoke might have appeared a strange choice of club. Although they had been one of the twelve original football league clubs, they had fallen on hard times. Attendances had dropped to an average of 3,000 but this was soon to change. Leigh was still determined to follow a medical career at some point and, in order to do this it was preferable to remain an amateur. Stoke agreed to pay Leigh his expenses, thereby allowing him to retain his amateur status. Moreover, Leigh could now stay in London and continue his work at Kings College Hospital, although he did have to relinquish his place on the degree course. He quickly became a favourite with the Stoke supporters, especially when he was largely instrumental in keeping the club in the First Division. Indeed this became a regular pattern and so, after three seasons and 144 league games including 40 clean sheets, Leigh began to reconsider his football future. He had put his medical studies on hold for three years so he decided to concentrate on his work and only play football on weekends. Everton signed him on this basis in November 1904.

Meanwhile, Leigh's international career went from strength to strength. In March 1902, he became the first Welsh goalkeeper to keep a clean sheet against England for twenty years. Against the same opposition in 1904, Leigh played on despite a fractured finger in his right hand in a performance in which *The Times* reported that "he was at his best throughout." Following a 2-0 win over Scotland, Leigh more than maintained his reputation stopping many awkward shots, gathering the ball with certainty and starting attacks as quickly as possible. International forwards were treated to the force of his fist as he became fully involved in goalmouth melees. The historian Geraint Jenkins talks of his "sharp eyesight, startling reflexes, competitive instinct and reckless bravery" and concluded that Leigh was indeed "an extraordinarily daunting opponent."

With Billy Meredith also approaching the peak years of his career, Wales could now seriously consider winning the Home International Championship for the first time. Meredith, of course, was the first 'superstar' of Welsh football. It is estimated that he played about 1,600 matches scoring 470 goals before he retired, aged nearly 50, in 1924 and during his remarkable career won FA Cup Winners medals with both Manchester City and Manchester United as well as two league championship medals while at Old Trafford. Meredith, with his thin spindly legs and slight physique looked nothing like a professional footballer while Roose standing over six foot and weighing thirteen stones was the perfect athlete but they were great friends, sharing a rebellious steak which sometimes landed them in trouble with the authorities. Both played against Ireland in 1906, the first international match to be filmed, a remarkable piece of historical evidence of spectator sport in the Edwardian era. Only two and a half minutes has survived but it proves that fanatical, committed crowds are nothing new.

Before this Leigh had received his highest honour in football when he accepted the captaincy of his country in March 1905. He oozed pride when he wrote the following year,

> To play for one's country is an honour, no matter how many times one is selected to appear. To captain one's country is however the honour of honours generating the kind of pride within a man that is difficult to define in words.

By 1907 Wales, despite not being able to field their strongest team in any of the matches, duly won their first title. Victories over Scotland and Ireland and a 1-1 draw with England were enough. Leigh had established a reputation that would outlive his career. *The Dictionary of Welsh Biography* said that Leigh had "been thoroughly grounded in the fundamentals of his art, and gave interpretation to them in the style and manner of a man of genius" while Sir Frederick Wall, Secretary of the FA, exclaimed that he was "a sensation as a goalkeeper." He went on to say that Leigh was,

> a clever man who had what is sometimes described as the eccentricity of genius. His daring was seen in the goal where he was often taking risks and emerging triumphant.

Leigh's stay at Everton was short but not without incident. He was now involved in a successful club team and for a while Everton looked as they could win the 'double' of league and cup. In the event they lost in the semi final of the FA Cup and a fixture pile up allowed Newcastle to beat them to the League title. Leigh blamed the club for allowing this to happen and, in temper, rejoined Stoke. At this point he decided to supplement his expenses by writing for *The Times* and the *Daily Mail* as well as the *Football Evening News*. His style was a little too intellectual for some of his readers, what his biographer, Spencer Vignes, called his "erudite style of writing," not a complaint one usually hears about the words of footballers. His stay at Stoke was, on this occasion, short lived. During a post match dinner following Stoke's fixture with Sunderland, the guest of a Sunderland director hurled insults at the Stoke team. One of the insults used described Stoke as "ten cads and a goalkeeper", a step too far for the Stoke keeper who promptly punched him in the face! This led to a fourteen day suspension and an eventual transfer to – Sunderland!

It was not the only occasion when Leigh was seen to possess a temper. At half time during the Wales v England international, Leigh had an unpleasant conversation with the England selectors who thought that his language was "not such as might be expected from a gentleman." The move to Sunderland, however, was a good one. He helped to keep Sunderland in Division 1 and the following season, 1908/9 they finished third. The highlight of this season came in December 1908 when local rivals Newcastle United, later to be crowned champions, were defeated 9-1 at St James's Park. It remains to this day Sunderland's biggest ever away win and Newcastle's heaviest home defeat.

Controversy followed Leigh whoever he played for but there can be no question that he provided entertainment. He was a real crowd pleaser, waving to the crowd or performing gymnastics on the crossbar when play was at the other end of the field. When playing for Everton he once sat on the crossbar during a break in the play. With his white gloves, twin peaked cap and padded knee bandages, Leigh was an unmistakable figure who insisted upon wearing a lucky undershirt which he never washed and dirty shorts which 'carried the scars of battle.' A great practical joker, Leigh was the spiritual ancestor of Bruce Grobbelaar, the highly successful Liverpool goalkeeper of the 1980s – particularly when wobbling his knees as the opposition player was about to take a penalty kick against him. Leigh had an impressive record of saving penalties. Thomas Richards, in a profile published in *Gwr o Athrylith*, describes the scene:

> I have always believed that Roose grew to his full height as a man in the purgatorial crisis of a penalty, drying off the clay around his feet, washing away the dross which entered his character with the gold. Arthur's sword against the bare fist. Then came the sword; the ball travelled like a bolt from the foot of the penalty taking forward, and in the blink of

> an eyelid, revolution, a thump and the ball landed in the heath and gorse of the 'Buarth'.

In his style of play Leigh resembled a modern day 'sweeper', always believing that a good goalkeeper would always come out to meet the danger, regardless of personal consequences. As he wrote in 1906, the keeper must "if necessary go head first into a pack into which many men would hesitate to insert a foot, and take the consequent gruelling like a Spartan." Goalkeepers don't come out of goal more often because "of their regard for personal consequences." Leigh believed strongly in goalkeepers adopting an innovative attitude, not being stereotypical in their approach, being "at liberty to cultivate anything" and that players prepared to do this would go far. Although he did get caught out occasionally, the *Bristol Times* could see the virtues of his approach,

> Few men exhibit their personality so vividly in their play as L.R. Roose…. He rarely stands listlessly by the goalpost even when the ball is at the other end of the enclosure, but is ever following the play keenly and closely. Directly his charge is threatened, he is on the move. He thinks nothing of dashing out 10 or 15 yards, even when his backs have as good a chance of clearing as he makes for himself. He will also rush along the touchline, field the ball, and get in a kick too, to keep the game going briskly.

Leigh also had great success when carrying the ball to the halfway line, which keepers were allowed to do, and launching an attack on the opposition goal. So successful was he that by 1912 the law had changed and goalkeepers were confined to their penalty area if they wished to handle the ball.

Off the field, Leigh was also a controversial character. While at Sunderland, the Football League took an interest in his travel expenses, encouraged, no doubt, by claims which read 'a pistol to ward off the opposition', using the toilet twice and a claim for the purchase of a coat and gloves to keep warm during matches. No charges were ever brought. While at Stoke, he once missed the train to Birmingham and charged the club £31 in expenses which he used in order to hire a private train. Around town Leigh cut a dashing figure, eating at the best restaurants, drinking at the best clubs and enjoying the company of the most attractive women. He bought his suits from Savile Row and his nephew clearly remembers him wearing full morning dress, including a top hat, when dining in Scott's Restaurant, Piccadilly. Towards the end of 1909, Leigh began a relationship with Marie Lloyd, the queen of the music halls and a very well known personality in her own right. She had been born in the slums of London's East End but was reputed to be earning £600 a week by the time she was a teenager. Her marriage to the singer Alec Hurley was in trouble and Leigh, one of Britain's most 'eligible bachelors', was on hand to provide comfort. For much of that season, 1909/10, they supported each other on the stage and playing field but by the end of the summer the affair had come to an end. Marie turned her gaze to jockey and Derby winner Bernard Dillon and, when Alec Hurley died in 1914, she married him. Both struggled with alcohol related problems and Marie died in 1922 after collapsing on stage with many in the audience thinking that it was part of the act. Reports confirm that 100,000 people attended her funeral.

Leigh's remarkable career was coming to an end. He broke his wrist in November 1909 and the following March played his 24th and last match for Wales, a 2-2 draw with Scotland. In 1911 he was released by Sunderland following a broken arm and Leigh wound his career down by making guest appearances for clubs such as Glasgow Celtic, Aston Villa, Huddersfield and Port Vale. He joined Arsenal as player-coach in December 1911 but played his last game in April 1912, just as the new law for goalkeepers, which he had made necessary, was being introduced. It was time to resume his medical commitments and join the after dinner speaker circuit.

With the outbreak of war in August 1914 Leigh had a decision to make. Despite his pacifist father's objections, it was a decision that Leigh was able to make quickly. His medical experience was bound to be extremely useful so Leigh had no trouble in joining the Royal Army Medical Corps and he was quickly despatched to Rouen to treat injured soldiers. He became part of the 'casualty evacuation chain', a series of hospitals treating casualties before they were transferred home. The historian Peter Hart describes graphically the work of this often overlooked unit;

> While the men on both sides sought to destroy the lives of

> their enemies, it was their task to try and patch up the results of the general mayhem. The crunching, flensing power of the splinters, the scything of machine guns, the sudden shattering impact of the snipers bullet all caused bodily wounds that needed urgent medical treatment.... Its work never ceased for a moment.

Hart goes on to say;

> Someone somewhere always needed to be swiftly diagnosed, tended, bandaged, splinted, vaccinated, stitched, operated upon, or simply drugged with morphine till all pain and life ebbed away.

The efforts of men such as Leigh Roose went largely unsung but were worthy of "earnest admiration."

At this point the story of Leigh Roose becomes shrouded in some mystery. It is known in April 1915 he was transferred to Gallipoli. The Dardanelles campaign was a disaster. Leigh continued to work in the hospitals and wrote of his experiences to friends. One such friend, George Holley the England and Sunderland inside forward, received a letter in June 1915 which describes vividly the conditions that those involved in the Gallipoli landings experienced;

> If ever there was a hell on this occasionally volatile planet then this oppressively hot, dusty, diseased place has to be it. If I have seen the fragments of one plucky youth whose body... or what there remains of it... has been swollen out of all proportion by the sun, I have seen several hundred. The bombardment is relentless to the extent that you become accustomed to its time, a permanent rata-tat-tat complemented by bursting shells... and yet at night the stars are so bright in this largest of skies that one cannot help but be pervaded with a feeling of serenity, peculiar as that appears.

It appears that he had even taken some injured soldiers to Egypt but, following the evacuation of Gallipoli, nothing more was heard of him. It appears that, on a return to London in July 1916, Leigh joined the 9th Battalion of the Royal Fusiliers as a private, probably in search of some real action. It has since been established by his biographer, Spencer Vignes, that the misspelling of his name as Rouse led to the confusion as to his whereabouts that, following Vignes' research, the events leading to his death are now known.

The 'real action' was not long in coming and in the summer of 1916 Leigh was sent to the Western Front to play his part on the Somme battlefield. And it proved to be an heroic part. After taking part in the capture of Ration Trench near Dainville, Leigh was amongst those who resisted the German counter attack and was awarded the Military Medal in the process. It was clear from the report in the *London Gazette* on September 21st that his goalkeeping skills – those of bravery and the ability to throw a ball great distances – had been put to good use;

> He managed to get back along the trench and, though nearly choked with fumes with his clothes burnt, refused to go to the dressing station. He continued to throw bombs until his arm gave out, and then, joining the covering party, used his rifle with great effect.

Following this success, Leigh got a break from the front line but by early October he was back in the action, this time for his final contribution. On 7th October, the 8th and 9th Royal Fusiliers were given the task of attacking two roads leading north west and north east out of the village of Guedecourt. During this fine, if rather damp windy day, the British Army had some successes. The advance on the Albert-Bapaume road led to the capture of Le Sars, while the French reached to within 200 yards of Sailly. For the 9th Royal Fusiliers, however, the day was a disaster with the loss of 332 officers and soldiers killed or injured. Leigh, in the second line of Fusiliers to go over the top, was seen, in No Man's Land, running towards the enemy firing his gun. The last sight of him was lying in a bomb crater, probably already dead. The attack had been a failure and one of Britain's greatest footballers had been lost. If he had been wearing his lucky undershirt, on this occasion it did him no good. His body was never found and his name, still misspelt, is with those of 72,000 others on the Thiepval Memorial. He was thirty-eight.

Leigh's loss was keenly felt by all who new him. The *Athletic Times*, acknowledging his temperament and character, described him as "dexterous though daring, valiant though volatile" and concluding that he was "a clever man undoubtedly, but one entirely unrestrained in word or action." While accepting the truth of this assessment, it is only part of the story. Leigh Richmond Roose, along with Billy Meredith, did more to put Welsh football on the map than any other player. That, coupled with his ability to entertain thousands of spectators, demands that he be remembered as a sportsman of real significance, one who died as bravely as he played.

'Our dusky friend' – The Remarkable Story of Walter Tull

Of the sportsman in this book, the story of Walter Tull is perhaps the most remarkable. As one of the first British born black army officers, the first black officer to lead British troops into battle and the first black outfield player to play professional football in England, Walter Tull merits his place in the cultural history of Britain. It is a contribution to British history that is finally being recognised through the publication of an excellent biography written by Phil Vasili, the making of a TV documentary and a series of articles published in historical magazines and on the internet. Walter Tull even warrants a place on the history curriculum followed in many schools. Walter Tull has finally arrived, and not before time.

Walter Tull was born on April 28th 1888 at Folkestone in Kent, the son of Daniel and Alice Tull. Daniel, a joiner, had been born in Barbados in 1856 and left home to settle in England in 1876. The couple appear to have had a happy 'mixed' marriage and it was not long before the children began to arrive. The first, a daughter, died in infancy but five more followed, three boys and two girls, Walter being the third boy and the fifth child in total. Unfortunately, tragedy was to hit the family for a second time when Alice died of breast cancer in 1895 leaving her husband with five children, all thirteen years or under, to raise. Daniel quickly remarried, the bride being Clara, the 26-year old niece of his first wife. The marriage was not entirely one of convenience as before long Miriam Victoria was born. However tragedy soon struck once again when, on 10th December 1897, Daniel died of heart disease. Clara was clearly going to find it difficult to cope with six children and no husband so it was inevitable that she would look for solutions that would ease her problems. A partial answer was found when the Methodist community agreed to sponsor an application for Walter and his brother Edward to move into a Children's Home and Orphanage in Bethnal Green, London. Clara's logic appeared to be that the two girls could help with the baby while William, the oldest boy at 15, would go out to work. As a result Walter (9 years old) and Edward (11 years old) moved to the orphanage on February 24th 1898.

Walter's time at the orphanage was, in the context of the time, reasonably successful. On moving in, he was examined and deemed to be physically fit, well equipped to be able to cope with the demands of being away from his family. Indeed, on occasions both he and Edward were allowed to visit the family for short periods. However it does not seem that Walter felt close to the rest of his family. When he joined the orphanage it was Edward who he named as next of kin. The orphanage introduced Walter to organised sport and both boys had the opportunity to display their considerable skills, particularly on the football field. For Edward though, the time spent at the orphanage was short lived. In 1900, he was adopted by the Warnock family and moved to Vincent Street, Glasgow where he began a lifetime journey of achievement to rival that of his brother. Edward's adoptive father was a qualified dentist and he was keen to train his new son for a life in that profession. In 1912 Edward Tull-Warnock became Britain's first black dentist as well as finding the time to play a respectable level of football in Scottish League Division 2 with Ayr Parkhouse and then Girvan Athletic. Walter found the orphanage more difficult when Edward left although it was not long before he was impressing in the football team, first as a left wing and later as left back. He also showed his talent for cricket. In 1905 he took his first steps towards a career when he became an apprentice in the printing department of the Children Homes and Orphanage. In 1907, with a job in printing before him, Walter moved out of the orphanage and into lodgings at Darnley Road Hostel.

It was now that Walter's football career began to take off. In October 1908, he had a trial with Clapton FC, then one of the strongest amateur sides in the country, and by the end of that season Walter had won the FA Amateur Cup, the London Senior Cup and the London County Cup with his new team. It was inevitable that he would attract interest from the professional clubs, not that Walter found it easy to reconcile the thought of professional football with his strongly held philosophy on life. Walter believed, according to Vasili, in the idea of 'muscular Christianity', that physical weakness is unnatural because it is a reflection of moral weakness and that people should try to become physically stronger through the living of good, moral Christian lives. Playing sport was about character building and developing an active mind through physical fitness. Playing for financial gain would make sport a commodity with profit as the ultimate objective with players as nothing more than paid labour. Nevertheless, despite these misgivings, Walter signed for Tottenham Hotspur for a £10 signing on fee and a weekly wage of £4, the maximum allowed at the time. He was taken on the club's summer tour where he impressed sufficiently to start 'Spurs' first season in Division 1 in season 1909/10.

It was not, however, to be a season which Walter would remember with any affection. The first game, against a strong Sunderland team containing Leigh Roose, was lost 3-1 and the press were critical of Walter's performance. Part of the problem was that Walter had replaced the gifted free scoring England centre forward Vivian Woodward who had moved to Chelsea. They were difficult boots to fill. The second match was lost 4-2 at Everton, although the *Daily Chronicle* did say that "Tull showed much promise." A 2-2 draw with Manchester United had the *Athletic News* talking of his coolness, passing ability, ball control and his ability to read the game. The *Daily Chronicle* also reported that in this match he was "a class superior to that shown by most of his colleagues" and concluded that his display "must have astounded everyone who saw it." But the widespread view was that Walter lacked pace and was prone to inconsistency. The crunch came in his seventh game, at Bristol City. Although reports of his performance in this game were generally good and talked of him being "as energetic as ever, responsible for some pretty work", it was in this game that Walter was first subjected to racial abuse.

Walter's ethnicity was obvious to all and was frequently referred to in newspaper reports. Following the Sunderland game, newspapers in the north east referred to the 'coloured man', and the *Football Star,* rather patronisingly, spoke of "our dusky friend with his clever footwork." Although attitude towards race was not as hostile as in the USA, black men were regarded as something very different and certainly not as 'equals', maybe more of a curiosity rather than a threat. Part of the problem was that there was no high profile forerunner to ease the pressure on Walter. Phil Vasili has shown us that there were 'men of colour' making their way in sport.

The first black footballer in England was the Preston North End goalkeeper Arthur Wharton in 1886 while in Scotland Robert 'Darkie' Walker played for Queens Park and Third Lanark in the 1870s. Andrew Watson, also of Queens Park, became a Scottish international in 1881 but neither Scotsman were professional players. Arthur 'Darkie' Wharton, as the first non-white footballer to earn a living from the game, is of particular interest. Initially intending to follow his father into the church, Wharton soon caught the 'sports bug' and played in goal for Darlington. He moved to Preston North End just before their 'golden', invincible years, leaving in 1887 in order to become a sprinter. As Patrick Barclay points out, it is strange that a goalkeeper should be a sprinter. Wharton, however won the Amateur Athletics Association 100 yards title in 1886 when he was only twenty years old, equalling the world record of 10 seconds in the process. The sprinting career did not last, however, and Wharton returned to football. He played for both Rotherham and Sheffield United, combining his football career with managing a pub, but developed a drinking problem. His career ended at Stockport County in 1902 and he worked as a haulage hand in a colliery near Doncaster until he died in 1930. Arthur Wharton remained a forgotten man lying in an unmarked cemetery for the next 71 years until a memorial stone was erected, followed by his induction, with Gary Lineker, Pat Jennings and Peter Schmeichel, into the English Football Hall of Fame.

It wasn't only football that saw the early examples of non-white competitors beginning to make their mark. James Peters, a Manchester born dockworker represented England at Rugby Union before turning to Rugby League while many black boxers plied their trade, particularly in the boxing booths. Even in boxing prejudice was rife – no black boxer was allowed to fight for a British title until Randolph Turpin in 1948. Even when black sportsmen did succeed in the early years of the century, some pointed to their physical advantages. The Revd. F.B. Meyer led a campaign arguing that matching black against white was unfair. In 1911 when the African-American boxer Jack Johnson was due to fight 'Bombardier' Billy Wells in London, Meyer believed that their "God given differences" made the contest invalid. Such attitudes made it almost impossible for Walter to be judged on his ability alone. As Vasili points out, K.S. Ranjitsinhji was a giant of both Victorian and Edwardian cricket but he was not a comparable figure. Playing with the style, beauty and grace of the Indian prince that he was, Ranji was evidence that class and cultural affiliation allowed a 'man of colour' to overcome any difficulty of race. Walter Tull had no such advantage.

The Bristol City match on 2nd October 1909 was very significant for Walter and his football future. That there was racist abuse directed at Walter is not in question. The correspondent of the *Football Star* reported "colour prejudice" and talked of "Bristol hooligans" while the *Northampton Echo* made it very clear that Walter was being abused.

> A section of the spectators made a cowardly attack on him in language lower than Billingsgate.... Tull is so clean in mind and method as to be a model for all white men who play football whether they be amateur or professional. In point of ability if not actual achievement, Tull was the best forward on the field.

There is no doubt as where that particular newspaper's sympathy lay but the Bristol press was strangely silent on the matter. Meanwhile, the 'Spurs' management reacted to the treatment dished out to Walter in a way that raises many questions. Over the next two years, Walter only played three more games for the first team. Possibly Walter was left traumatised by the experience but it could also be argued that 'Spurs' did little to support him. The following season, 1910/11, the Reserves won their League and Walter contributed 10 goals to the cause but his time at Tottenham was coming to an end. In October 1911 Walter was signed by Northampton Town for 'a substantial fee' plus Charlie Brittain moving in the opposite direction.

The move to Northampton was a good one for Walter. It is likely that a move to a more parochial, less intense environment helped Walter to play his best football. He also came under the influence of the man who signed him, the revolutionary Herbert Chapman, one of the greatest, if not the greatest English football manager in history. Chapman had begun his managerial career at Northampton in 1907 and went on to build both Huddersfield Town and Arsenal into the best teams of their era. Chapman left for Leeds City the following year but Walter stayed until the outbreak of war, scoring 9 goals in 110 league appearances. Most of his football was now being played at wing half rather than inside forward, more of a midfield role where his lack of pace was not such a problem. By 1914 Walter was Northampton's biggest star and it appears likely that he was on the verge of signing for Glasgow Rangers.

The outbreak of war was to change everything for Walter. A letter sent by the Secretary of the F.A., Fred Wall, might have played a part in his decision to volunteer. The letter, sent to all clubs south of the River Trent, informed footballers of the 17th (Service) Battalion, Middlesex Regiment and encouraged all unmarried players, along with officials and supporters, to join. On 21st December 1914 Walter took the plunge and joined up. By November 1915 his training was complete and he was on his way to the Western Front. Here Walter was quickly into the action in the front line between La Basse and Loos and for the next five months he was in and out of the action around the Givenchy/Bethune region of Northern France. The troops alternated between the front line, second line, reserve line and rest over periods of four weeks and it appears that Walter adapted well to this routine. However, nine continuous days of shelling in April 1916 gave him shell shock and led to his removal from the front line. Walter was admitted to the Anglo-American Hospital at Wimereux on 28th April and by the 9th May he was on the hospital ship *St Denis* sailing for home. He was not alone. Vasili tells us that 50,000 men were treated for nervous complaints in the second half of 1916 while around 200,000 soldiers were discharged from the Army on psychiatric grounds during the war. Vasili also tells us that Walter was likely to have been a patient at Sandgate Military Hospital in Folkestone but this is unconfirmed. What is certain, however, is that Walter had spent seven months at the Front without leave. Nevertheless, in August, fit and able once again, he was with the 27th and 6th Battalions of the Middlesex Regiments and back in combat by 29th October. He now spent the next three weeks fighting on the Somme.

It was at this point that Walter became attracted to the idea of becoming an officer. That he saw himself in this way should not surprise us. Perhaps his experience in the orphanage had prepared him well for life in the army. Moreover, Walter's laid back temperament coupled with a single minded determination would be an asset in an officer. During his career to date, both as a footballer and as an army private, Walter had earned the respect of those around him. There were plenty of opportunities for advancement – it has been calculated that 14.6% of officers lost their lives in the War. On the 25th November 1916, supported by references from Northampton Football Club, Walter submitted his application. By February 1917, following his departure from the Somme as a result of trench-foot, Walter had begun his training. Normally it could take up to two years but Walter completed his officer training in a little over three months a reflection of the desperate need for replacement officers as much as of Walter's undoubted suitability for the role. All practical tests and exams successfully completed, Walter graduated on 29th May 1917, first as a Sergeant, then Lieutenant, and finally a 2nd Lieutenant in the Special Reserve of Officers, the first black infantry officer in the British Army. He now had the unenviable job of ensuring discipline and raising morale and, although Walter now had more influence and the reward of privileges such as better food and drink, there was an expectation that he would show initiative when on the battlefield.

There were prejudices to be overcome before Walter could achieve this position. As recently as 1886 Lord Wolseley at the War Office had said,

> Let us keep our British Regiments strictly British.... If ever we begin to fill our ranks with alien races our downfall will most surely follow.

Indeed Vasili reminds us that, according to the *Manual of Military Law*, black soldiers of any rank were not desirable. Military Chiefs of Staff, supported by government ministers, believed that white soldiers would not take orders from black officers or 'men of colour' and that in no circumstances would it be appropriate for black soldiers to serve on the front line. The horrors of World War 1 was to change that, albeit slowly. By 1918 the Army had officially allowed the colour bar to be broken.

It wasn't very long before Walter's leadership skills were being put to the test. Between 7th and 15th June he was fighting in the Battle of Messines using explosives to destroy German trenches but before long the battalion became involved in the nightmare that was

Passchendaele. There was some initial success for Walter and his troops at the Battle of Menin Ridge Road but at the cost of 15 killed and 23 missing, losses which contributed to the average cost of 37,000 casualties lost for each kilometre of land captured, land that was all lost in the Spring Offensive of March 1918.

Walter continued to be involved in action after Passchendaele and fought in Italy during the winter of 1917/18. It was here that, on Christmas Eve, Walter led a reconnaissance raid across the fast flowing River Piave, the first documented evidence of a black officer leading British troops into action. New Years Day 1918 saw Walter once again leading troops into action, on this occasion taking German prisoners without incurring casualties. For this success, Walter was cited for his bravery by his commanding officer Major General Lawford. (It is interesting to note that after the war Lawford settled in Florida where his only son, Peter, became an actor, a member of the infamous 'Rat Pack', friend of Marilyn Monroe and brother-in-law of US President John F Kennedy.) With the onset of the Spring Offensive in March, Walter, back on the Western Front, was at the heart of attempts to repel the German advance. In the desperate retreat across the Arras-Bapaume Road on 25th March, Walter was killed when a machine gun bullet pierced his neck. He had spent five months in continuous action and not had any leave since the previous summer. His devastated men made several attempts to recover his body but, in the face of enemy fire, repeatedly failed. Walter's body was never recovered. After surviving the first Battle of the Somme it is somewhat ironic that he should die in the second.

Tributes were not long in coming. On 12th April the *Rushden Echo* reported,

> The deceased sportsman was an officer and a gentleman every inch of him, and the news of his death will come as a great shock to his many Rushden friends.

Second Lieutenant Pickard wrote to Walter's devastated brother Edward,

> Allow me to say how popular he was throughout the Battalion He was brave and conscientious; he had been

> recommended for The Military Cross and had certainly earned it; the commanding Officer had every confidence in him and he was liked by his Men… personally I have lost a friend.

This reference to the Military Cross is the first in a battle for recognition which was resumed ninety years later. In recent years, as interest in Walter has intensified, memorials to his memory have appeared. He is, of course, named on the Arras Memorial but, in more recent times, Northampton in particular has begun to give Walter the recognition that he deserves. Sixfields Stadium, the home of Northampton Town, has a memorial which stands in a Garden of Remembrance. The inscription reads

> Through his actions, WDJ Tull ridiculed the barriers of ignorance that tried to deny people of colour equality with their contemporaries. His life stands testament to a determination to confront those people and those obstacles that sought to diminish him and the world in which he lived. It reveals a man, though rendered breathless in his prime, whose strong heart still beats loudly. This memorial marks an area of reflective space as a Garden of Remembrance.

This is an appropriate, if somewhat belated, tribute to a man who has a significant place in British social history and the battle for equality. The road leading to the stadium has been re-named Walter Tull Way while the headquarters of the Northampton Probation Service is now Walter Tull House. Since 2009, moves have been made to ensure that, if and when Tottenham Hotspur move to a new stadium, a statue of Walter should be erected in his memory, an attempt perhaps to make good the lack of support given to Walter a century ago. In Dover, his mother's home town, Walter's name now appears on the town's War Memorial.

The battle to gain military recognition for Walter's bravery on the battlefield has proved to be more difficult. That Walter deserves recognition is beyond question. By leading his men in the situations that he did, particularly when leading them back to safety without incurring casualties, he accomplished deeds that have been recognised when performed by others. Walter had twice led his Company across the River Piave on a raid and returned them to safety. He had been Mentioned in Despatches for his 'gallantry and coolness' under fire. The Military Cross is awarded for those who 'distinguished themselves in battle' and, according to the letters written by Major Poole and Second Lieutenant Pickard, Walter meets this criteria. The Ministry of Defence have continued to use every possible argument to deny Walter this honour, from a fear that it will open the floodgates to the rule that a Military Cross cannot be awarded more than five years after the event. His supporters, who include the MP's Brian Binley (Northampton), David Lammy (Tottenham) and Glenda Jackson, have argued that men who did similar heroic deeds in battle have been honoured but, as yet, the Ministry have refused to bend. Perseverance with this campaign must surely bring its reward. It would be a fitting tribute to a remarkable man if, a century after his death, a way could be found to honour one of the most significant figures in the struggle for racial equality.

"Don't mess with me" – The Controversial Career of Sandy Turnbull

Among the most interesting characters to emerge in this book is Manchester United footballer Sandy Turnbull, the first of a series of lowland, working class Scotsmen who have played a significant role in the history of one of the world's leading football clubs. Followed by Matt Busby and Alex Ferguson, Sandy Turnbull became an important figure in the first great Manchester United team. If Sandy had played one hundred years later he would have been a multi millionaire and a regular headliner on the back pages. He would also have been a front page tabloid villain. His career was surrounded by controversy and came to an end in the ignominy of a lifetime ban from the game he loved, before his life was ended in confusion and mystery at the Battle of Arras in May 1917. His story is almost worth a book on its own.

Sandy was born in the small village of Hurlford near Kilmarnock on 30th July 1884, the second of seven children. His father, James, a miner in the local Ayrshire coalfield, died at the age of 41 when Sandy was sixteen, leaving him as the main breadwinner. Sandy was already working underground and had been since leaving school at 14 but he was also showing promise as a young footballer. Each Saturday afternoon he would exchange the dirt and the dust of the colliery for the escapism of the football field turning out for his local team Hurlford Thistle. The 1901 census shows Sandy still employed underground but by then following year the scouts were calling and Sandy was offered professional terms. At this time young Scottish boys were as sought after by the big English clubs much as the Brazilian, Italian and Spanish youngsters a hundred years later and it was inevitable that the tough competitive striker would head south in search of fame and fortune. When Manchester City offered him £3 a week, treble his wages in the mines and equivalent to £250 a week today, it proved an impossible offer to turn down.

Sandy made an immediate impact and, by the end of his first season in Manchester, City had won the 2nd Division title with their new Scottish striker contributing 12 goals. The club's first season back in the top division, 1903/4, was spectacular and only two defeats at the end of the season, to Aston Villa and Everton, allowed Sheffield Wednesday to pip them to the title by three points. The game with Villa gave Sandy his first taste of notoriety. During a tempestuous battle Sandy became embroiled in a dispute with the Villa captain Alex Leake. Sandy had been giving the English international a torrid time leading to the frustrated Leake throwing mud at his opponent. Sandy reacted with a two-fingered gesture so Leake punched him. A fight ensued. Somehow both players stayed on the pitch but at the end of the game Sandy was dragged into the Villa changing room where he was given what can best be described as a 'going over' emerging looking much the worse for the experience.

There was, however, to be some consolation when, on the Saturday before City's final league game, nineteen year old Sandy was part of an FA Cup winning team for the first time. In the first all Lancashire final, City defeated 2nd Division Bolton 1-0 with Billy Meredith, the 'Welsh Wizard', scoring the only goal of the game. There was qualified praise for the victors with *The Times* offering the opinion that the lack of a southern team being involved had led to there being less interest than usual in the final. Meredith, they reported, did little other than score the goal although "Turnbull made some fine runs". City, it was said, played the more "scientific football" and Bolton adopted a much more "kick and rush" style of playing. Not that City worried much about any of this when, after being entertained by "The Association of Lancastrians", they returned to Manchester with the Cup.

Scandal was soon to follow. Following the notorious Villa-City game at the end of the season, Alex Leake claimed that Billy Meredith had offered him £10 to throw the game, thereby giving City a chance of winning the title. Meredith was found guilty and suspended for eighteen months as well as being fined. When City refused to help him financially, Meredith went public over illegal payments being made to players. In October 1904, just six months after the Cup Final triumph, a consultative committee of the FA, amazed by the club's rapid improvement over recent years, began an investigation into the affairs of Manchester City. The investigation included scrutiny into their transfer activities. It was discovered that negotiations relating to certain players had been concluded outside FA regulations and that City's directors had attempted to conceal some of the facts. By the spring of 1905 it had emerged that Meredith's claims had substance and that City were paying some players £6-£7 a week, nearly double the agreed maximum wage. The Club Secretary and directors were given bans and the offending footballers, including Sandy, were suspended from playing organised football until 1st January 1907. The manager, Tom Maley, was banned for life. Despite a supporting petition containing 4,182 signatures being presented to the FA, their pleas for a review of this penalty was flatly rejected. Five directors resigned and all the offending players were put up for sale, proceeds to go towards paying the fines imposed on the club. City arranged an auction at the Queens Hotel, Manchester for the players and offered an open invitation to secretaries of Football League and Southern League clubs to attend. The Manchester United manager/secretary Ernest Mangnall, in a move that would match any of the dealings later carried out by Ferguson or Busby, took advantage of his close proximity to affairs to steal a march on his rivals. Recently promoted, United needed to strengthen their resources and it is likely that Mangnall conducted negotiations beforehand. When the 'pub auction' was held, Sandy, 'Welsh Wizard' Meredith and two other of City's best players, Herbert Burgess and Jimmy Bannister, were on their way across the city to United. On the 1st January 1907 Sandy Turnbull became a Manchester United footballer.

Sandy's time at United proved to be even more successful and even more controversial. The controversy came first when, on 21st December 1907 at United's Bank Street ground, he became the first player ever to be sent off in a Manchester derby. The *Manchester Guardian* takes up the story,

> Sandy Turnbull and Bill Eadie made themselves ridiculous early in the game by repeatedly making grimaces at each other and, in the second half Turnbull lost self control so far as to strike George Dorsett to the ground. He was promptly ordered off the field by the referee.

There is no doubt that Sandy had a combative side to his character. In an article written by John Litchfield one hundred years later, he describes the brutal, ill-disciplined side of his make up:

> He stares out from the old team pictures unsmiling, hair receding, robust knees pulled together, one eye brow quizzically raised. He looks like and was a bruising character.... Something in his expression says 'Don't mess with me!'

It could almost be a description of Wayne Rooney, who Sandy with his stocky build physically resembles. For many supporters, Sandy was exactly what they looked for in a player. Litchfield describes him as a player who, in his own way, represented the man on the terraces:

> a working man's hero in the time of straw boaters and cloth caps, when the rise of professional sport foretold the rise of the common man"

Sandy had become a firm favourite with the fans, a status confirmed when at the end of his first full season, 1907/8, the club won their first ever League title. Sandy made a massive contribution with 25 goals in 30 league games and a total of 27 goals in 35 matches in all competitions.

Manchester United were not then the club that they are today – crowds of 7,000 to watch them play Bury and 10,000 to see the clinching 5-1 win over Sunderland confirm that – but this was the first significant step on their journey. The days of the Busby Babes, Best, Law and Charlton and the remarkable era of Alex Ferguson were decades into the future but the team of which Sandy was a part were the first to alert the world as to what was possible. The *Manchester Evening News* had no doubts about Sandy's contribution;

> A man of big shoulders and quick feet and active brain, Sandy is a great player, and a more unselfish inside man I never saw. A great opportunist with class written all over his football.

The *Manchester Guardian* columnist 'An Old International' agreed, citing the partnership with Meredith as crucial to United's success.

> When Meredith lifts the ball across the goal there are invariably three of his partners in a line ready to receive it and generally it is Sandy Turnbull who puts the finishing touch to Meredith's artistry.

This first title was only the beginning. The following season, 1908/9, saw Manchester United win the FA Cup for the first time when they defeated Bristol City 1-0 at Crystal Palace. Before the game there was a serious doubt as to whether or not Sandy would play. A recent knee injury was giving him pain but he was desperate to play in what had now become the showpiece game of the season. Fortunately his captain, Charlie Roberts, agreed. "Let him play," argued Roberts, "he might get a goal and if he does we can afford to carry him." United were on top throughout the game and looked like winners from the start. The only goal came when a Harold Halse shot caught the underside of the cross bar and rebounded to Sandy who "with toe kept well down, sent in a sharp 'grounder' quite beyond the reach of Clay in the Bristol City goal." The captain's hunch had proved correct and United had won their first FA Cup. The following Monday the *Athletic News* printed the supporters song paying tribute to their hero,

> Why we thought you were 'crocked'
> Dashing Sandy,
> That to fame your road was blocked,
> Hard lines Sandy,
> But you came up to scratch
> Made an effort for THE match
> When Halse hit the shiv-ring bar,
> Lucky Sandy
> There were groans heard near and far,
> Deep ones Sandy,
> But the ball was on the bound,
> And your boot was safe and sound,
> When the net your great shot found,
> Champion Sandy...

Manchester United was now a force to be reckoned with and in February1910 their new status was confirmed when they moved to a new ground, Old Trafford. The first game to be played in what was to become one of the most famous venues in football was against Liverpool on 19th February and Sandy achieved the honour of scoring the opening goal in front of a capacity 45,000 crowd. The *Manchester Guardian* reported that Sandy met a cross only "a foot or two off the ground... with that extra durable head of his and drove it hard into the goal." Although United led 2-0 and then 3-1 they managed to lose the game 4-3 but Sandy had added further to his reputation for scoring on the big occasion. Another championship followed in 1910/11 when Aston Villa missed out by a single point. Sandy scored 19 league goals from his 38 appearances and United could reasonably claim to be the most successful team in the country.

There was still controversy however. Sandy, with Billy Meredith, was at the forefront of efforts to form the Association Footballers Union following the authorities' failure to award compensation to the family of Thomas Blackstock, a fellow United player, who died after heading a ball. The United players refused to leave the Union and were briefly banned after posing for a picture entitled 'The Outcasts'. When other professionals supported the cause the Football League gave way. Sandy still incurred the anger of some directors after showing 'insubordinate behaviour', not helped after the Cup Final when the missing lid from the trophy was discovered in Sandy's jacket pocket. It is possible that it was Sandy's reputation as something of a trouble maker that cost him the opportunity of playing for Scotland. For a striker with his record not to have been given the chance of gaining international honours is surprising and can only be explained by Sandy's ability to attract scandal. The biggest scandal, however, came as Sandy's colourful career was running down. Following their league title win in 1911, United reverted to being a mid-table team, finishing 13th, 4th and 14th in the league between 1912 and the outbreak of war. Sandy was given a joint testimonial in 1914 with United full back George Stacey and the pair shared gate receipts of £1,216 following a match against Manchester City, a sizable sum at the time. Yet the career of a footballer was a brief one with none of the opportunities for work available today. A full house at Old Trafford could result in total takings of up to £3,000, only about £50 of which went to players and officials in a normal game, leaving them feeling very undervalued. The making of a little money through 'illicit' means therefore was always a temptation for the players. It was clear that, with the war showing no sign of ending any time soon, the future was unclear for professional footballers. Perhaps their careers were about to end for good. On Good Friday, 2nd April 1915, as the season drew to a close, Manchester United beat Liverpool 2-0 at Old Trafford, a result which confirmed United's place in the First Division while doing nothing to harm Liverpool's mid table position. A couple of weeks later a letter appeared in the *Sporting Chronicle* signed 'Football King' on behalf of a firm of bookmakers asking if anyone could help with information relating to a betting scam. The letter alleged that several players from both teams had bet on a 2-0 win for United. Sandy, although not playing in the game, was one of those under suspicion.

The game itself appears to have been a strange affair. The *Sporting Chronicle* described it as "the most uninteresting game ever seen at the ground" while the United manager, John Robson, was so disgusted with the performance of both teams that he left the ground before the final whistle. A committee was assembled by the Football League to examine the situation. The referee, John Sharp, told the committee that he suspected that something was amiss but decided to carry on with the game although it was the most extraordinary match that he had ever officiated over. It emerged that Jackie Sheldon, the ex-United, Liverpool player, had met Sandy with his teammates Arthur Whalley and Enoch West in the Dog and Partridge pub near the ground on the morning of the match. They agreed on a 2-0 win for United with a goal in each half. The players pleaded their innocence but Liverpool's missed penalty and Billy Meredith's claims that nobody would pass the ball to him did nothing to help their case. When Liverpool's Fred Pagnam hit the bar late in the game, his teammates were furious as a goal would have ruined the result. On 27th December 1915, three Manchester United players, Sandy, Enoch West and Arthur Whalley along with four Liverpool players, ringleader Sheldon, Tom Miller, Bob Pursell and Thomas Fairfoul, were banned from playing for life. Enoch West continued to plead his innocence and even tried suing the FA for libel. His reward was to remain banned when all the others were reinstated in 1919 as recognition 'of their service to the country' during the war. West was finally reinstated in 1945. For Sandy however, the lifting of the ban came too late for him even to see his reputation restored.

With Sandy's football career seemingly over he, along with Sheldon and Whalley, joined the footballer's battalion of the Middlesex Regiment in early 1916. Also joining the Middlesex Regiment 1st 'Football Battalion' was an ex teammate of Sandy's, Oscar Linkson. Oscar had played a total of 59 games for Manchester United between 1908-1913 after joining them from his home town club, Barnet Alston. He was the youngest of five boys, three of whom died in infancy and another of disease as a result of serving in the Boer War, and he also had four sisters, three of whom survived into adulthood.

Oscar was a tough right full back who once played over half a match with a broken jaw and was described by the *Athletic News* as "a nicely built lad, nimble on his feet, and kicks well ...has the makings of a fine back". He was signed by United when they came across him during a tour of central Europe in the summer of 1908. Oscar, a part time footballer and part time factory worker (making artificial teeth) was also on tour playing with an amateur invitation team, The Pirates. So well did he play on this tour that he was offered the chance to play permanently in Hungary. On hearing this Ernest Mangnall acted quickly and secured his signature. The twenty-year old Oscar made his debut on 24th October 1908 against Nottingham Forest, a game which ended 2-2 with Sandy scoring both of United's goals. Oscar, a committed family man, continued to live in Barnet and it took a number of years for him to establish himself. He played no part in United's cup success in 1909 and did not play enough games to be awarded a league champions medal in 1911 but he remained a popular member of the squad. Leaving his 17-year old pregnant wife Olive at home, he was transferred to Shelbourne in Ireland in 1913. At Shelbourne he won the Leinster Senior Cup (1913) and the Gold Cup (1914) but Oscar's career was at something of a crossroads when war broke out. A second baby arrived in 1914 but, nevertheless, Oscar decided to make his contribution to the war effort in 1915.

By the time Sandy was due to leave for France, he had left Oscar and the Middlesex Regiment and been drafted into the 8th Battalion of the East Surreys. The date of this transfer cannot be verified as the records were destroyed in the Blitz during World War Two but it is known that by 15th July Sandy was fighting on the Somme battlefield. The 8th East Surreys are famous for Captain Billy Nevill's decision to lead his men 'over the top' kicking footballs, as they advanced. Private L.S. Price described the scene,

> As the gun-fire died away I saw an infantryman climb onto the parapet into No Man's Land beckoning others to follow. As he did so he kicked off a football: a good kick, the ball

> rose and travelled well towards the German line. That seemed to be the signal to advance.

Nevill had been concerned as to how his raw, inexperienced young troops would react to their first, and as he suspected, possibly last taste of battle so he had obtained four footballs, one for each platoon. He offered a prize to the first platoon to kick a ball the 400 yards to the German trenches in the face of machine gun fire. One platoon inscribed their ball as follows;

The Great European Cup
The Final
East Surreys v Bavarians
Kick Off at Zero

The action was sanctioned on condition that the men didn't chase the ball but only kicked it when it came to them. It was partially successful as, despite the heavy losses Nevill feared, Dantzig Alley and Mountauban were captured. Nevill himself was killed just short of the German wire but the Surrey's were immortalized in the *Daily Mail*.

> On through the hail and slaughter,
> Where gallant comrades fall,
> Where blood is powered like water,
> They drove the trickling ball.
> The fear of death before them,
> Is but an empty name
> True to the land that bore them,
> The SURREYS played the game.

Sandy, it would appear missed the early exchanges on the Somme although he appears to have been involved near Erquinghem Lys in August. Oscar Linkson was not so lucky. His battalion suffered heavy losses at Delville Wood and at Guillemont where Oscar was killed on 8th August. His body was never found. He was 28 years old and left a young wife with two baby children. Sandy on the other hand was promoted to Lance Corporal and, following a break when he played for the battalion football team, he was back in Regina Trench, a German construction near to the German fortifications at Thiepval in October. After winning the Divisional Cup Final on 1st January 1917, Sandy was moved back to the frontline on the Somme at Grandcourt. In April they were moved north to Arras.

The action that took place at Arras was to be among the most significant of the war, and was heavily backed by the new British Prime Minister, David Lloyd George. The plan was to provide some relief to the French armies further south. The British Army had been on a steep learning curve and was now ready to fight on a front of 24 kilometres using far more effective firepower. 2.7 million shells were fired at Arras, a million more than on the Somme, and 99% of them detonated and exploded on impact. There was much more success in cutting the barbed wire so it was more likely that the British would make progress. The Germans, defending with their usual tenacity, were forced to pull more troops into the area, thus relieving the pressure elsewhere on the front, just as the British had hoped. The result was another drawn out battle with heavy casualties, an average of 4,070 a day between 9th April and 17th May.

Sandy's unit were given the task of capturing the village of Cherisy, ten miles east of Arras where the German frontline was now situated. In this area, close to where the A1 motorway from Paris to the north now stands, the Battle of Arras was fought. Following a bombardment on 3rd May, the British captured Cherisy with relatively few casualties. The units either side of the main British thrust did not, however, fare so well. Possibly confused by having to fight in the open rather than in the enclosed trenches, Sandy's unit became stranded and subjected to a German counter attack. Of the 500 men who fought with Sandy, 90 were killed, 175 wounded and at least 100 captured in action that lasted eight hours. What happened to Sandy is unclear although for a time it was thought that he had been captured. If so, he probably died in captivity and was buried in a grave later overrun by the fighting. It is possible that he was just left to his fate. Richard Van Emden has quoted the experience of A/Lance Corporal Cecil Withers of the 7th East Surrey Regiment at Arras who tells of there being so many wounded soldiers that there were not enough men left to attend them. He was told to carry the wounded himself as there were no stretcher bearers. He goes on to describe how men were collapsing with sheer exhaustion, unable to carry on. The only hard evidence regarding Sandy's whereabouts was uncovered by East Ayrshire community historian Anne Geddes who discovered an article in the *Kilmarnock Herald* which reported that Sandy had been wounded and taken prisoner. She quoted a letter, published in the article, which had been written by a comrade and sent to Sandy's wife Florence. In this letter Sandy is referred to as 'Alec'.

> I am writing to try to explain what has happened to your dear husband Alec. He was wounded, and much to our sorrow, fell into German hands, so I hope you will hear from him. After Alec was wounded he 'carried on' and led his men for a mile playing the game until the last we saw of him. We loved him, and he was a father to all of us and the most popular man in the regiment. All here send our deepest sympathy.

A second correspondence was even less optimistic.

> Turnbull was missing during an attack on the Germans. I have very little hope of him being alive. I spoke to him when he got his first wound and asked him if he was badly done. 'No', he said, and from all accounts he must have continued going along with us, and when last seen had four separate wounds.

Sandy was never seen, dead or alive, again.

Lance Sergeant Sandy Turnbull, one of the most successful, best known and controversial footballers of his generation is remembered on the massive twenty foot high, fifty yard long Arras Memorial, on the section dedicated to the East Surrey Regiment. His 1909 FA Cup Final shirt is displayed in the Manchester United museum at Old Trafford. Strangely for one so well known, his death appears not to have been reported in the national press. Yet he died leaving a real legacy at Manchester United. In scoring a total of 101 goals for United in 247 appearances he is placed, at the time of writing, 19th on the all time list of scorers between United legends Cristiano Ronaldo (18th with 118 goals) and Bryan Robson (22nd with 99 goals). When the controversy is put to one side there remains a brave and popular soldier whose sacrifice left Florence and their four children mourning for one of Manchester United's first true greats.

Jimmy Speirs – Cup Final Hero

Sandy Turnbull was not the only Scottish footballer to score the winning goal in an FA Cup final and then lose his life on the Western Front. Jimmy Speirs, captain of the best team ever to represent Bradford City, met the same fate on a wet August day in the mud of Passchendaele. Jimmy, a skilful inside forward, was a Scottish international who, as well as thriving at Bradford, enjoyed a successful career with Glasgow Rangers, Clyde and Leeds City. He was also to be decorated on the battlefield, an honour which he and his family prized above all his other achievements.

James Hamilton Speirs was born the sixth of seven children on 22nd March 1886 in Govan, Glasgow. He was the son of another James Hamilton Speirs, a forty year old ex-miner working as a boilermaker, and Janet who successfully brought six of their children to adulthood, one having died in infancy. Use of the name Hamilton was to become something of a family tradition having originated through Jimmy's paternal grandmother. The family background was one of coal mining and went back at least as far as Jimmy's great-grandfather before Jimmy's father left the industry, thereby breaking the mould. In early adulthood Jimmy was recorded as being a valuator's clerk, a job not usually associated with would-be Scottish footballers from Govan. Surprisingly, given Jimmy's success as a professional footballer, he continued to list his profession as that of a valuators clerk even on the birth certificates of his children. By the age of twenty Jimmy had married Bessie Mabon, a photographer's assistant and a year later she gave birth to a son, another James Hamilton Speirs. A daughter Elizabeth, known as Betty, followed in 1912.

By the time of his marriage Jimmy was making an impression on the football field and his life was about to change when he left his junior club Annandale in order to play for Maryhill Football Club in the Glasgow League. Maryhill were a top club in the junior leagues and half of this particular team went on to have successful careers in top flight football. By the spring of 1905 Jimmy had won both the Glasgow Cup and the Glasgow Charity Cup and, although he had only played in nine matches, Glasgow Rangers had seen enough. They signed him that summer.

Jimmy made his debut for Rangers on the 25th September 1905 but it proved to be a very difficult introduction as he suffered the ignominy of being on the end of a 5-0 thrashing. Things did improve and Jimmy scored 6 goals in the 18 games that he played during the season. His time at Rangers was successful and his strike rate improved so that in a total of 67 games he scored 35 goals, a very healthy strike rate for an inside forward who brought attributes to his game other than that of a goal scorer. His time at Rangers only lacked one thing – trophies. During the three years that Jimmy was a Rangers player the only trophy that Jimmy ever won was the Glasgow Merchants Charity Cup. During these years it was bitter rivals Glasgow Celtic who had a hold on the Scottish League and Cup. Two third place finishes was the best that Rangers could do and, so, in the summer of 1908, Jimmy moved to Clyde. In the one season that he was at the club, Clyde had their best season ever finishing third behind (ironically) the champions Rangers. Jimmy scored 11 goals in his 24 matches but was offered the chance to further his career in the more competitive English league with Bradford City. By this time Jimmy had won his only Scottish cap when he played in the 2-1 victory over Wales in March 1908.

The move to Bradford was a good one as they were one of the most improved teams in England. They were about to begin their second season in the top division when Jimmy arrived and, although they lost the opening game of the season 1-0 to the FA Cup holders Manchester United (Sandy Turnbull included), they recovered to finish the season in seventh place. Jimmy established himself as a regular playing a total of 40 league and cup games during the season and his contribution was quickly recognised by the *Yorkshire Post*:

> No finer footwork has ever been seen at Valley Parade than that which Speirs provides, and his unselfishness is appreciated by all. He is one of those forwards of whom it is said his partner cannot help playing well, so splendidly is he nursed. Off the field Jimmy is one of the quietest and gentlemanly of men, and his popularity is as great as it is well deserved.

Jimmy was making a mark in another way. Just before his 22nd birthday, while playing for Clyde, Jimmy had become involved in Freemasonry. He had been proposed by John McNee of the Wholesale Whiskey Merchants of Glasgow where it is possible he worked during the close season. In 1909 Jimmy became a Master Mason and was made a Life Member on 12th February 1913. Something of an entrepreneur, Jimmy is thought to have made a substantial amount of money by trading shares in rubber before he left Clyde. He became an active member of the Association Football Players Union, the same organisation that had led to difficulties for Sandy Turnbull and Billy Meredith, although in Jimmy's case his involvement does not appear to have caused him any problems. Life appeared to be pretty good and in 1911 it was about to get better.

Season 1910/11, Jimmy's second season at the club and first as captain, was to be the greatest in Bradford's history and remained so, certainly until the club's promotion to the Premier League in 1999, or maybe until their storming run to the League Cup Final 101 years after winning their only major trophy. That Bradford won the Cup in 1911 in some ways should be no surprise as they finished 5th in the league, three places above their opponents Newcastle United. Newcastle, however, were the current holders of the Cup and had won the League Championship three times since 1905, so the Press gave Bradford little chance. On the day of the final *The Times*, after lamenting that the match was being played too late in the season when the players were tired, praised Newcastle, so confident of their success that they didn't even mention Bradford until the end of a very long second paragraph. They praised Newcastle captain Colin Veitch as a wonderful sportsman and concluded that "Newcastle United ought, of course, to win" and that Bradford were "untrained in the subtleties of combination". There was talk of Bradford's "kick and rush tactics". Before the game, Jimmy wrote to Veitch and, in the words of his opposing captain, "expressed in sound terms the true spirit of comradeship, and the proper sentiments one would expect to see associated with the sportsman and the sport". Jimmy never lost his belief in fair play and respect for his opponent, characteristics which ensured his lasting popularity within the sport. But if this sporting, Master Mason conjures up the picture of a rather serious, almost too good to be true young man, then the family website paints a picture of a fun loving teammate, fond of a good story and a joke, a "popular peacock" as one publication found on that website describes him, with "an abundance of humour". While avoiding any of the antics of fellow cup final hero, Sandy Turnbull, Jimmy was always full of fun as long as there was no malice involved, a trait that seems to have run throughout the Bradford team.

The final itself was a largely dull and uneventful game. The 70,000 crowd at Crystal Palace witnessed a boring 0-0 draw. Bob Torrance replaced an injured fellow Scot, Willie Gildea, for the replay at Old Trafford and his heroic defensive display inspired Bradford to a 1-0 victory in front of a crowd of 66,646. Before the replay Torrance had only played in 36 league games in the three years since joining Bradford from his home town club, Kirkintilloch Rob Roy for the princely sum of £5. It was to prove to be an inspired signing and the first confirmation of that came in the much more exciting replay. Jimmy grabbed the all important goal in the first half when playing against a very strong wind. Bradford's style of playing long balls to the wings, along with what *The Times* describes as "rough and ready" tackling, proved more suitable to the conditions than Newcastle's "sophisticated" short passing game. The Bradford team, containing eight Scots, held out magnificently, not that *The Times* wanted to give them much credit. In their match report Jimmy, the scorer of the goal and captain, did not even warrant a mention. Neither did 'man of the match' Bob Torrance. The only player referred to by name was Veitch. Not that this bothered Bradford as they celebrated in the Lord Mayors civic reception. An estimated 100,000 people flooded onto the streets to welcome the triumphal team home. The *Leeds Mercury* was ecstatic with the result.

> The Cup has come home and Bradford has gone mad with delight. In the long history of the city there has never been anything to equal the extraordinary scenes that took place this evening.

It was the high point of Jimmy's football career. The following season he spent six months on the sideline with injuries and, although he recovered, his position in the club had become much less secure. Details are unclear but there does appear to have been a falling out of some kind – player/manager/club disputes were much less likely to find their way into the media during the Edwardian era. Whatever the reason for Jimmy's departure from the cup holders, the recent captain and the hero of Bradford's greatest day was soon on his way. In December 1912 Jimmy left Bradford for Leeds City. Leeds manager, Herbert Chapman, was looking to build a side using proven players as his core so he was willing to pay the relatively high fee of £1,400 for Jimmy. The signing was seen as a major step forward for Leeds. After all, Jimmy Speirs was an international footballer, who although only having gained one cap, had played in a number of international trials and represented the Anglo Scots against the Home Scots. He was still seen as a hero by Bradford City supporters, captain and goal-scorer in the biggest match in the English calendar. The local press were pleased with his arrival and pointed out that his thinning hair was not evidence of a player necessarily past his best. Leeds City were moving up in the world and Jimmy's signing was further evidence of their ambition. Leeds was the last major city in England to produce a team fit to join the Football League (in 1905/6) but, when the impressive Chapman arrived, things began to happen. Jimmy was seen by Chapman as a crucial figure on this journey.

With Jimmy as captain, Leeds finished 4th in the Second Division in 1913/14 and won the West Riding Cup, Jimmy scoring the only goal in the victory over Hull. This was to be the only trophy ever won by Leeds City and Chapman would have to look elsewhere if he was to make history. Leeds City were dissolved in 1919 following financial irregularities and Chapman moved on to remarkable success at Huddersfield Town and Arsenal. Leeds United arose out of the ashes of Leeds City and joined the league in 1919/20, although it would be nearly half a century before they became a major force in English (and European) football. Jimmy, meanwhile, played his last game in April 1915 at the end of a mediocre season in which he scored ten goals. Jimmy's career figures were more impressive. In 255 league and cup games he had scored 104 goals as well as setting up numerous opportunities for others, a career of which he could be very proud.

At the end of the 1914/15 season, Jimmy headed straight back to Glasgow. As the father of two young children, he was under no obligation to join the fray but on 17th May 1915 Jimmy enlisted in the 3rd Battalion Cameron Highlanders. He was soon made a Lance Corporal but Jimmy would also have been delighted to discover that the battalion had a successful football team. His new teammates were equally excited and the regiment's magazine, *79th News*, reflected this.

> The battalion is fortunate in having the services of L/Cpl Speirs who played for Bradford City and Glasgow Rangers. He plays inside left and is a tower of strength to the side. With a little more practice in playing together, the 3rd Cameron's should prove capable of holding their own against any team or combination of teams thrown against them.

Twenty-nine year old Jimmy, at five feet ten inches and eleven and a half stone, larger than the average young man of his generation, was in the prime of life and his ability and experience was an asset to any team.

Football, however, soon had to take a back seat. Heavy losses being suffered in France meant that the 3rd Battalion was sent to join the 7th Battalion at the end of March 1916. In July, Jimmy was made a corporal and was seeing action. The Battalion War Diary reported that "he was wounded in the heavy fighting of autumn 1916 but was not fortunate enough to be sent to a home hospital. He rejoined his regiment after convalescence." The injury was to the shoulder but months later Jimmy was back in action at the 2nd Battle of Arras. It was here, between the 22nd and 27th April 1917, that Jimmy achieved his greatest military success when he won the Military Medal. The reports are not very specific as to how he achieved this distinction but it appears likely that Jimmy was in charge of a Lewis Gun Section which attacked Guemappe, part of a wider attack on the Hindenburg Line, on 23rd April. A number of Military Medals were won in this action.

Jimmy's success was recognised at home. His Lodge reported that his medal was awarded for "conspicuous conduct in the field" while a local newspaper ran the headline 'A Gallant Sergeant'. The reporter informed the readers that Jimmy had come through a "big engagement unscathed" and went on to say that he was,

> …an old friend of mine, for whom I have always had the highest regard. Both on and off the field Jimmy Speirs is a gentleman and there are few I would place before him in this respect.

Another reporter understood exactly how much this honour would mean to Jimmy when he wrote that "among all the honours won by him on the field of play none will be more prized than this latest award for gallant conduct." Jimmy now returned for a short break, newly promoted to the rank of sergeant, but back on the Western Front in the wettest August in living memory, the build up for Passchendaele had begun.

On 20th August, Jimmy's battalion moved up to the front to relieve the 8th Battalion Worcester Regiment and two days later, at 4.45am, he, along with 14 other officers and 450 men of other ranks, went 'over the top'. What exactly happened is still unclear but the *Bradford Daily Telegraph* reported on 8th September that Jimmy's wife Bessie had been contacted by another sergeant saying that Jimmy had been wounded and was now missing. Five days later the paper was reporting that he had been wounded in the thigh, had crawled into a shell hole and not been seen since. His body was eventually found almost a year after the cessation of hostilities, in October 1919. Jimmy's remains were found on Hill 35, west of Iberian Farm where the battalion had succeeded in sweeping the Germans off the rising gradient. There had been heavy fighting in this area on 22nd August so it is perfectly possible that this is when he was killed although his death is officially recorded as being two days earlier. Jimmy is buried at Dochy Farm, New British Cemetery. In the Bradford City Football Club Museum the following tribute, written by Lieutenant Colonel A.M. Cumming OBE of the Regimental Headquarters, The Highlanders is displayed;

> A remarkable man… to have played for Scotland, won the FA Cup, scored the winning goal and won a Military Medal is remarkable by any standards.

A remarkable man indeed. Jimmy was one of nine footballers who had represented Bradford City, six first team players and three reserves, to die on the battlefield. This is one of the most tragic examples of loss of life for an English club in the war, comparable with both Hearts and Celtic in Scotland. Life, however, goes on even after events as traumatic as the Great War. Thirty-one year old Jimmy had left his wife Bessie with their two young children, James and Betty. Eventually Bessie remarried and later gave birth to a second daughter while James emigrated to Canada. He returned to Europe during World War Two when he served in the Royal Canadian Artillery Regiment. Bessie was widowed for a second time in 1974 and died in 1981 aged ninety-three. In 2003 Jimmy's medals were auctioned and the FA Cup medal was sold for £26,210. Fortunately, it was bought by a Bradford City fan, Mark Lawn, who later became chairman and allowed the medal to be put on display, thereby ensuring that Jimmy Speirs will never be forgotten by the Bradford faithful.

What of that other hero of the 1911 Cup Final, Bob Torrance? As a munitions worker he had been excused military service but, keen to play his part, in March 1917, he enlisted as a Gunner with 'A' battery 162nd Brigade Royal Field Artillery. In the Spring Offensive of March 1918 Bob was thrust into the action. During the severe fighting he lost an arm and was taken to the field hospital but even here there was no escape from the ferocity of the German attack. The hospital was bombed and Bob was killed, his body never to be found. This magnificent centre half, veteran of 161 league games and now recognised as possibly Bradford's finest ever defender, is one of 11,954 names on the Tyne Cot Memorial. He joins Jimmy Speirs as the most eminent of the nine Bradford City footballers killed in the war, the two heroes of the greatest day in their club's history.

Two England Internationals – Lintott and Latheron

Footballers, as we have already seen, played a significant role on the battlefield. Players such as Jimmy Speirs and Leigh Roose had been decorated for their bravery and both paid the ultimate price for their actions. The experiences of Donald Bell and Willie Angus are recounted later. However it is noticeable that English international footballers have not featured thus far. The stories of Jimmy Speirs and Leigh Roose are both inspiring and tragic but these are tales of a Scottish and Welsh international respectively. Sandy Turnbull was probably the best known footballer to die in the Great War but he failed to gain the international recognition that his ability warranted. Walter Tull, remarkable man though he was, never produced the prowess on the football field that attracted the attention of the international selectors. In this respect football was unlike both cricket and particularly rugby where high profile fatalities were more commonplace. The two exceptions to this are Evelyn Lintott and Eddie Latheron.

Evelyn Henry Lintott was one of the nine Bradford City footballers to die in the Great War. Born on 2nd November 1883 into a wealthy family from Godalming in Surrey, he possessed a true 'Corinthian spirit' and, during his successful career, he became one of the most respected players in the game.

Evelyn's family earned their comfortable living through trading cattle and this allowed the five children, four boys and a girl, to benefit from a good education. Evelyn, the second son, combined his studies with a love of football in which he began to excel as an enthusiastic, talented half back. After completing his education at the Royal Grammar School, Guildford, he moved to St Lukes College, Exeter where he trained to be a teacher, and it was during his time at Exeter that his football career began to take off. He had already played regularly for Woking, making his debut as a sixteen year old centre forward in the 1899/1900 season and he continued to do so when home on holiday. He also represented Surrey in this period, helped by his versatility which was seen to its best effect when he moved to centre half.

Evelyn's other love was teaching, and in the 1901 census he is listed as a pupil-teacher. After leaving St Lukes and embarking on a teaching career, Evelyn made two appearances for Plymouth Argyle as an amateur player. In 1907, Evelyn took a teaching job at Oldfield Road School in Willesdon, London and he joined Queens Park Rangers, a club, like his previous teams, playing their football in the Southern League. During his first season, 1907/8, QPR won the Southern League championship, a success which resulted in them playing in the first ever Charity (now Community) Shield on 27th April. As champions of the Southern League, QPR faced Manchester United, the league champions, a side which included both Billy Meredith and Sandy Turnbull. Following a tough 1-1 draw at Stamford Bridge, QPR were soundly beaten 4-0 in the replay two days later, a game which Sandy Turnbull missed but in which his namesake Jimmy Turnbull scored a hat trick. Despite this defeat Evelyn, settled by now at right half, had entered into the defining years of his career.

As early as 1906, Evelyn had made his debut on the international stage, in the amateur England XI which went on a continental tour that year. The amateur international team had only just been formed and in their first game the England team, with Evelyn at left half, proved embarrassingly strong for France. They won 15-0 with the great Vivian Woodward scoring eight, an early indication of a spectacular future career.

Woodward was a remarkable man in many ways. He practised as an architect while still a footballer and remained amateur, never claiming expenses except when playing overseas. He captained Great Britain to gold medal success in both the 1908 and 1912 Olympic Games and achieved a remarkable scoring record in international football, 29 goals in 23 full international matches and 44 goals in 30 amateur internationals. His scoring record for Spurs and Chelsea is also impressive, a goal every other game for the former and one in three for the latter. With the outbreak of war, Woodward became an ideal recruiting aid and he quickly joined the 17th Service Battalion (1st Football) of the Middlesex Regiment. A second lieutenant, supporters were very keen to fight alongside him. When he reached the front, Woodward was injured in the thigh by a grenade but returned to fight at the Somme. He was lucky to survive and ended the war coaching the army football team. After the war he designed the football stadium to be used in the 1920 Olympic Games at Antwerp before leaving architecture for dairy farming. After World War Two, Woodward became more and more lonely. He had never married and ended his days in an Ealing nursing home in 1954. He remains one of England's finest footballers, and one who in 1914 was influential in encouraging sportsmen to join the forces.

However, to return to Evelyn, a similarly respected footballer, who proceeded to win five amateur caps and was never on the losing side. Such was his success, both with England and QPR, that in January 1908 Evelyn was invited to take part in the North v South full England trial. Representing the South, Evelyn gave a good enough account of himself, despite being part of a team which sacrificed a 4-1 lead to draw 4-4. The solidly built half back (by now he stood at five foot ten inches and weighed twelve stone) had impressed with what the football writer Ivan Sharpe called his "bubbling enthusiasm, enterprise and brilliance" and it was no surprise when Evelyn took his place alongside fellow amateur Woodward and their professional colleagues for England's match against Ireland on February 15th in Belfast. Evelyn had created a piece of history as the first QPR footballer to play in an international. *The Times* reported that he "made a promising first appearance in international football" and it was no surprise when he kept his place for the games against Wales and Scotland.

The game against Wales, winners of the Home International Championship in 1907 and one of that competition's strongest teams, proved to be something of a sensation. England won 7-1 with the irrepressible Woodward scoring another hat trick. Leigh Roose was the Welsh goalkeeper but had to be replaced during the game due to injury. Billy Meredith, the other 'Welsh superstar', had to witness the beating to the end. Evelyn had been given the task of marking him out of the game and Sir Frederick Wall, secretary of the FA, recorded the extent of Evelyn's dominance over Meredith:

> He clung to him like an affectionate brother. At last the patience of Meredith gave out and he turned on Lintott with these words 'Go away you confounded schoolboy. Go away!

> Do you hear? You have got seven cursed goals, how many more do you want?' Lintott was silent but he continued to haunt his jaded adversary.

One suspects that Meredith's outburst might well have been phrased in more colourful language. Evelyn, according to J.A.H. Catton in his book *The Story of Association Football* (1926) says that "he carried out his orders so loyally and rigidly that Meredith could not move." Man to man marking was probably not the sort of task to appeal to Evelyn as he was much more likely to want to match skill with skill. Nevertheless there is no doubt that this most sporting of opponents did an effective job on the mercurial Meredith. A 1-1 draw with Scotland followed, allowing the two countries to share the championship, a title Evelyn was to help England win outright the following year. In that season Evelyn played in four more internationals, against Ireland, Scotland and two against Hungary, each match resulting in an England victory thereby maintaining his record of never having played in a losing England team either in the amateur or full international team. His final international game against Hungary resulted in an 8-2 victory for England, with Woodward getting four, and meant that, in his seven international matches, England had scored 29 goals and conceded 7. This was a record of which Evelyn could justifiably be very proud.

During these years Evelyn was also earning respect off the field. Although he was an amateur player, he showed solidarity with his professional teammates when he joined the Association Football Players Union. As a man of conscience, Evelyn felt that it was important to stand together and, such was the high esteem in which he was held that he was elected Chairman in the 1910/11 season. Evelyn also carried out some lay preaching on Sundays, further establishing his credentials as one of the most respected sportsmen of his time. When QPR ran into some financial problems in November 1908, Evelyn agreed to turn professional and be sold to Bradford City for £1,000. This fee for a player who had played only 35 matches for the club but who was a current international went a long way to solving QPR's financial problems. He was offered a job at Sports and Pastimes, a company who made Bradford's shirts but preferred to take a teaching job at Dudley Hall. In his first season Evelyn played a part in helping Bradford avoid relegation which they did by defeating cup winners Manchester United on the last day of the season and kept his place in the England team. But as Bradford improved, finishing seventh and fifth in the next two seasons, Evelyn's career in the top flight began to run down. He lost his place in the England team and played no part in Bradford's 'Jimmy Speirs inspired' Cup win in 1911, a bad injury against Bolton earlier in the season denying him the opportunity to play his part in Bradford's finest hour. After 57 games for Bradford he accepted Herbert Chapman's offer to join second division Leeds City in June 1912.

Evelyn's time at Leeds, although brief, did make an impact on those connected with the club. Herbert Chapman agreed to pay him a full year's salary of £208 although only ten months of the year was left. This was above the maximum wage and meant that Evelyn was possibly the highest paid footballer in the country although he continued to live in a modest terraced house in Bradford. That a man such as Chapman rated him so highly is testament enough to his ability. The history of Leeds United Football Club describes Evelyn as follows,

> He was a gifted and astute footballer, sound and resolute in defence, always ready to spring an attacking move with accurate, controlled passing from the rear and adept and powerful in the air, the perfect embodiment of what was expected of a centre half in the Edwardian period.

Evelyn was made club captain and, in his first season Leeds, finished sixth in the division. The local press took to him immediately. After his debut, a 4-0 defeat at Fulham, the *Yorkshire Evening Post* reported enthusiastically that "there was no more energetic man on the field than he" while the *Mercury* added that he played magnificently, strong in defence and at the heart of Leeds best attacks. The *Mercury* continued this theme after his second game, a 2-0 win over Barnsley

> Lintott gave a fine display of clean tackling, smart headwork and clever placing. He worked with untiring energy and to a large extent was responsible for the ineffectiveness of the Barnsley forwards. Lintott looks like proving an ideal captain and, in him Leeds City have certainly found a treasure. He

> is the sort of leader who by his play and general conduct on the field encourages and inspires his colleagues.

This was an excellent reference for a future officer in the British Army. There was even talk of an international recall. However, the following season Evelyn was moved to right half and, following an injury, lost his place never to regain it. With the outbreak of war, the patriotic Evelyn joined the 15th Battalion West Yorkshire Regiment ('Leeds Pals') on 14th September 1914. After 45 games for Leeds City, his illustrious football career ended.

It is quite likely that Evelyn had already taken the decision to end his career before the outbreak of war. A succession of injuries followed by the loss of the captaincy to Jimmy Speirs, coupled with the team's failure to gain promotion, sapped Evelyn's appetite to continue in the game. The outbreak of war gave him the opportunity to do something different. On joining the Army he listed his occupation as that of a teacher rather than as a footballer. Nevertheless, he was one of the first footballers, certainly the first high profile footballer, to join up in the initial flush of enthusiasm for the war, a feeling confirmed by Arthur Dalby who served in the same battalion when he described how he joined

> I saw this lot in the paper and it said it was all Leeds people, and I joined up, I didn't even know that infantry walked to be quite truthful with you, I didn't know anything about soldiers.... I've never regretted a moment of it really, because I never met a finer lot of fellows in my life.

When the 'Leeds Pals' left for their initial training in the Yorkshire Dales, 20,000 people saw them off from Leeds station. Unsurprisingly, Evelyn was quickly promoted to the rank of sergeant and, on 20th December 1914, he was made a Lieutenant, the first footballer to obtain a commission. In June 1915 the battalion moved to Ripon to continue their training and on 7th December they left Liverpool for Egypt in order to guard the Suez Canal. Evelyn wrote home expressing his embarrassment at being described as being 'on active service' as he was so bored. This was soon to change and, by March 1916, they had been directed to the Western Front in order to take part in the great offensive of July 1916. After landing at Marseilles, the 'Leeds Pals' headed for the Somme.

The first day of the Somme was a desperate day for the British Army and the 'Leeds Pals' were not spared the full horrors of battle, horrors that will be described in greater detail in Chapter 15 with the story of Major Booth, the England cricketer, who was in the same regiment. As the sun rose on that beautiful morning 'Kitchener's Army' went 'over the top'. By 3.00pm Evelyn Lintott was dead. The first word of his death was given by Private David Spink who reported that "Lt. Lintott killed by machine gun at 3pm in the advance. He was struck in the chest". A letter published in the *Yorkshire Post* a week later gave more details:

> Lt Lintott's end was particularly gallant. Tragically he was killed leading his platoon of the 15th West Yorkshire Regiment, the 'Leeds Pals', over the top. He led his men with great dash and when hit the first time declined to take the count. Instead he drew his revolver and called for further effort. Again he was hit but struggled on but a third shot finally bowled him over.

Evelyn's body was never found and his name joined the 72,000 others on the Thiepval Memorial. He had never married and left only £78 and a few personal effects – books, photos and postcards – be dealt with by his brother, a journalist on the *Bradford Daily Telegraph* and editor of the *Football Player Magazin*e. Yet he left much more – the memory of a fine English international footballer and a true sporting gentleman.

The second English international footballer to lose his life in the Great War was the diminutive Blackburn Rovers inside forward Eddie Latheron. The seventh of eight children born to signalman John Summerson and his wife Martha, Edwin Gladstone Latheron is listed as being born on 22nd December 1887 near Middlesbrough, although this date has since been challenged and it now appears that some time earlier that year is more likely to be correct. It is not clear why Eddie did not use his father's surname (his mother's maiden name was Brampton) and details of his early life are very sketchy. Nevertheless, Eddie had a domestic career which demands that he be remembered. Few players, certainly in the history of Blackburn Rovers, have commanded such affection from the supporters. Known as 'Pinkie' on the terraces due to his red hair and fair complexion, Eddie was the complete inside forward, both a creator and scorer of goals. Two league titles bear testament to Eddie's contribution to Blackburn's proud history.

Eddie was discovered playing for his local club, Grangetown Athletic, in the Northern League in 1906. Having journeyed to Grangetown in order to watch another player the Blackburn secretary/manager, Robert Middleton, was captivated by Eddie – eighteen years old, five foot five inches tall – and quickly paid the £25 necessary to take him to Blackburn. Middleton recognised that, despite his size, Eddie was comfortable on either side of the field and that he possessed the speed of thought and quickness of eye to open up defences. The Blackburn press, however needed to be convinced as the glut of new signings struggled to make any impact. The *Blackburn Times* suggested that "the second rate players might advantageously be reduced and the money thus saved be utilized in paying the maximum wage to first class men". The appointment by Middleton of Bob Holmes, the former Preston North End 'invincible', as trainer in 1909 changed everything. In the next two years Blackburn finished 4th and 3rd in the league and in 1911 reached the semi-final of the FA Cup where they lost to the eventual winners, Jimmy Speirs' Bradford City.

By now Eddie was developing into a top player. A gifted playmaker and accomplished goalscorer, Eddie combined these skills with an unquenchable enthusiasm and a dogged tenacity which made him extremely popular with the fans. He was in modern parlance 'a box to box' player, never afraid to do the 'fetching and carrying' for other players. Despite his lack of height, Eddie was good in the air with excellent ball control and a powerful shot which resulted in him scoring plenty of goals, in spite of an unselfishness which saw him as happy to create goals for others as to score himself. The result was Blackburn's first league title being won in the 1911/12 season. Eddie had missed a part of the season due to injury but in the run-in his goals were vital as Blackburn held off Everton's challenge by three points. The following season, despite a long unbeaten run that didn't see their first defeat until Christmas, Blackburn could only finish fifth, but for Eddie there was compensation in his call up to the full England team.

Eddie made his international debut alongside three other Blackburn players at Ashton Gate, Bristol on 17th March 1913. Only 8,000 supporters turned up to see a thrilling game in which England beat Wales 4-3. He scored England's second goal after only twenty-five minutes of play and appeared to have made a good start to his international career. His second cap though did not come until nearly a year later. On 14th February 1914, in his home town of Middlesbrough in front of a crowd of 25,000, England were soundly beaten 3-0 by an Irish team claiming its first ever Home International Championship. Eddie never wore the England shirt again. Nevertheless, later that season Blackburn claimed their second title with Eddie contributing 13 goals, one of his best returns. The following season, the first year of war, Eddie did even better with 17 goals as Blackburn finished third. One cannot help but think that, without the interruption of the war, Eddie would have returned to the England squad. After all, he was still only 27 years old.

Eddie did not join up immediately and played on until the cessation of competitive football and the introduction of conscription. He played in wartime competitions such as the Lancashire Section of the Northern Competition 1915/16 and played as a guest for Blackpool when Blackburn ceased playing that year. He eventually joined the Royal Field Artillery as a gunner and, after his final game for his beloved Blackburn, a 2-2 draw with Bury on 17th March 1917, he went to France leaving behind his wife Bertha and son Walter. It was not long before he was involved in some of the worst action of the war, the 3rd Ypres, the Battle of Passchendaele. British High Command was determined to keep the German Army occupied at Ypres to allow the French to attack Champagne on 23rd October as well as to allow the Allies to prepare for an alternative operation at Cambrai in mid November. Haig was therefore of the opinion that he needed to keep the Ypres operation running for as long as possible and hopefully take Passchendaele Ridge before the winter set in. Haig stuck to this plan despite the exceptionally heavy rain of early October and the advice of generals such as Gough and Plumer who counselled that enough was enough. Indeed, officers were of the opinion that no operations should take place until the conditions improved and until more guns could be moved through the horrendous mud nearer to the front. Haig, however, would not back down. With the rain continuing to pour from the heavens, Eddie was killed on 14th October, just after he had pulled a comrade to safety. In the manner of his death he was luckier than some. Wounded soldiers had, in some cases, been left where Eddie had died and drowned in the rising water of the flooded shell holes. Others, clinging to the muddy sides of craters, were succumbed to exposure. In the twenty-four hour period when Eddie died, 13,000 Allied troops were killed. The rain finally stopped the following day.

The loss of Eddie Latheron was never forgotten in Blackburn. As a one club man, he commanded great loyalty from the fans, some of whom were telling their grandchildren of his special talents as late as the 1960s. In 303 games Eddie had scored 120 goals for his club and is still the fourth highest scorer in their history. He is buried at Vlamertinge New Military Cemetery, one of three Latheron sons to be killed in the slaughter of the Great War. Private Walter Latheron had already been killed at Sanctuary Wood, Ypres in 1915 while Private Peter Latheron was to lose his life in October 1918 when serving with the Green Howards, the Yorkshire Regiment. On 14th October 2007, ninety years to the day after his death, Belgian supporters of Blackburn Rovers held a memorial service and placed flowers on Eddie's grave. As the history of Blackburn Rovers records, "the memory of his special talent would continue to glow in the hearts of the Blackburn public long after the guns had been silenced".

1905 and all that
The 1905 All Blacks, Their Captain Dave Gallaher and Welshman Charlie Pritchard

As we have seen the growth of Rugby Union in the latter years of the nineteenth century and the establishing of the game in the fabric of British society. However if there was one event that cemented the sport as having a pivotal role in the British sporting calendar it was the 1905 New Zealand All Blacks tour of the British Isles and France. This was particularly true in Wales where the emergence of a strong national team about to embark on Welsh rugby's first 'Golden Age' came up against a New Zealand team determined to establish itself as the leading power in world rugby and give that proud country a status which defied the rather patronising attitude that the British establishment showed towards this particular 'colony'. No Welsh schoolboy brought up in the 1960s, as this author experienced first hand, could fail to know of the intense rivalry that existed between two small countries intent on establishing its own identity and the importance of rugby to how they viewed themselves. Even the unbroken success enjoyed by New Zealand against Wales since 1953 hasn't doused the fire and the excitement felt in the South Wales valleys when the All Blacks arrive. In the absence of any victory at international level since 1953, club triumphs involving Newport and Llanelli and successes enjoyed by the British Lions and the Barbarians containing a healthy Welsh representation, are seized upon by the Welsh public, hungry to prolong the rivalry so dramatically forged in 1905. Central to the birth of this rivalry is the career of the New Zealand captain in 1905, David Gallaher and his Welsh opponent Charlie Pritchard.

Dave Gallaher was born at Ramelton, County Donegal, on 30th October 1873, the seventh of fourteen children (three of whom died in infancy), born to James and Maria Gallagher. His father was a sixty-nine year old shop-keeper and his mother a much younger twenty-nine year old teacher who decided, in May 1878, to embark on a new life in Bay of Plenty, New Zealand. James, who by now had changed the family name to Gallaher in order to avoid confusion over spelling and pronunciation, was expecting to be employed as an agent for the Donegal Knitting Company but when this post failed to materialize the family fell on hard times. One child, Patrick had been left in Ireland, being deemed to be too sick to travel and he died in 1880, but Maria gave birth to her final four children in the years immediately following their arrival in New Zealand. With James aging and finding it difficult to find work, Maria returned to teaching to become the main breadwinner. However her health began to fail and the thirteen-year-old David left school to work with his older brothers as a local stock and station agent. In September 1887 Maria died of cancer leaving her oldest children to support the family. In order to do this the family moved to Auckland.

It was here, despite spending some time in hospital being treated for a curvature of the spine, that Dave began to develop his sporting interests, playing both junior rugby and cricket. When the family moved again, this time to Freemans Bay, he joined the Ponsonby District Rugby Club, and his fitness improved through his constant handling of animal carcasses when working for the Auckland Farmers' Freezing Company. By now Dave had developed into the solid six foot, thirteen stone specimen that would prove the ideal build for an All Black forward. In August 1896, he won his place in the Auckland provincial team and was part of the Ponsonby team that won the Auckland championship the following year.

In January 1901, with his rugby career going well, Dave made a decision which may seem surprising a century on – he enlisted with the New Zealand contingents of Mounted Rifles and spent the next eighteen months serving in South Africa during the Boer War. As well as reaching the impressive rank of squadron sergeant major and receiving the Imperial South African War Medal, Dave captained the New Zealand military team which won the forces championship while in South Africa. On his return to New Zealand in August 1902, Dave resumed his place in the Auckland team and in 1903, when nearly thirty years old, was selected for the national team's tour of Australia, where New Zealand were due to play their first ever test match at Sydney. Selected as what we would recognise as a wing forward, (his first five matches on tour had been played at hooker), Dave contributed to the 22-3 victory and kept his place exactly one year later when New Zealand played their second international fixture, this time against the 1904 British Lions. Another victory, this time 9-3, failed to impress the Lions captain David Bedell-Sivright who predicted defeats against the Home Nations when New Zealand toured the following year. How wrong he was proved to be!

With the benefit of hindsight it is much clearer to see why New Zealand were so successful in 1905 and Dave Gallaher, both as player and captain, is central to the success. In only his second international, already vice-captain under Billy Stead, Dave had caused confusion in the Lions ranks. His interpretation of the wing forward role (to use modern terminology) was controversial and not appreciated by his opponents. New Zealand had devised the method of packing down only seven forwards in the scrum against the eight used by their opponents. By using only two forwards in the front row, one of the opposition was left redundant pushing against a non-existent opponent. The spare wing forward would be free of scrimmaging duties and could act as a scrum half or a 'rover' when his side won the ball. When the opposition scrum half had the ball he was forced to run around the wing forward who would be doing his best to disrupt and obstruct him. Technically, in the modern game, this would mean him being off side but in the early 1900s the tactic was perfectly legal and remained so until 1930. It was extremely frustrating for opponents, and in many eyes was nothing more than cheating. The Newport, and later Wales, scrum half Tommy Vile played in the Lions test against New Zealand in 1904. Later an international referee and rugby administrator of some note, Vile has articulated better than anybody the chaos that this tactic of blocking the scrum half caused. He said,

> I had no idea what he was going to do or how he was going to do it, and it took me some time to realise what he was there for and what part he took in the play. I had no possible chance of getting on to the opposing half back because Gallaher simply stood there and blocked my way.

Not that Tommy Vile was prepared to take it lying down.

> He was bullicking me as I went round the scrummage and I was letting him have it, but there was something quite fatherly in his mild rebuke. However he did not stop at obstructing me.

He goes on to show his sneaking regard for this frustrating opponent.

> No player on the NZ side came in for so much criticism, but I think he must have been a kind-hearted man, for I remember how he dealt with me in the test match.... I was desperately annoyed by his tactics, and showed it by word and action, but he put his hand on my head and said to me in a paternal way 'now don't worry, don't lose your temper. It will be alright'.

Yet in the end Tommy Vile reached the conclusion that was very much in keeping with those of his defeated teammates.

> At the same time, I must say that I think his tactics were deliberately obstructive and contrary to the spirit of the rugby game. They undoubtedly created ill-feelings in this country, as they did with the British team out there.

The controversy that seemed to have attached itself to Dave's All Black career did not end with his interpretation of the wing forward role. His rather surprising appointment as All Black captain for the 1905 tour, where he swapped roles with his vice captain Billy Stead, did not meet with unanimous approval. At the end of the 1904 season Dave had been suspended from playing due to a disagreement over a claim for expenses submitted to Auckland Rugby Union. Although the matter had been resolved when he repaid the amount, the incident did not exactly endear him to the rugby hierarchy. A New Zealand team had been sent to Australia prior to the departure for Europe and Dave had not even been selected to go, let alone as captain. Some have recognised an anti-Auckland bias in New Zealand rugby at this time and on the forty day voyage to Britain both Dave and Billy Stead resigned their positions. It took a 17-12 vote to persuade them to change their minds but the decision was to prove crucial in the history of New Zealand rugby. Tommy Vile had his doubts but offered his own explanation as to why his old adversary was leading the attempt to prove Bedell-Sivright wrong:

> It has been difficult to understand why he was made captain

> of the All Blacks. I think Stead was the brains of the team. But evidently the players liked him. Some fellows are 'men's men', liked by other men, and perhaps that was why the choice fell upon Gallaher. He must have been liked or he would never have kept the team together as he did.

Whatever the reason, the combination of Billy Stead's' knowhow and Dave Gallaher's popularity, leadership skills and ability to disrupt the opposition was to prove a powerful blend. They worked together to put rivalry and factions behind them to form a tough, professional almost unbeatable unit – 'The Originals'.

The tour got off to an unexpected start. It was not only Bedell-Sivright who harboured doubts and, as they lined up for their first match against the English county champions Devon, the press predicted a tight close hard fought encounter. By the time the All Blacks had destroyed the opposition to the tune of 55-4 British rugby had a better idea of what to expect. One Devon official seemed in awe of both the team and their captain. Gallaher, he said, was "a sort of blooming hermaphrodite, forward and half back too". Questions were asked about Dave's role but the whole 2-3-2 diamond formation of the pack with the roving and disruptive wing forward was bemusing the English teams. In their first eleven matches the All Blacks scored 408 points and conceded only 7. Since a try was worth only three points as opposed to five in the modern game, the achievement seems even more remarkable. Surrey managed to keep the score to 11-0 but only with the aid of a referee who refused to let the game flow. By the 28th November E.T. Gurden, an ex-international and past president of the RU, concluded that the NZ success was due to "fitness and quickness, superb backup and finely judged kicking". He said that they proved the value of straight running and not passing "for passing sake" and that the English game, which was deteriorating, would benefit from the All Black success. Critics began to question, according to Smith and Williams, whether the "decadence of the English athlete really has set in".

The internationals did prove to be much tougher for the tourists. The first one saw Scotland, one of the strongest of the home nations, lead 7-6 with ten minutes to go only to concede two late tries in a 12-7 defeat. Scotland's effective use of the foot rush and a dense fog caused problems for the All Blacks but they still to scored four tries. Dave missed the following international against Ireland due to injury, a severe disappointment to him on his return to his homeland, but it made little difference as the All Blacks ran out 15-0 winners having scored three converted tries despite a plucky performance from the Irish pack. With their captain restored to the team the All Blacks ran in five unconverted tries without response against England, a defeat that would have been even heavier but for the pitch being something of a quagmire.

And so to the fixture with Wales – the World Championship of Rugby as it was seen in the Principality. In many respects it was even more than this. Both countries recognised in the other that rugby union was the way in which they defined themselves to the outside world. The game in Wales had developed to be inclusive, a means of forging an identity from the thousands of immigrants who had flocked into the valleys seeking work in the mines and iron works from all corners of the United Kingdom but particularly from the west country, the Midlands, Ireland and rural Wales. Gareth Williams has expressed the view that rugby in Wales was "a pre-eminent expression of Welsh consciousness, a signifier of Welsh nationhood". New Zealanders harboured similar sentiments. The country had broken away from British rule five years earlier and was well on its way to achieving the dominion status which was finally confirmed two years later. New Zealand was a dynamic young country keen to prove itself, benefiting from an annual population growth of 23 per 1,000 in the forty years between 1881 and 1921, the highest in the world at that time. Moreover, New Zealand saw itself as a go ahead modern country. It had introduced women's suffrage in 1893 and old age pensions in 1898, two innovations that were causing headaches for British politicians at this time. This clash of the rugby giants was more than a rugby match – it was a clash of two cultures which placed success on the rugby field at the forefront of their search to confirm a national identity. These teams were not playing for what today's media irritatingly term 'bragging rights'. It was something much more. Recognising in one another their dedication to the sport of Rugby Union and its place in their society, they were playing for a nation's pride. In one way or another this clash can lay claim to be the most important game of rugby ever played.

The press, completely seduced by the sensational performances of the All Blacks to date, gave Wales little chance. *The Times* felt the Welsh backs to be slower than in previous years and the forwards to lack the necessary strength, concluding that "the defeat of the visitors is an unthinkable contingency". Wales had, however, prepared thoroughly. In order to counter the problems posed by Dave's disruptive presence, the selectors had decided to pick a 'rover' of their own, Cliff Pritchard of Pontypool. A regular centre three-quarter, he now became the extra back in a Welsh back division oozing experience and flair. Playing an extra back however, would put extra demands on the pack. One forward in particular was to rise to this challenge and play the game of his life.

Charles Meyrick Pritchard was born in Newport on 30th September 1882. Educated at Newport Intermediate School and at Long Ashton School, a private school in Bristol, Charlie grew up to take his place in the family wine and spirit business. By 1901 this six foot, thirteen and a half stone forward had joined Newport Rugby Club and made his debut against another leading Welsh club, Swansea, on the 25th January 1902 in front of 12,000 spectators. It was no surprise that Charlie joined Newport as his father John, a well known local cricketer, had been one of the founding members of the club. By 1903, he was a travelling reserve with the Welsh team and the following year he gained the first of his fourteen caps when he was picked to play in the back row against Ireland in Belfast, a game that Wales, rather unluckily, lost 14-12. However this disappointing result was not the end of Charlie's international career and the following year Charlie played his part in a Welsh Triple Crown, although he missed the deciding match against Ireland through injury. By the time the All Blacks rugby machine rolled up in Cardiff, Charlie Pritchard was an automatic choice in the Welsh back row.

One look at any picture of the Wales team that took to the field on 16th December, sees Charlie at his best. With his fine physique and his strong features, he looks like a man who others would follow, a player who would command respect. Wayne Thomas has written,

> He was like a lion on the field; off it he was extremely gentle, tender and lovable. In his play he was an untiring worker with almost inexhaustible energy. Although not a specialist, he more often than not played in the back row. He played

> with great fire and exuberance and was a very difficult player to stop. He had an excellent swerve in open play and always seemed to sustain a resolute forward momentum in the mauls and tight play. His passing was excellent while he could dribble and scrummage as well as any player. But his most important asset was his deadly tackling.

It was this tackling by the gentle, kind hearted and charming Charlie that was to prove so crucial in the game to follow.

On the morning of the game the hordes of Welsh supporters poured into Cardiff. It is worth remembering the differences in the preparation for this crucial encounter when compared to the modern era. Gwyn Nicholls, the vastly experienced Welsh captain who had reversed his decision to retire, due to the importance of this game, and his brother-in-law Bert Winfield, the highly regarded Welsh full back who would frustrate New Zealand with his superb line kicking, had completed a morning shift at the laundry that they jointly owned before making their way to Cardiff. The referee John Dallas, at twenty-seven younger than both captains and who was to play such a vital and controversial part in the proceedings, was said to have taken to the field in street clothes and ordinary walking boots. The less than impressed New Zealanders later referred to this ex-Scottish international forward as an "old man in a long jacket", clearly not seeing him as the man to take charge of such a significant encounter. This image has since been discredited as an attempt by some New Zealanders to undermine the referee. John Dallas refereed the game wearing the attire common to referees of this period but the New Zealand attitude confirms the importance that they attached to this game. So too the Welsh. 47,000 supporters packed the ground and the gates were closed at 1.30, an hour before kick off. No tickets were issued in advance and so spectators travelled, in the words of Williams and Smith, "more in hope than expectation".

As they waited the terraces swayed, the new stands creaked and the trees outside the ground held hundreds of those unlucky enough to be denied entry. It was then that the crowd began to sing. When the teams took the field Dave Gallaher led his team in the 'Haka', a performance which the *Western Mail* described as "not very musical but… very impressive" and listened to in respectful silence by the excited yet tense crowd. Teddy Morgan, the Welsh wing who was about to pass into immortality, led the Welsh response. When 'Hen Wlad Fy Nhadau' was struck up by the band the crowd and players picked it up quickly creating a 'wall of sound' sixty years before Phil Spector ever coined the phrase. The *Lyttelton Times*, the most popular newspaper in New Zealand, reported six weeks later,

> The scene at the ground was unique in the New Zealander's experience.... The Welsh... were there to sing and to cheer their champions to victory.... Imagine some 40,000 people singing their National Anthem with all the fervour of which the Celtic heart is capable.... It was the most impressive incident I have ever witnessed on a football field. It gave a semi-religious solemnity to this memorable contest... was intensely thrilling, even awe-inspiring. It was a wonderful revelation of the serious spirit in which the Welsh take their football.

The journalist was not the only one to be moved. The New Zealand captain himself later said that he had never been more impressed in his life as when the crowd sang the chorus. The atmosphere at the kick off was electric. There was no need for the rather contrived excitement of flares, loud music and over-excited public address announcer, just genuine rugby supporters hardly able to contain their excitement as the two leading rugby nations clashed for the first time.

The game itself can be dealt with briefly. As expected, Dave's destructive (or obstructive) role angered the partisan crowd who barracked him constantly but Wales, with their extra back, were able to combat the tactic and allow their own backs to cause problems. *The Times* later reported that the "football was the hardest imaginable" but Wales had a definite advantage. When Teddy Morgan raced over for what would prove to be the only score, it was no more than Wales deserved. History, of course, has given great attention to the disallowed try by All Black centre Bob Deans but the debate as to whether or not the inappropriately attired referee kept up with play enough to see what happened is of no concern here. Wales were considered to be worthy winners and the country celebrated in style. Dave acknowledged the Welsh win with a magnanimous tribute,

> It was a rattling good game, played out to the bitter end, with the result that the better team won, and I am content. I have always made it a point never to express a view regarding the referee in any match in which I have played.

Charlie, with his tireless work rate and deadly tackling was feted as a hero, particularly by his teammates who were, perhaps, more aware than the supporters of his magnificent contribution. George Travers, club colleague and fellow Welsh hero, said that Charlie had "knocked 'em down like ninepins" and believed that he had been the pick of the Welsh forwards that day. This was confirmed by the other players who referred to him as the 'star' player on the day and 'always in the thick of the fight', throwing himself at his opponents in an attempt to disrupt their rhythm.

Celebrations went on well into the night with bars, pubs and hotels full within fifteen minutes of the final whistle. The players were expected to make their own way home after the game and ecstatic supporters waited at every station to greet them. Cliff Pritchard was met at Pontypool station after midnight and carried shoulder high through the town, serenaded by 'Men of Harlech', 'Sospan Fach' and 'Land of My Fathers'. The press meanwhile were forced to eat some humble pie. *The Times*, which on the morning of the match predicted "an inevitable defeat", admitted that Wales deserved to win. The *Lyttelton Times* said that the game had been a "Homeric contest of skill, endurance, pace and sheer brute strength – the hardest, keenest struggle I can ever remember". The strength of Welsh rugby was confirmed when, in subsequent weeks, New Zealand struggled to beat the leading Welsh club sides. Newport, captained by Charlie, only lost by 6-3 after dominating the second half, Cardiff were beaten 10-8, their only defeat of the season, while Swansea were beaten 4-3, one drop goal being a superior score to the one try scored by the hosts. The tourists then left for France, followed by a return home via the USA and British Columbia with the magnificent record of played 35, won 34, lost 1. The tour tally was 976 against 59 with 243 tries (including the matches in France and British Columbia but not in the USA). In the 32 matches played in the British Isles the point difference was 830 against 39, a record that will never be equalled. 'The Originals' were very nearly 'The Invincibles'.

It was the pinnacle of Charlie Pritchard's rugby career. He played a further ten matches for Wales amassing fourteen caps, a significant number when international matches were much fewer in number than they are today. Gwyn Prescott, in his book *Call Them to Remembrance*, suggests that Charlie would have won a further ten caps were it not for injury. Included in those games in which he did play were contributions to the 1906 championship winning side, scoring a try in the 16-3 victory over England, being one of only a few Welsh players to enhance their reputation in the disappointing defeat to the 1906 Springboks, and playing a part in the Grand Slam of 1908 (he missed the 1909 Grand Slam due to injury). But nothing could surpass his triumph in 1905. Charlie captained Newport for three years between 1906 and 1909 but knee injuries began to take their toll and he missed most of the 1908/9 season. Charlie played his last game for Wales against England in 1910. He was selected for the following match against Scotland but withdrew with a rib injury, making way for his clubmate Ernie Jenkins. Jenkins, despite having a successful club career, had never been capped and some suggested that Charlie pulled out with a relatively minor injury so as to allow his clubmate the opportunity to gain a deserved cap. Wales won and Jenkins kept his place. Charlie's international career was over and his last game for Newport followed a year later. He was, however, remembered with affection. Tommy Vile recalled that

> Charlie Pritchard, although very popular, may not have been the best captain but he was a great player. On the field he was a lion and off it he was a gentleman with a quality of gentleness in his manner and a note of affection in his voice.

Charlie Pritchard's reputation as one of Newport rugby's greatest servants was safe.

Dave Gallaher took his now legendry team to France and led it to a convincing 38-8 victory but this was to prove his last appearance for the All Blacks in international rugby. He played thirty-six times in an All Black shirt, twenty-seven of them as captain and scored six tries, setting the template for all future All Black captains. On the journey to British Columbia at the end of the tour, along with Billy Stead, he wrote *The Complete Rugby Footballer*, which is regarded as one of the most influential books on rugby ever written. In its 322 pages, (most, it must be said, written by Stead), the authors raised the technical discussion about the game to a new level. On his arrival back in New Zealand Dave announced his retirement and moved into coaching grade rugby teams and Auckland Grammar School. In 1906, he became the sole Auckland selector, a position he held until 1916, and he was a respected national selector between 1907 and 1914, a period when only one test match was lost. The nomadic Dave ensured that his personal life became more stable and happy when, on 10th October 1906, he married Nellie Francis, the sister of dual-code rugby international Arthur Francis. Their daughter Nora was born in September 1908. The future appeared to be very bright.

Playing alongside Dave in his final international was another All Black representing his country for the last time. Eric Tristan Gerald Harper was one of the most interesting, if little used, players on the tour. Born on 1st December 1877, Eric was an outstanding sportsman who was the national champion in both the 440 yards hurdles (1901) and 880 yards hurdles (1902) and represented Canterbury at cricket. At a shade under six foot tall and weighing in at just below thirteen stones, Eric was a strong running centre or wing three-quarter. Born at Papanui, Christchurch to a pioneering Canterbury family, his grandfather, Henry Harper, was the first Anglican Bishop of Canterbury and the first European, along with Eric's Uncle Leonard, to cross the Southern Alps. This instilled in the family a love of mountaineering which resulted in Eric and Leonard's son Arthur, a well known naturalist, exploring together. In 1908 Eric negotiated the 6,500 foot Denniston Pass and had a creek named after him while in 1913 he and Arthur scaled the 2,280 foot Mt Davie in the Waimakariri Valley.

Before becoming involved in the dangerous hobby of exploration and mountaineering Eric focused on his rugby and his career as a lawyer. Described as a "fine centre three-quarter, sure with his kicks, a good tackler, plenty of pace, a 'potter' of goals, and a place kick", Eric established himself in the Canterbury team in 1900 and represented the South Island in 1902. By the 1904 British Lions tour he was knocking on the door of the All Blacks and, following an appearance against the Lions for Canterbury/ West Coast XV, he was selected in the centre for his first cap. Although making little impact in the game, Eric did enough to warrant selection for the 1905 tour, which was to prove disappointing for the talented Eric as he played in fewer than half of the matches. Known as 'aristocratic Eric' due to his wealthy background and his insistence on wearing a full dinner suit to all the formal functions on the tour, it is possible that he didn't quite fit in with his teammates. One of the few players from the South Island and the only player with a recognised profession, Eric stood out as being a little different. He put his money to good use, however, when, along with five or six other of the wealthier players, he put £2 each week into a fund to support those players who were struggling financially.

There is no record of Eric picking up any serious injuries on the tour but he played in only four of the first seventeen matches. He was particularly disappointed, one would imagine, not to be picked to play against Ireland when injuries meant that Simon Mynott, a first five-eighth, had to play in the three-quarter line although he was inexperienced in the position. After scoring a try against Charlie Pritchard's spirited Newport side, Eric was finally picked for his second cap against France. His rugby career ended on a high when he ran in two tries at the Parc des Princes but he never played first class rugby again. Overall on the tour, Eric played in ten matches scoring six tries and three conversions.

Following his retirement from rugby, and alongside his adventures in the mountains, Eric practiced in the law. He worked for his father's legal firm as a barrister and settled in West Christchurch with his wife and two children, a comfortable upper middle class, settled existence which promised years of happiness and success. However, the military had always interested him and appealed to his adventurous nature so he carried out voluntary military service in the years before the war. On the outbreak of war, Eric was rejected by the military on the grounds of having varicose veins. Given Eric's character, this was never going to keep him out of the action. Following an operation, Eric reapplied, falsifying his age and no doubt spurred on by his brother Gordon's injuries in Gallipoli. Gordon, already a DCM, was later killed in Romani, Egypt, in August 1916, where he fought alongside another brother, Robin. Finally accepted into the Canterbury Mounted Rifles, Eric quickly reached the rank of Sergeant Major and left Wellington on 31st May 1917 for Suez. The New Zealand Expeditionary Forces attempted to capture Damascus after being forced to retreat from Amman, low on morale and with numerous casualties. Eric's division were involved in the attack on Turkish positions at Shunet Nimrin, a part of the 7,000 strong Allied attack known as the Second Action of Es Salt or the Second Battle of the Jordan. Eric's unit came under severe bombardment and, while attempting to quieten the horses, the forty-year-old ex-All Black was killed, an early victim among the 1,784 casualties, in this unsuccessful venture. His name is engraved on the Jerusalem Memorial.

With the outbreak of war, Charlie Pritchard was quick to enlist and 'do his bit' as part of Kitchener's army. He joined the South Wales Borderers as a temporary Second Lieutenant in May 1915, was promoted to lieutenant at the end of July and was made a captain in the 12th Battalion the following October. Following a period of training, Charlie arrived on the Western Front in June 1916 in time for the Somme offensive and he was quickly into the action. He wrote to a friend, Mr Horrace Trust, in a letter published after his death, that he had experienced a "rummy" time when being caught in an Allied bombing attack when on patrol. He and his men had been forced to take cover in the long grass from their own bombs and struggled to avoid the German searchlights while listening to the trumpets that the Germans always blew when something unusual was happening. On the night of 12th/13th August Charlie was instructed to lead a raiding party on the German trenches with a view to taking as many prisoners as possible. He led his men into the trenches showing exceptional bravery in the process and, despite being wounded in the wrist, continued to encourage and lead his men in what was to prove to be a successful raid. Tragically the wrist injury proved to be the least of his wounds. The official report is quoted in Steve Lewis's history of Newport Rugby Club

> He himself took one of the enemy prisoner and forced him to ascend the ladder, following him over the parapet. He was then again badly wounded and handed the prisoner over to another officer of his party. He was finally brought back to our parapet in a state of collapse, owing to his many wounds. The success of the enterprise was largely due to his gallant leadership and devotion to duty.

Weak from loss of blood, Charlie was taken back to the British front line and then to No 1 Casualty Clearing Station shortly before dawn on the wet morning of August 13th. Here his concern for the success of the raid and his devotion to duty came to the fore asking, "Have they got the Hun?" "Yes" he was told, "Well I have done my bit," Charlie replied, the last words that he was known to speak. He died without ever leaving the Clearing Station on 14th August 1916.

Following his death, his commanding officer, Lieutenant Colonel Alexander wrote a heartfelt and sincere letter to the family saying that, although operation was otherwise successful, Charlie's death had "cast a gloom" and that he had been as "brave as a lion". On August 18th, just four days after his death, the *South Wales Argus* said that "it was impossible to say what we thought and felt" and that Charlie was "near to our hearts". George Boots, a fellow Newport player, spoke of "Charlie the Lion heart" who "was chivalrous and generous" and who would pick opponents up off the floor after he had grounded them with one of his thumping tackles. In private, he said, Charlie had "a private tenderness" and a "depth of affection". Charlie's family fought for him to be awarded the Distinguished Order but were told that his death prevented this. Despite acrimonious correspondence with the War Office, the family had to settle for a Mention in Dispatches. The South African international Major J.E.C. Partridge, a former Newport teammate and opponent, wrote to Charlie's family in a letter quoted by Nigel McCrery,

> I have never met a man who played more in the spirit of the game.... He was a fine example of what a British sportsman should be, and was loved by all who came into contact with him.

Charlie was buried in Choeques Military Cemetery, one of 86 members of Newport Athletic Club who lost their lives in The Great War and remembered on the Memorial Gates at Rodney Parade. He left, in Llwynderi Road, Newport, a grieving widow with two young boys and the legacy of a true Welsh rugby hero.

What of Dave Gallaher? Due to his age, Dave was exempt from conscription but, nevertheless, on 25th July 1916, he enlisted and was made a Corporal in the 2nd Battalion of the Auckland Infantry

Regiment, part of the New Zealand Expeditionary Force. In order to ensure that he would be accepted, Dave had taken three years off his age but his past record in the Boer War undoubtedly helped create the right impression and probably helped him gain rapid promotion. In October he was promoted to the rank of Sergeant and in January 1917 he was promoted again, this time to Company Sergeant Major. Part of Dave's motivation is said to have come from the loss of his brother Douglas at Laventie in June 1916, although it is highly unlikely that Dave, with his army experience and leadership skills, would have been happy sitting at home. Further tragedy hit the family when another brother, Henry, was killed in action in April 1917. Dave, no doubt driven by a wish to avenge the loss of his brothers, was now thrown into the action at the 3rd Ypres, Passchendaele.

We have already seen, in an earlier chapter, something of the horrors of Passchendaele, a monumental exercise in futility, overconfidence in artillery and a serious underestimation of the difficulties imposed by the unforgiving terrain. The very name has become a symbol for the horrors of the Western Front. The historian Lyn MacDonald has quoted the soldiers view, "We died in Hell – they called it Passchendaele". On July 16th a ten day artillery bombardment began but heavy rain turned the battlefield into a quagmire. One soldier, Sergeant Berry of the 1st Battalion Rifle Brigade recalls,

> We heard screaming coming from another crater a bit away. I went over to investigate with a couple of the lads. It was a big hole and there was a fellow of the 8th Suffolk's in it up to his shoulders. So I said 'Get your rifles, one man in the middle to stretch them out, make a chain and let him get hold of it'. But it was no use. It was too far to stretch, we couldn't get any force on it and the more he struggled the further he seemed to go down. He went down gradually. He kept begging us to shoot him. But we couldn't shoot him. Who could shoot him? We stayed with him watching him go down in the mud. And he died. He wasn't the only one. There must have been thousands up there who died in the mud.

Dave and his men marched through Ypres on October 1st and

by the 3rd they were camped at St Julian-Langemark in order to prepare for battle. The New Zealand regiments were due to attack the Abraham Heights and Gravenstafel Ridge at 6.00am the following day. By 5.30 a German barrage opened up and the shells began to rain in. Rum rations were issued and, with the rain becoming heavier and the temperature falling, Dave led the second wave of attack. He was wounded as shrapnel pierced his helmet early in the attack and, despite being evacuated to the Dressing Station at Abraham Heights and then being transferred to Poperinge, he died there of his wounds, one of the 250,000 British and Allied casualties killed, wounded or missing between August and November in the Ypres salient alone.

Even with such hideous losses, Dave's death was a huge event in New Zealand. As early as 1922 the Provincial Championship in Auckland was renamed the 'Gallaher Shield' and two years later the 1924 All Blacks visited his grave at Nine Elms British Cemetery in Belgium. Terry MacLean, the great New Zealand rugby writer, was of the opinion that "In death he acquired a mystique" and this recognition has continued into the twenty-first century. In 2000 the Dave Gallaher Trophy was contested between New Zealand and France and in 2005 Letterkenny RFC, the club closest to his birthplace, renamed their ground after him. A plaque was put up in his birthplace and members of the 2005 All Blacks were present to witness the unveiling. One of the local players, Jeremy Worth, wrote a moving poem about Ireland's greatest export to New Zealand, keen to acknowledge Dave's Irish roots. The poem reads as follows,

Through the mists of time a figure stands tall
An All Black legend from Donegal
This man had power poise and pace
An iron man with an honest face
Smart as a fox he soon rose to fame
A soldier's instinct in a magnificent game
Hard as nails and strong and fast
A super human with an unlikely past
The name of Gallaher still rings aloud
A century on from the original crowd
Dave was a hero, a leader of men
As men would follow again and again
A family man respected by all

A tragic loss with a heroic fall
A nation inspired history made
An Irish Kiwi in Belgium laid
One hundred years later his presence still felt
A child inspired wears a tag rugby belt
His gift to rugby is still very clear
Ireland's gift to New Zealand still held so dear.

A moving and lasting memorial. In 2010, the Dave Gallaher Park was opened in Ramelton and finally, the following year, a bronze statue was unveiled at one of the entrances to Eden Park, Auckland, one of the greatest All Black captains permanently remembered at the home of New Zealand rugby.

David Bedell-Sivright and the 1904 British Lions

The concept of the British and Irish Lions has survived the many changes that have taken place in rugby over the last one hundred and twenty five years. On numerous occasions critics have predicted the idea to be an anachronism, never more so since rugby union first introduced a World Cup in 1987 and embraced professionalism in 1995. Yet as I write, the Lions have just completed a most successful tour of Australia and the interest in such adventures has never been greater. The Lions are big business. That this should be so is due, in no small part, to the roots planted in the years preceding the Great War. One man at the heart of this creation was David Revell Bedell-Sivright, the captain of the 1904 British Lions team in Australia and New Zealand.

David Bedell-Sivright was one of the early heroes of Scottish rugby and he remains to this day the only Scottish player to play in three Triple Crown winning teams. He is also remembered as one of the real characters of the sport, a man who played as hard as anyone but who fully understood and embraced the idea of amateur rugby. Such is the reputation of the charismatic leader uniformly known as 'Darkie', that it is very often difficult to separate fact from fiction. Born in Edinburgh on 8th December 1880, the impressively built rather swarthy handsome all round sportsman was clearly destined to make his mark on life one way or another. Educated at one of Britain's finest public schools, Fettes College, he won a place at Trinity College Cambridge to read medicine in 1899. There David won four rugby Blues as well as making his debut for Scotland in 1900 in the 12-3 defeat to Wales at St Helen's, Swansea. Rugby, by this time, was taking precedence and on completing his first degree, David put his studies on hold in 1903 while he toured South Africa under the leadership of fellow Scot Mark Morrison. Although enjoying a successful tour and even serving on the Match Committee as a senior player, he was not selected for any of the international/test matches.

It should be remembered that participation in Lions tours during the early years was heavily dependant on availability. As was the case with many amateur cricketers, (C.B. Fry and Stanley Jackson leap to mind), some leading players never took part in an overseas tour. The early tours tended to be either unofficial, organised by commercial promoters, or semi-official and tolerated by the national unions. Often the teams were made up of a generous helping of Oxbridge Blues and gentlemen of private means. Yet it is somewhat surprising that, when the selection of the team to tour Australia and New Zealand was made only one year later, David 'Darkie' Bedell-Sivright was the only player common to both teams. Even more surprising perhaps is that the twenty-three year old hard tackling back row forward was named as captain, that that invitation came from the English Rugby Union was even more surprising. There was very little 'hype' around the selection at all and it was very low key compared to the modern day media circus. The press referred to the "British Isles team to tour the colonies", reminding us that the term 'British Lions' did not appear until 1924, and that in many respects this was an 'invitation' side. When it was decided to add the extra leg of the tour, a visit to New Zealand, an open invitation for some more forwards was issued by the selection committee giving them five days (8th to 13th April) to respond. On the 18th April, the 'invitation squad' of twenty-four players, the highest number to embark on a tour of this nature so far, was announced from the City Liberal Club and consisted of ten current internationals and four players who would later represent their country.

The man chosen to lead this team was certainly a formidable character. Clem Thomas, a Welsh international back row forward of a similar ilk, writing in his history of the British Lions, described him as

> ...a man after my own heart, being a rough handful as a player. He was one of the first in a long line of Scottish forwards to master the art of wing-forward play.

David was widely accepted as being the roughest and toughest forward of his day who has been quoted as saying "When I go on to the rugby field I only see the ball, and should someone be in the road, that is his look out". Off the field, although never aggressive,

'Darkie' was in the thick of the action. He is reputed to have tackled a carthorse to the ground in Princes Street following the celebrations of a Scottish victory and also, on one occasion, lay on the tram tracks for an hour in order to hold up the traffic. No policeman, it is said, would go near him.

The touring party left the Charing Cross Hotel in early May and, after a five week voyage on the Royal Mail Ship the *Ormuz*, arrived in Australia on June 13th. Like with all successful touring parties, the seeds of its success were sown through the team spirit engineered in the early weeks. Tommy Vile, chosen as an uncapped Welsh scrum half, talked of the comradeship of the players on the tour. He put this down to David's leadership and in particular his serious attitude to training. Training began at the start of the long voyage, when the weather was at its hottest. Vile tells us,

> We rose at 7.30 and had half an hour's shadow exercise, then a walk round deck, a cold bath and breakfast. Between breakfast and lunch there was a deck game such as deck cricket or quoits. In the afternoon there was skipping practice scrummage practice, passing with sandbags and walking. Afternoon training started quietly but became heavier as we neared Australia.

This level of preparation, although not comparable with Warren Gatland's Polish training camps with its use of a deep freeze cryogenic centre, was a great deal more advanced than anything previously experienced by British touring parties. And, in Australia at least, it worked. David's British Lions won all fourteen matches, including the three test matches. Although not as strong as they would become by 1908, this Australian side were no pushover, styling themselves on neighbouring New Zealand. However the Lions hit the ground running with their fitness and stamina showing from the first game. The three tests were won 17-0; 17-3; and 16-0 although David, for reasons that are unclear, played in only the first of these, Teddy Morgan taking over as captain. Tommy Vile, once again, is a reliable source for this tour. He was keen to sing the praises of the Welsh backs (of which he was one!) but in particular of his outside half Percy Bush and the three-quarters Rhys Gabe, Willie Llewellyn and Teddy Morgan, the very men who defeated

New Zealand in 1905. Not that these events were widely reported back home. Even *The Times*, a keen rugby newspaper, reported only the final score. There is no mention of who played or who scored. The Australian press, however were impressed. The *Sydney Morning Herald* was of the opinion that,

> Our British visitors have shown… the rugby game in its perfection, shown it as calling forth the highest power of the athlete in the avoidance of danger as well as in the overcoming of obstacles.

New Zealand, however, was a different matter with only two of the five matches won, with one drawn and two defeats, including the only test match. Matters weren't helped by the serious leg injury that David received in the first match in New Zealand which prevented him from contributing his aggressive game to the British cause. Tommy Vile, reflecting on events on this leg of the tour, felt that the rugby supporters at home had no idea just how good New Zealand were. He considered them to be "tremendously fast… individually clever and their combinations… perfect". David, however thought the New Zealand tactics (use of the 'rover') to be unfair. His attitude to the hosts was considered by New Zealanders to be patronizing, saying that the colonials would dare not come to Britain where they would succeed only against 'the underdog' teams and would lose the international matches. While accepting that in the test match New Zealand (with both Dave Gallaher and Eric Harper) had been the better team, much of this was due to the fatigue experienced by the tourists and a lack of competitive rugby while playing in Australia. He even saw the, in his eyes, lavish and even excessive hospitality offered by the hosts as detrimental to his teams efforts to beat the All Blacks. This attitude did nothing to endear David to New Zealanders.

However the incident that has become remembered in relation to David's leadership took place during the Australian leg of the tour, in Newcastle, New South Wales where the British Isles played the Northern Districts. Although not playing in the game, the whole incident confirms his strength of character and his fearless determination to stick up for what was right. One of the British Isles players, Fred Jowett, had left the field with an injury caused by the

Australian international No 8 Pat Walsh. In the days before substitutes any loss of a player had serious consequences for a team and the British players were none too pleased with Walsh, so much so that he became a heavily marked man. When a penalty was awarded against the British team following play involving Walsh by the referee Harry Dolan, one of the players, the England international forward Denys Dobson, was sent from the field for uttering "words not used in polite society". The British team, knowing Dobson as a very mild mannered civil servant, Oxford educated and, according to Tommy Vile, the most popular player on the tour, found it difficult to accept that he had become the first British rugby player to be sent off on an overseas tour. To put it bluntly, they did not believe the referee and would not accept his decision. David, watching from the stands, promptly ran onto the field and led the team back to the changing rooms where they stayed for twenty minutes while frantic discussions took place. David regarded the referee's action as an insult to Dobson and the team. Dobson, he said, was "one of the quietest and most gentlemanly members of the team" and anyway the referee had his back to the play and couldn't have seen the incident. David later told reporters, eager for the full story, that "he regarded Mr Dolan as an incompetent referee".

Although the team eventually returned to the pitch (minus Dobson) and won the game 17-3, the matter did not end there. David insisted that his action was not about challenging the right of the referee to make a decision but something far more important, personal honour. The team were prepared to put up with the referee's incompetence as long as it only affected them in their play but "when he chose to take up a position which reflected on their personal honour, they thought it time to show their resentment," he said. An inquiry was conducted by the New South Wales Rugby Union which concluded that no further action be taken against Dobson for his 'improper expression'. It emerged that Dobson's improper expression was no more than the question "What the devil was that for?" which had been enough to upset the clearly sensitive Mr Dolan, who never refereed a first class fixture again. Pat Walsh never represented Australia in Rugby Union again but switched codes to Rugby League and toured Britain in 1908. On the outbreak of war, Walsh joined the Australian 12th Light Horse and successfully served in Gallipoli, Egypt and Palestine where he was mentioned in dispatches. Unfortunately he ended the war with serious leg injuries but lived until 1953. Denys Dobson was not so lucky. A successful international career which included six England caps, in which he scored three tries, and four Lions test matches, was now over. He joined the Colonial Civil Service and was District Resident in Nyasaland where he was in charge of Sleeping Sickness Operations. On 10th July 1916, he was fatally gored by a charging rhinoceros, not an official war casualty but none the less tragic for that. It is said that, on hearing the news one of his old lecturers at Oxford exclaimed that "he always did have a weak hand off" although one hopes this is an apocryphal story.

For all David's difficulties with southern hemisphere referees and the controversy that he encountered, the 1904 tour was considered extremely successful. The superb team spirit, encouraged during David's ruthless training sessions, lived on and there were reunions at the Charing Cross Hotel on one international weekend each year. Even as late as 1958, when only five of the players were still alive, reunions still took place. Looking back it can be seen as one of the most significant overseas tours and one that did much to pave the way for the 'Lions' tours of later years where players fondly experienced the meaning of being 'a Lion'. There was something about Australia and the people that appealed to David and, with teammates Blair Swannell and Sid Crowther, he remained 'down under' at the end of the tour. For the next year David worked in stock rearing but eventually became bored and returned to Edinburgh to complete his medical studies and become a surgeon. Following a period in Japan, David finally left Sydney on 3rd June 1905, on the *Ormuz*, the very ship that had brought his team to Australia the year before.

On his return the All Blacks soon had the opportunity to prove to David how seriously he had underestimated them a year earlier. As we have seen, Scotland, with David very much involved, was beaten in November 1905, but relations were far from cordial. New Zealand's victory was received in stony silence. The Scottish authorities were less than hospitable to their visitors, resulting in them using an Australasian club for the post match celebrations, and objected to them receiving a share of the gate receipts, arguing that it amounted to professionalism. Such was the strength of feeling that even nineteen years later, on the next All Blacks tour to Britain, Scotland refused to play New Zealand. David's rugby career, however, continued to flourish. In November 1906, he was part of the Scottish team that defeated a South African side who had won their previous fifteen games and later that season was part of a Triple Crown winning team for the third time. He gained his last cap in 1908 but, far from seeing this as the end of his sporting career, David now took up boxing. By 1909 he was the Scottish amateur heavyweight champion employing a style that relied on raw punching power rather than technique, before settling down as a fully qualified surgeon from 1910. With his sporting career now largely behind him, David could look forward to a successful professional career and face the future with confidence.

Sid Crowther also decided to return from Australia. Born in 1875 in Bromley, Kent, the son of a solicitor, he had been a talented pupil at Warwick School where he first played rugby. The fourth of five children, Sid grew up at Holly Lodge, Chatham in Kent. On leaving school he headed to London and Westminster Hospital where he trained as a doctor and played his rugby with the Surrey team, Lennox, as well as with a very strong Westminster Hospital team. By 1903, he had qualified and consequently felt free to become one of the fourteen uncapped players invited to tour with Bedell-Sivright's team in 1904, one of two doctors and five medical students in the party. Sid, a forward, played in eighteen matches on the tour, including all four tests and can be considered to be one of the successes of the trip, his reputation enhanced. Staying on after the tour, Sid put his medical skills to use working as the ships doctor on board *The Empire* where he was reunited with Bedell-Sivright who was returning to Australia after spending time in Japan and Hong Kong. On returning to England, Sid worked at Brookwood Hospital, Woking, the second county asylum before moving to the new Surrey Asylum at Netherne, a pioneering force in the treatment of mental illness. Here patients were given a higher standard of care and were encouraged to work on the estate and also to enjoy leisure activities. Sid, as a Senior Assistant, was at the heart of this forward thinking institution and was rewarded when made Superintendent Elect just before the outbreak of war.

Blair Swannell, on the other hand, did not return to Britain. Unlike his two colleagues he continued his rugby career Down

Under. Blair Inskip Swannell had been born the son of a farmer in Weston Underwood, Buckinghamshire in August 1875. After completing his education at Repton he attended Thames Nautical Training College where he successfully graduated as a second mate. In 1897 Blair first went to Australia as a mate on a schooner and on his return joined the British Army and fought in the Second Boer War, serving with 37th (Buckinghamshire) Company, 10th Battalion Imperial Yeomanry and was soon recommended for a commission. He reached the rank of Lieutenant before resigning in 1903.

This might appear to be an exciting enough life but it did not prevent Blair, a keen self-promoter, from embellishing his experiences to another level. In his own words he had fought insurrectionists in Uruguay, hunted seal around the American coast, Cape Horn and Labrador as well as playing rugby in France, Germany, India, South Africa and North and South America. None of this can be substantiated but what is clear is that Blair Swannell had a remarkable rugby career. Playing most of his rugby for Northampton where his mother now lived, Blair was selected to tour Australia in 1899 with Matthew Mullineux's British Isles team despite having no international experience. Blair played in the three test wins in the back row, missing only the first test defeat. This success, however did nothing to endear him to his teammates. They were appalled at his low level of personal hygiene, not helped perhaps by his years at sea, and unimpressed with the football breeches which he refused to wash and wore in every match. Blair was a hard, uncompromising player who, although undoubtedly seen as a player to have on your side, was considered to be too violent in his play. Whereas 'Darkie' Sivright was considered to be an extremely hard, no nonsense forward who would take no prisoners, Blair was seen by many as a 'dirty' player in all senses of the word. Clem Thomas says, in his history of the British Lions, that Blair was "renowned for unsavoury play and unusual hygiene" and had been known to turn up in a dirty, once white sweater with badges and dates of all the countries that he had represented on it. Turning up in unwashed kit appears to have been standard behaviour for Blair but it did not prevent his selection for the 1904 tour. Here he played in all four tests, scoring a try in the third test against Australia and putting himself on the line in the defeat to New Zealand where he left the field with two black eyes and covered in blood. Clearly New Zealand had decided to match fire with fire!

Staying on in Australia, Blair continued to play rugby. In many respects he reflected the modern stereotype of the Australian sportsman, brash, confident, physically imposing, never taking a backward step and with an attitude that says winning is everything and second is nowhere. Such was his success that he was selected for his new country in the 14-3 defeat to the 1905 All Blacks, although not everyone was impressed. The Wallaby captain, Herbert Moran, was of the opinion that "Swannell was, for a number of years, a bad influence in Sydney football... his conception of rugby was one of trained violence". Nevertheless, Blair became an important figure in Australian rugby.

In retirement, Blair turned to coaching both rugby and hockey as well as becoming vice president of the local swimming club. He had great success as coach of St Joseph's College, the team winning several championships. Blair also took responsibility for training senior military cadets for examinations in life saving, his adventures and rather nomadic lifestyle an asset. Indeed, journalists who had previously been critical of his methods now looked to him as an authority, particularly on the art of forward play where Blair believed all games were won and lost. In 1908 the *Star* newspaper hired him to write articles on scrummaging and the importance of forward dominance, articles which the *Sydney Morning Herald* said were "couched in language understandable to the average footballer". In 1910 Blair was made Secretary of the Metropolitan Rugby Union and paid a salary of £250 a year, a healthy sum at the time. The following year he moved into refereeing and by the end of the season was being described in the press as one of the best in the country. From unpromising beginnings Blair Swannell had, by 1914, become one of the most respected, if not universally loved, figures in Australian rugby.

The outbreak of war in 1914 had grave consequences for all three British Lions. Dr Sid Crowther was still waiting to take up his new post at Netherne when he enlisted in the British Army. He was assigned to the 2nd Signal Troop of the Royal Engineers as a motorcycle dispatch rider and given the rank of corporal, but sadly his war was to be brief. On the 18th October 1914 at L'Epinette near Armentieres Sid was killed in action. Details of his death are few but he is commemorated on the Le Touret War Memorial, Pas de Calais.

In Australia, Blair was in the process of joining the Australian Imperial Force as a captain in the 1st Battalion. He quickly passed the examinations to be promoted to the rank of major and was soon heading, with many other Australian soldiers, via Egypt to the Dardanelles and confrontation with the Turks. The initial feeling about this expedition was that it was an easier option than fighting in the hell that was now the Western Front but, in truth, the expedition, encouraged by Winston Churchill as a means of breaking the stalemate in France and Belgium, never had much chance of success. The plan focussed on attacking the narrow Dardanelles strait, thereby opening the route to Constantinople. In theory the plan had something to commend it but insufficient resources were made available to ensure success. Bombardments began on 19th February and minesweeping followed. Nevertheless three Allied battleships were sunk and three more damaged, though this did not prevent the land expedition putting ashore, where they faced the most horrendous conditions. The heat caused almost as much difficulty as the damage caused by the Turkish soldiers picking off the Allied troops from the cliffs above. Fresh troops landing in the unbearable heat of early August made little difference, although it took until November for the High Command to admit total failure. The evacuation, begun in December 1915, was complete by the end of January the following year but 200,000 dead comrades had been left behind and Churchill's political career was in tatters. He left the Cabinet in November 1915.

Blair Swannell's part in the action was all too brief. As part of the first landings of 25th April, Blair, who had been diverted to reinforce the 12th Battalion, fought in the battle for Baby 700, a hill nearly 700 feet above sea level which was key to the Anzac position. The battle here was intense and the hill changed hands five times during the afternoon. Blair and his colleagues were keen to be involved having spent months of rather tedious training but very quickly they became frustrated when realising the real nature of the fight. Steel and Hart quote one soldier as saying, "There was no co-ordinated effort about it. We were just a crowd of Diggers working with each other trusting each other blind." With no artillery support heavy casualties were inevitable. Besides the Turks, better co-ordinated, were determined to defend their homeland against what they considered the infidel invader. At some point during the day

Blair, while demonstrating to his men the best way to aim their rifles, was shot in the head. He lies buried in Baby 700 Cemetery. At the end of the war a plaque was laid in Weston Underwood Church, where he had been born nearly forty years before. The obituaries published in Australia recognised Blair's contribution but the *Evening Post* could not resist reminding its readers that he had been "the roughest player" in the British team, a reputation that would never leave him.

Two months later, on 28th June, another member of Bedell-Sivright's 1904 tourists also lost his life on the beaches of Gallipoli. Ronald Joseph Rogers was a little remembered front row forward who, although never capped by England, successfully plied his trade with both Bath and Somerset. Records show that Ron served as a captain in the 14th Battalion Rifle Brigade and died at Krithia on 28th June 1915, although the exact circumstances are unclear. The Third Battle of Krithia was fought on 4th June, in the Helles war zone but the main period of fighting was over by the end of the day so what happened to Ron over three weeks later is difficult to determine. What can be confirmed is that on the 1904 tour the twenty one year old Ron, after six appearances, forced his way into the test team for the first ever meeting with the All Blacks. As we already know, in front of 25,000 eager spectators in perfect conditions, the British Isles surprisingly succumbed 9-3 to the rapidly emerging All Blacks. This was Ron's only experience of international rugby, hence his almost total disappearance from sporting history. He is, however, remembered on Panel 196 of the Helles Memorial, one of more than 21,000 names contained there.

What became of the captain of the successful British Lions tour of 1904? At the beginning of the war David was commissioned as a surgeon in the Royal Navy and very soon was also on his way to Gallipoli. He was posted to the Hawke Battalion of the Royal Naval Division in March 1915, loaned to the Royal Scots Fusiliers during June and finally posted to the Portsmouth Battalion of the Royal Marine Light Infantry from 20th June. By now he was working at an advanced dressing station treating soldiers wounded in the exchanges. The nature of the job frustrated David, who was keen to be involved in the direct action. Nigel McCrery quotes a letter written by David to a friend around this time,

> It makes me swear that I am a medico. I'd be ten times more useful with a parcel of jam-tin bombs and a few Turks in front of me than as a sort of qualified vet.

Despite these rather dismissive comments about his work the conditions in which David worked and the situations with which he had to deal were truly appalling. Illness was as much a problem as wounds. Max Arthur, the historian, quotes the experience of Fusilier Harold Pilling paints an even more horrific picture of experiences onshore.

> If you looked in the latrines you'd have been sickened. You'd think people had parted with their stomachs or their insides. It was awful. You had to cover it and dig another. It hadn't to be so high or else you could fall down. There were no supports or anything, it was just an open trench, but it was fairly deep.

That David would have witnessed such dreadful experiences there can be no doubt. He would also have been expected to treat men suffering the most appalling of injuries with very little support. Steel and Hart tell of the experiences of a midshipman, Eric Longley Cook who says that,

> I was asked by the army to take this lighter load of perhaps 100 wounded men off to the hospital ship. The hospital ship was easily marked and when I got there they just waved me away. I said 'well, look I have got dying men here' and they were screaming with pain. The hospital ship said 'We are absolutely full up and cannot take any more wounded'. So then I went to one, two, three, four of the transports. The same story everywhere.

Eventually Cook took them to his own ship, *The Prince of Wales*, where three doctors and three sick bay stewards did the best that they could to help them. One problem was the shortage of hospital ships. On the day of the landings there were only two such ships and they could only take between 400-500 of the seriously wounded soldiers so other ships were converted into auxiliary hospital ships. By the evening of 25th April, these too were overflowing.

On the 3rd September, David was on one of these ships, *HMHS Dunluce Castle*, not as a working surgeon but as a seriously sick patient. Days earlier he had been bitten by what is now thought to have been a brown recluse spider, which bears a potentially deadly hemotoxic venom. Complaining of fatigue, David was taken to the ship but died two days later of what was diagnosed as acute septicaemia. Although, like his three lost teammates, he was mourned by his colleagues, it is surprising that the life of 'Darkie' Sivright is not remembered and honoured more frequently. As one of the most successful of 'Lions' captains and a three time Triple Crown winner, he had achieved great things on the rugby field and achieved successes that no other Scotsman has matched. David was also a remarkable character who put as much into his successful medical career as he did his rugby, enjoying life to the full. Buried at sea, his name is to be found on the Portsmouth Naval Memorial.

Five England Rugby Union Captains

After chapters on New Zealand, Wales and Scotland players it would be very misleading to think that English losses were less significant. Twenty-seven English rugby internationals lost their life in the Great War a figure which does not include uncapped British Lions like Sid Crowther and Ron Rogers. Only Scotland lost more capped players. These heavy losses should not be a surprise. In England rugby was a game adopted by the public schools and the boys who played very often served as commissioned officers on the Western Front. English public schools invariably had some form of military training as part of the curriculum, an experience which was, understandably, seen as advantageous to would-be officers. The proportion of officers killed in the war was high, particularly junior officers – first and second lieutenants and captains. Estimates of life expectancy for junior officers on the Western Front vary and it is almost impossible to be accurate but the most common figure quoted is six weeks, although some historians put the figure at as little as fourteen days. Whatever the true figure there can be no doubt that young officers faced almost unimaginable difficulties and that the losses of such men were heavy. What is also unsurprising is that many of these men were rugby players and that some were among the most distinguished players of the time.

One player in particular stands out as an icon of the time. It is hard not to warm to the special gifts of Ronald Poulton-Palmer, England's rugby captain at the outbreak of war and the man who four months earlier had led his team to their second consecutive Grand Slam. Such is the character and sporting ability of this player that he transcends any suggested or imagined preconceptions or prejudice. Ronald Poulton-Palmer was a true sporting icon of his time and remains one of England's finest rugby players.

Ronald William Poulton, born on the 12th September 1889 in Headington on the outskirts of Oxford, was son of Sir Edward Bagnell Poulton, a distinguished zoologist and lecturer at Jesus College, and Emily Palmer-Poulton, the daughter of the wealthy

Reading family who had founded the Palmer biscuit empire. Ronnie was the fourth of five children, who grew up in the comfortable surroundings of Wykeham House, Oxford. Following a period at the Dragon School, a prep school in North Oxford, Ronnie attended Rugby School, steeped in the history of rugby and William Webb Ellis, where his sporting prowess, first spotted at prep school, came fully to the fore. It was not only rugby that captured his interest. Ronnie was a true all round sportsman who also excelled in hockey, cricket, tennis and gymnastics. Although being something of a chatterbox in the classroom, the young Ronnie was academically bright and secured a place at Balliol College Oxford in 1908 to study Engineering. His impact on the rugby scene was immediate although he was surprisingly left out of the Oxford team for the varsity match against Cambridge that December. Oxford, it appears, had a full set of 'international' Blues already and he was considered to be a risk not worth taking despite his already well-documented talent. In 1907, when barely eighteen years old, *The Meteor* described Ronnie, the ten and a half stone and shade under six foot centre, as "a really good three quarter with plenty of pace… has an excellent swerving run and makes good openings". Although "inclined to pass somewhat wildly," Ronnie "gathers the ball beautifully, holding the ball with both hands at arms length, swerving forward, combining excellently with those around him." They concluded that "if his tackling improves he will become a truly great player". His tackling certainly improved but throughout his career, and particularly in his early years, Ronnie was criticised as too much of an individualist and not as successful in combining with others. The counter argument to this is that teammates often did not have the ability to read his intentions.

The England selectors had no such reservations. With his interests in other sports now largely put on hold, rugby took centre stage. During his first year at Oxford he was offered an England trial and on 30th January 1909, only weeks after the varsity match for which he was not required, Ronnie was playing in the centre for England in front of 15,000 spectators at Welford Road, Leicester in the 22-0 victory over France. Although he didn't score, he kept his place for the remaining two games against Ireland, an 11-5 victory at Lansdowne Road Dublin, and against Scotland at the Athletic Ground Richmond. There was much press discussion as to whether he would be more effective as a wing, where he had played during his term at Oxford, but it was as a centre that he first lit up the international stage. On the eve of his third cap, the 18-8 defeat to a strong Scottish side, *The Times* was of the opinion that he was "a brilliant player with a beautiful swerve" and that, although he lacked experience, "he will be a great player in a year or two." Indeed in that defeat, Ronnie was "often doing good things" and all agreed that the future looked to be very bright indeed.

And so it proved. The following season there was no talk of leaving him out of the Oxford team to play Cambridge. Oxford won comfortably with Ronnie scoring five tries, a remarkable personal achievement which has never been repeated. It was the start of Ronnie's rise to national prominence as the 'Golden Boy' of English rugby. By the start of what had now become the Five Nations championship *The Times* was calling him the "Jessop of rugby football", a reference to the cricketer Gilbert Jessop, a big hitting, free scoring all rounder much glamorised by the English press following his heroics in the 1902 Ashes series. In the 1910 championship Ronnie played on the wing in the 11-6 victory over a strong Welsh team in the middle of their 'Golden Era'. This was his and Wales first international at Twickenham but he was missing for the rest of the championship, not representing his country again until March 1911, once again at English rugby's new headquarters, in the 13-8 win over Scotland. Why he missed over a year of international rugby is unclear but there is a suggestion that he put his studies first for a while. Two more tries in the 1910 varsity match and another one in 1911 when he was captain, both Oxford victories, kept him in the public eye as the 'glamour boy' of English rugby. Among latter day English three-quarters he could be compared to Jeremy Guscott or David Duckham, in particular the latter with his ability to play either centre or wing three-quarter. However neither of these modern greats has been written about in the way that Gareth Williams has described Ronnie Poulton. He sees him as rugby's Rupert Brooke with his striking good looks, "the wondrous Poulton… fleet and flaxen, a golden haired Apollo". Indeed Ronnie knew the poet Brooke from his time at Rugby, although there is no evidence that they moved in the same circles. Thirty ears later Prince Alexander Obolensky certainly had the glamour but much of this is due to his exotic Russian origins and his sensational debut against the 1936 All Blacks. However Prince Obolensky won only four caps for England and his period in the limelight was brief. For the sustained quality of his rugby in the next three years, Ronnie must have the edge. It is ironic that both these glamorous rugby players were killed during a World War. Prince Obolensky was killed in an RAF training accident while flying in World War Two.

In the summer of 1911 Ronnie left Oxford, after securing a Hockey Blue to add to the three gained on the rugby field, and secured a position at his uncle's cake and biscuit factory. His uncle, George Palmer, was a substantial shareholder in Huntley and Palmer Ltd in Reading, a very successful business. Ronnie was keen to experience the various aspects of the business including the engineering and manufacturing. To this end he trained both in Reading and in their factories in Manchester thereby giving him the chance to meet and work with a variety of people, an experience which in turn helped him to bond with his men in the trenches. The future looked extremely bright when George decided to leave his share of the business to Ronnie on condition that he took the name Palmer, which he did by royal licence on his uncle's death in 1913. Although Ronnie is often called Poulton Palmer strictly speaking this was never his real name. He was Ronald Poulton until 1913 and Ronald Palmer afterwards.

Now Ronnie's rugby career really did take off. When working in Reading he played regularly for the Harlequins and fell under the influence of Adrian Stoop. Six years older than Ronnie and another ex pupil of Rugby School, Stoop is credited with revolutionising English back play by formulizing the positions of inside and outside half in the way already done in Wales and New Zealand. Ronnie benefited from this development he found that playing outside Stoop enabled him to show his natural flair and put many of the new ideas into practice. In effect he became Stoop's able lieutenant and this relationship with the fifteen cap England captain did his international prospects no harm at all. In January 1912, on the eve of the new Five Nations Championship, *The Times* was of the opinion that "it will be many a year, let us hope, before Poulton can be left out of the National Fifteen". Victories over Wales (8-0) and Ireland (15-0), where Ronnie scored his first try for his country, set up England for a Calcutta Cup clash with Scotland. Although England were beaten 8-3, Ronnie had his best match yet and showed how much his all round game had improved. *The Times* said,

> His tackling and touch-kicking were admirable and he was half the English defence throughout. He made what he could of a bewildering variety of sloppy passes, and on several occasions one of his short swerving runs would have set a dangerous attack going but for the blunders of the other backs.

The following season continued in much the same vein for Ronnie with the added bonus of almost uninterrupted success for his country. Despite Ronnie's try against South Africa in January 1913 and his almost scoring two more, England lost 9-3 in a game which according to *The Times* was "memorable because of his great runs". But this was England's last reverse before the Great War. Eight consecutive wins gave England their first back to back Grand Slams, with Ronnie at the heart of it. Two weeks after the defeat to South Africa, England gained their first win at Cardiff Arms Park and Ronnie contributed by dropping a goal. England were on their way, clinching the Grand Slam with a rather scrappy 3-0 over Scotland. Despite a less confident performance in this game, Ronnie was now being recognised everywhere as the great player that he undoubtedly was. In 1948 W.J. Townsend Collins remembered clearly the outstanding talent of England's leading three-quarter.

> In every sphere of effort there is a distinction between genius and talent; geniuses are few. He was one of them. .... Usually he seemed a man apart. He had great individual gifts... could do brilliantly everything a centre three-quarter was expected to do; but over and above the power and the willingness to do the obvious was a quality of unexpectedness which played havoc with the defence.

His last season, 1913/14, was probably Ronnie's best as he now captained England to the Grand Slam once again. The first three games were extremely tight with England beating Wales 10-9, Ireland 17-12 and Scotland 16-15 but Ronnie's contribution was immense. Following the Wales game *The Times* was fulsome in its praise

> ...England's victory was alone made possible by the soundness and resource of the greatest three-quarter back that this country has had for a quarter of a century... did ever a man do as much for his side as Poulton? ....Wales, the better team on the day, retired beaten by fate and Poulton.

The Grand Slam was clinched on 13th April at Colombes where Ronnie gave his finest performance in what was, unbeknown to him, his last international match. In a 39-13 victory Ronnie scored four tries, the last of which was a superb individual effort, part of an unstoppable second half performance. The *Rugby Football Annual* remembered later that year that,

> As a three-quarter back he is unique and his name will be handed down as an epoch maker in that part of the game. He is a born leader, never over confident and never flurried.

D.R. Gent, the Welsh-born, England scrum half, remembers his distinctive style when writing in J.B. Marriot's *Rugby Football* that "the very mention of swerving sends ones own thoughts to... Ronald Poulton, the swerver par excellence...swerving and Poulton are almost synonymous terms". The respected writer A.A. Thompson who, as an impressionable teenager saw Ronnie play at Twickenham in 1912, wrote that he was "without exception the most beautiful player I ever saw" and "a cavalier, a supreme artist, a dazzler of dazzlers.... There have been few like him, none quite like him". "It is," wrote Thompson, "difficult for a young lad not to have an idol and Poulton was mine."

With the triumphant season over Ronnie's life was about to take a dramatic turn. As early as April 1912 he had joined the Royal Berkshire Regiment and began service as a Second Lieutenant in the 4th Battalion, Territorial Force. While at Oxford Ronnie had served with the University Officer Training Corps and consequently had the right background. He enjoyed the experience and encouraged workmates at Huntley and Palmer that they too should join the Territorials. The outbreak of war took Ronnie's army experience to a new level. In August 1914 his battalion was mobilized and, following a period of training, he left for France on 30th March 1915, ironically on the same ship that took him to France for what turned out to be his final, memorable international a year earlier. By now a Lieutenant he led 13th Battalion of 'D' Company into the trenches on the 10th April and a day later they experienced their first bombardment. On the 15th April they were moved up the line to Ploegsteert, known as 'Plugstreet' by British soldiers, 15 km south of Ypres. This was a quiet wooded area at this point, although the constant smell of decomposing bodies and the continuing threat of enemy snipers ensured that soldiers did not forget where they were or the dangers that they faced. The lull gave Ronnie the opportunity to write letters home in which he described the conditions faced by the men. Ronnie talks of the atmosphere as being "tainted with the smell of death" but constantly praises his men for their hard work and determination. Yet he was also alert to their apprehension, noticing how quiet they were on the voyage to France. Ronnie, an intelligent, sensitive man, could also see the irony of British and German working parties a matter of a hundred yards apart and able to hear one another talk, laugh and shout but take no action that could be interpreted as 'warlike'.

Tragically Ronnie's active service was short. On 5th May he was supervising working parties repairing dugouts and trenches near to Antons Farm. As he climbed out onto the roof of a dugout in order to examine what progress was being made, Ronnie was shot in the chest by a sniper, watching him through the dark and the mist. Death was instantaneous. It has been said that his men "wept to a man" and the letters certainly confirm their sense of loss. One soldier wrote that "we would have followed him into the jaws of death for he was a brave soldier and a gentleman", while another recalled that "it cut me up terribly the more so that we saw him carried back through our lines". Ronnie was buried at the Royal Berkshire Cemetery, Hyde Park Corner on the Messines Road. Just twenty-five years old, no England rugby captain has lived a shorter life.

Any study of Ronnie Poulton reveals that he was much more than his success on the rugby field: he was a man of great social conscience, always looking to help others within his community. Although interested in politics, Ronnie was never a 'party man', his rather liberal leanings tending to be used in ensuring a better life for others rather than to advance a personal agenda. His attitude towards his men confirms this. A memorial service held for him in

Oxford a few weeks after his death, quoted in Harris and Whippy, reminded everyone that "His rugby career was a mere fraction of his activity and had he lived I am sure he would have been known for far greater things". His friends were devastated. One, Army Chaplain Dirk Dugdale, also quoted in Harris and Whippy, wrote home, "You know I loved him more than anybody else" and this sentiment was repeated in the numerous letters sent to the family following their terrible loss.

However it is as a rugby player that he will be remembered best by succeeding generations. H.B.T. Wakeham, the rugby author and journalist conveys the awe in which he was held.

> I have only to shut my eyes to see him again, with his head flung back, his fair hair waving, threading his way through the opposing defence as if they were mere stationery obstacles in a gymkhana, and though I, being rather of the humbler fry, cannot claim ever to have had a close personal relationship with him, I knew him well enough to realise that his skill at football and most other games was only a small part in the make up of a wonderful personality.

W.J.A. Davies, one of the few men to play international rugby both before and after the Great War, said that Ronnie Poulton was the best player that he ever played with or saw play. He also thought him to be the best captain and man that he ever met. Perhaps it was A.A. Thompson who said it best. Thompson, who died in 1968, is probably best remembered as a highly regarded cricket writer, worshipped Ronnie as his own particular hero. He likened him to cricketer Victor Trumper, a player who radiated excitement and caught the breath every time you watched him play. Thompson wrote,

> When you saw Poulton flying through a defensive gap that had not been there a split second before, you instantly had the feeling that the opposition did not really exist. He went through a ruck of players as the prince in some fairy tale might pass by a touch of his magic sword through a castle wall.

Thompson talks of Ronnie's "rhythmic stride" and swerve as he approached the opposition full back only to leave him "clutching the air" giving spectators the "optical illusion of seeing him go, not past the full back but right through him". The loss of this dashing young England captain was the greatest suffered by rugby union during a conflict that saw seventy-nine English, Welsh, Scottish and Irish internationals make the ultimate sacrifice.

Although Ronnie Poulton was the most high profile English rugby international to be killed he was not even the only England captain lost in the conflict. The second captain lost was also a high profile player. Edgar Mobbs was born the third of six children on 29th June 1882 in Northampton. Unlike many English rugby players, Edgar was not a product of public school and Oxbridge but attended Bedford Modern School. He started playing rugby for a team of under 10s but was forced to give up at sixteen due to a knee injury, taking up hockey and cricket instead. On leaving school Edgar followed his father into the motor industry and worked for Pytchley Auto Car Company at Market Harborough. When he was eighteen his mother died and the family had to learn to cope without her. In 1903, Edgar decided to resume his rugby career.

Edgar began his senior rugby career playing for Olney, Weston Turks and Northampton Heathens and it was not long before this six foot one, fair haired three-quarter was noticed by bigger clubs. This should not surprise us as it was unusual for such a big, strong man to be capable of running 100 yards in a little over ten seconds as Edgar was. In 1905 he joined Northampton and, despite being dropped from the team to play the 1905 All Blacks, (although he did face them when he was asked to play for Bedford in a 41-0 defeat), by 1907 he was captain. Although it took a few years, the strong running wing/centre with the powerful hand-off eventually impressed the England selectors enough to pick him to play Australia at Blackheath in January 1909. Although England lost, Edgar made a good impression and capped his performance with a try after "a splendid bit of football", the first scored by his country against Australia. Indeed, with the exception of the game at Cardiff where he missed a good chance to score, Edgar had a successful first season, scoring in the wins over France and Ireland as well as in the defeat to Scotland. Against France he played on both wings at different times in the match and, despite playing outside a disappointing Ronnie Poulton making his debut, played well in a 22-0 victory. Against Scotland, this time on the left wing, Edgar impressed once again with *The Times* informing its readers that "he is a determined runner with a strong hand off, and whenever he got the ball he seemed dangerous". Four tries in his first five matches seem to confirm this analysis.

Surprisingly, Edgar's international career was relatively short. He did not play in the 11-6 victory over Wales but was back for the 0-0 draw with Ireland although he had to leave the field injured. The following match against France saw Edgar awarded the highest accolade, the captaincy of his country, and played his part in the 11-3 victory as a strong running, high striding centre. He did not represent his country again. Why this should be the case is difficult to understand, although Edgar was known to be a strong willed man of principle not afraid to take on the establishment. Indeed, during the 1909/10 season Edgar was called before the RFU to answer charges of professionalism in Midlands, especially Northampton, rugby. The club were exonerated but officials had been made aware of his determination in defending the players. Two years later Edgar criticised the RFU for their treatment of the South African tourists in matters of hospitality including sub standard accommodation. So grateful were the touring party that Edgar received a signed photograph of the squad. It is unlikely that the RFU were as pleased with his actions and it is very possible that, by expressing his views, Edgar was denied further games for England. It is not as though his playing career had come to an end. He played for Toulouse where his pace and strength won him many French admirers and forced some of his immediate opponents to wear a protective cap when facing him. In the 1912 County Championship, he and Ronnie Poulton formed a very intimidating centre partnership which could have served England well. However it was not to be and in 1913 Edgar Mobbs retired.

When war broke out Edgar was keen to be involved as soon as possible: every inch the man of action, he saw it as his duty to join up. One can only imagine his disappointment, even anger, when he was refused a commission on the grounds of age. Thirty-two when war began and a fit man, Edgar found this situation difficult to accept. He was also conscious that, as a well known international rugby player, he could encourage others to join the armed forces. During one game at Franklyn Gardens, his old home ground, Edgar, now a sergeant and soon to be a captain, addressed the crowd wearing his straw boater hat. In a short simple speech he talked about the need and process of recruitment and asked if men would join him. The following Monday four hundred rugby supporters and players turned up and two hundred and sixty four were passed fit for active service. 'Mobbs Own' were integrated into the auspices of the Northampton Regiment, D company of the 7th Battalion. Players who joined Edgar included the captain of Devon, E.R. Butcher and the captain of Bedford, H. Willett.

Arriving in France in September 1915, it was not long before this particular band of brothers saw action. On the 25th the company was engaged in the Battle of Loos where Edgar fought bravely, rallying his men and leading charges against the enemy. Although half the men became casualties Edgar's efforts had not gone unnoticed. In the next fifteen months he would be promoted first to major in 1916 and later to lieutenant colonel where he was given full command of the battalion. From Loos, Edgar moved to the Somme where he saw action at Guillemont in August 1916, becoming one of the two hundred and fifty wounded soldiers when hit by shrapnel. He was lucky. Fifty of his men were killed with another fifty missing. Edgar's efforts continued to be recognised and during 1916 he was twice mentioned in dispatches and was awarded the Distinguished Service Order in the New Years Honours list of January 1917. Following participation in the Battle of Arras in April 1917 where the 7th Battalion suffered severe casualties, Edgar was wounded again at Messines on the 7th June and again on the 10th when an exploding shell left him with serious neck injuries. He returned to his men three weeks later. Like his fellow Northampton citizen Walter Tull, Edgar seemed to appear wherever the action was at it's thickest but he was being worn down by his efforts.

There was to be no let up as Edgar and his men prepared for Passchendaele. Following ten days of continual bombardment, Edgar became involved at the outset of the attack from an area called Shrewsbury Forest. Due to the heavy losses suffered by his officers, Edgar decided that he would lead from the front. As the commanding officer there was no requirement for him to do this and he could, perhaps should, have delegated this task. However that was not Edgar's way. Perhaps he was not thinking clearly or maybe his judgement was clouded after the intensity of his war experience. Maybe he just felt an overwhelming compulsion to lead by example. Whatever the reason the decision had a predictably tragic outcome. On 31st July Edgar led his men in an assault on a machine gun which had trapped a detachment of his Battalion at Lower Star Post. The exact details of how he was killed are unclear. Some reports say that, single-handed, he attacked the trench while others say that he had successfully secured the first trench and was in the process of marshalling his men for an attack on a second trench when he was killed. It has also been said that one of the ploys that Edgar used when leading his men into battle was to punt a rugby ball into No Man's Land and encourage his men to follow it up. This was a tactic reminiscent of Captain Nevill and his footballs on the Somme, although there is no evidence that the tactic was used on this occasion. However his death occurred, Edgar's body was never recovered. The Battalion history offers the opinion that

> The fact that his body could not be recovered and buried, as all ranks would have wished, was perhaps a good thing, as it helped keep alive his memory in the Battalion, and inspired in everyone the resolve to avenge his death and to end the war that had already caused so much misery and suffering.

Edgar Mobbs was certainly not forgotten. In addition to having his name inscribed on the Menin Gate, a memorial was unveiled in 1921 at the north end of Market Square, Northampton, although by 1937 it had been moved to Abington Square. The memorial, which is a robed female figure representing the Goddess of Fame with a bust of Edgar at its base, has a moving inscription reminding us of how instrumental he had been in inspiring and leading others. Mobbs Memorial reads,

> In memory of Edgar R Mobbs DSO, erected by subscriptions of admirers the world over, to the memory of a great and gallant soldier sportsman. When the Great War broke out he founded 'Mobbs Company', joined as a private and rose to command a battalion to which it belonged. He did his duty even unto death.

'Edgar Mobbs Way' is, since 2006, to be discovered in a newly redeveloped part of Northampton which is linked to the A45 road. The Mobbs Memorial Match has been played since1921 and for many years was played between East Midlands and the Barbarians. In recent years that fixture was overtaken by the demands of professional rugby and the match, although still known as the Mobbs Memorial Match, has been played, since 2008, between the East Midlands and Bedford Blues. The proceeds of the fixture help with the development of youth rugby in the area, a use of which Edgar would surely approve. Although the Battalion carried on after Edgar's death, it continued to suffer significant losses. They were badly hit by both the Spring Offensive of 1918 and the flu epidemic that followed. It is estimated that of the four hundred men who eventually served in 'Mobbs Own', only eighty-five survived.

Ronnie Poulton and Edgar Mobbs are certainly the two most acclaimed of the England rugby captains killed in the war but three more England captains perished, each with a strong connection to the city of Liverpool. It might seem surprising to us today but in the early years of the twentieth century Liverpool was a very significant rugby club. Indeed, three players from the club represented England in the first rugby international ever played, England against Scotland in 1871, and it is said that Liverpool Rugby Club is the oldest in the world. In the same year as that first international was held, nearby in the Wirral, Birkenhead Park Rugby Club was formed. Two of the other remaining English captains, Harry Alexander and Percy Kendall, played for Birkenhead, while Lancelot Slocock played for Liverpool. In total fifty-seven Liverpool players and members were killed in the Great War.

Lancelot Andrew Noel Slocock was born the third son of the Revd. F.H. Slocock and his wife Judith Emily on Christmas Day 1886 in the village of Wootton Wawen, Warwickshire. The young Lancelot, also known as Andrew or Noel on occasion, was educated at Marlborough College where he was a contemporary of Siegfried Sassoon, the future war poet. At school Lancelot showed his all round sporting prowess but it was rugby that really captured his imagination and he made an impact in the school team. On Leaving Marlborough, Lancelot went into the cotton trade and joined Liverpool

Rugby Club where he established his reputation as a lineout forward. By the autumn of 1906, not yet twenty years old, Lancelot was selected to play for the North against the South in a trial match, after which the England team to play South Africa would be picked. Lancelot did his chances of selection no harm in the trial but there was a rather bizarre twist when the team was announced. Selected to play in the second row for England was a medical student from Guy's Hospital, Arnold Alcock, a useful forward but some way short of international class. It appears to have been an administrative error and that Lancelot was the intended forward. It is possible that he was known as Andrew Slocock at this point so it is not difficult to see how the error occurred. Alcock played adequately in the 3-3 draw but was never selected again. He did, however, put a great deal back into the sport that he clearly enjoyed. On becoming a GP in Gloucester, Alcock joined the local club and was president of Gloucester RFC between 1924 and 1969. He died in 1973 aged ninety-one and the last survivor of the team that drew with South Africa. Lancelot, although playing for Lancashire against South Africa (and scoring a try) a few days later and finally winning his first cap in January 1907, was not so lucky. His life was to be cut horribly short.

Lancelot was to play eight times for his country. He made a try-scoring in front of a modest crowd of 6,000 at the Athletic Ground Richmond on the 5th January 1907, in a 41-13 victory over France. A week later he found life much more difficult as England crashed to a 22-0 defeat to a strong Welsh team on the verge of greatness. *The Times* however was quick to praise Lancelot who they felt "deserved a better fate". He kept his place in the team and scored a try against Ireland, although this match, a hard forward battle, and the final one against Scotland were both lost. The following season, 1907/8, was not much more successful, although there were two victories and Lancelot achieved his greatest honour in rugby. France was easily defeated 19-0 and Ireland tamed 13-3 but another defeat, this time by 28-18, was handed out by Wales. For their last match of the season at Inverleith the selectors changed the captain and Lancelot was given the job. In front of a crowd of 20,000, he did not let anybody down and even scored a try but England lost 16-10 and his international career was over. His successful career in the cotton industry took him abroad on a regular basis, especially to the United States. His career reminds us that rugby was an amateur sport and business definitely took priority over rugby, so much so that after marrying Lena in 1912, Lancelot moved the family to Savannah, Georgia. A son, Anthony, was born in 1914 but with the outbreak of war Lancelot headed home.

Lancelot was commissioned as a Second Lieutenant in the 10th Battalion of the King's (Liverpool) Regiment and arrived in France in January 1916, in plenty of time for the 'big push' in the summer of that year. The Battalion was to be involved in the attacks to prepare the way for a creeping artillery barrage and subsequent infantry advance along the Somme. The particular area where Lancelot was involved was the village of Guillemont, a place that was a central objective of the military planners. The attack on 8th August failed but on the following day, in temperatures that reached 84 degrees, Lancelot led his men over the top. Before the end of the day he was dead, one of 82,000 casualties of this part of the campaign that had seen an Allied advance of 1,000 yards. A fellow international, Lance Corporal J.A. King, died in the same offensive, part of the same battalion.

John King was a lock forward or hooker who won twelve caps for England between 1911 and 1913. Ironically he only joined the Liverpool Scottish, as they were known, following a chance meeting with Lancelot when John expressed his wish to experience more action than he was seeing in the Yorkshire Hussars. Both players are commemorated on the Thiepval Memorial, their bodies never found. This was not the end of the suffering for the Slocock family. Lancelot's brother, Cyprian Henry Benson Slocock of the Oxford and Bucks Light Infantry 3rd Battalion died of wounds on April 3rd 1918 and is buried in Boulogne Eastern Cemetery, yet another example of a family who had sacrificed more than one son to the horrors of The Great War.

The two remaining England rugby captains to die in the conflict both had strong connections with Liverpool having played for Birkenhead Park. Born within five months of each other, Percy Kendall, (born 21st August 1878), and Harry Alexander, (born 6th January 1879), had brief careers as England's captain but were highly regarded players in the early years of the century.

Harry Alexander was born at Oxton, Cheshire and quickly

proved to be talented both academically and on the sports field. By the time he had left Uppingham School in Rutland, to attend Oxford University, Harry had shown his skills at rugby, hockey and golf. He became a county hockey player and a scratch golfer as well as showing ability in the little known sport of 'bandy', a hybrid of field hockey and ice hockey played on a rink the size of a football pitch. Harry was also a good singer who even fulfilled some professional engagements.

But it was on the rugby field that he made his mark. Playing in the pack, Harry won his Blue in 1897 and retained his place a year later. On leaving Oxford, Harry played for Birkenhead Park and by February 1900 he was in the England team to face Ireland as a goal kicking forward, the first of seven caps. It began well, with Harry contributing a conversion in a 15-4 victory. Despite England's indifferent record during the next few years, (they won only two and drew one of Harry's seven games), he was to keep his place in the team for the remainder of the season and the whole of the next even though all three games in the 1901 championship were lost. Indeed, not only was Harry a regular in the England team, he was also the designated choirmaster. In 1902 Harry took a job teaching in Stanmore Park Preparatory School in North London and joined Richmond who played on the same Athletic Ground where he had made his England debut two years earlier. In the opening game of the 1902 international championship Harry was made England captain against Wales. The game appeared to be going well for England helped by Harry's conversion of one of two English tries but, what could have been a winning start and the beginning of a successful period of captaincy, was thwarted in the last minute. With England leading 8-6 Wales made their final assault into England's territory and forced Harry's team to concede a penalty in front of their own posts. The goal was duly kicked by the full back Strand-Jones to give Wales a 9-8 victory and Harry's reign as captain was over. He kept his place in the England pack for the next match against Ireland at Blackheath but, although England won 6-3, it was the end of his international duties. Harry continued to play a high standard of rugby and remained with Richmond for the rest of his career, becoming captain in 1905/6 when he led his club against the 1905 All Blacks. That year Harry also represented the Barbarians in matches against Newport and Cardiff.

Playing with Harry Alexander in the final match of the 1901 championship was a talented half back, Percy 'Toggie' Kendall. Born in Prescot on the Liverpool side of the Mersey, Percy was educated at Elleray School, New Brighton and then Tonbridge School, where he played scrum half, before reading Law at Cambridge. Although he represented the university on a number of occasions Percy surprisingly never won a Blue, but his rugby career began in earnest after leaving Cambridge. During his university days he had already turned out for Blackheath, one of the leading English clubs, and now, on obtaining articles in London, he played for them regularly. By Boxing Day 1899, he was representing the Barbarians in their match against Cardiff, the first of nine occasions that he was to wear the black and white hooped jersey, and his rugby career was beginning to take off. Returning north to practice as a solicitor, Percy joined Birkenhead Park where he represented his club with distinction and became a mainstay of the Cheshire County XV.

International honours were soon to follow. Following successive England defeats to Wales and Ireland in the 1901 championship, Percy was selected for the final match of the season against Scotland at Blackheath on March 9th. Playing behind a beaten pack it proved to be a difficult debut for Percy. *The Times* reported that the English half backs were "slow in getting the ball and uncertain in passing" and "never really gave their three-quarters a chance." Playing against a Scottish side containing David Bedell-Sivright, the England team was well beaten 18-3 in a game which gave Scotland the Triple Crown and championship. Nevertheless when the 1902 championship got under way Percy was still in the England team. He had played very well in the England trial earlier in the season when he had scored an excellent try playing for England against the Rest. This enabled him to keep his place in the opening match of the championship. This was the close fought game in which Harry Alexander led England to a last minute defeat to the eventual champions, Wales. Once again *The Times* was less than complimentary reporting that "Kendall of Cheshire did not distinguish himself at half for England." Part of the problem for Percy was that the England selectors choose not to specialise at half back, expecting scrum halves and outside halves to interchange. At Birkenhead Park Percy, a scrum half, and his half back partner Frank Hulme were specialists and were considered to be the best available to England. However, when playing for England the demands were different and Percy wasn't at his best. Following this, his second cap, Percy was dropped.

The following season saw England struggle once again and Percy was recalled for the final match, this time as captain. Ironically his club partner, Frank Hulme, having played in the two previous games, was now dropped. Despite an improved performance England was defeated 10-6 in front of a crowd of over 25,000 at Richmond by a Scottish team which regained the title and Triple Crown. Although on this occasion he gave a more effective performance, Percy Kendall was dropped the final time. He continued to play for both club and county including captaining Cheshire against the 1905 All Blacks, a game in which *The Times* reported him as being "energetic and extremely useful", but his time in the limelight was over. He played on occasionally and coached the younger generation at Birkenhead Park right up to 1914. He was also vice-president of the Cheshire Union.

With the outbreak of war in 1914 schoolteacher Harry and solicitor Percy were quick to enlist. Percy volunteered within twelve hours of war being declared, joining the King's Liverpool Regiment, just as Lancelot Slocock was to do a year later, and was commissioned as a Lieutenant on October 14th 1914. Between 1914 and 1916, the King's Liverpool Regiment could boast seven rugby internationals in its ranks. Percy was soon heading to the Ypres salient where the first battle of Ypres had ended in November 1914. Before the second Ypres began in April 1915, the soldiers had to come to terms with the horrors of trench warfare where they embarked on futile attacks on well-defended German lines and risked the dangers posed by snipers. With a shortage of troops, supplies and ammunition, losses were inevitable and on 25th January 1915 the thirty-six year old Percy, now an Acting Captain, became a victim of a German sniper. He left a wife, Katherine and two children and is commemorated in Kemmel Churchyard, Heuvelland, West-Vlaanderen in Belgium. The *Birkenhead News* paid a tribute on 30th January 1915, referring to him as "a man of the true type of English gentleman." A few days later this newspaper added that "his ideals were not acquired, they were inbred, and he was one of nature's own gentlemen." Birkenhead Park had, they said, produced many great men in the forty-five years of its existence but "few have gained a higher rank of excellence than P.D. Kendall."

Harry Alexander was not long in joining Percy on the roll of war dead. He had enlisted in the 1st Battalion of the Grenadier Guards in 1914 as a Second Lieutenant and was also soon on his way to Ypres, following a period of training in both London and Marlow. The Grenadier Guards had been in action in Ypres since the autumn of 1914 and by the summer of 1915 had lost all but four of their officers and two hundred men. Harry did not take part in any of the action during this period but on just his thirteenth day of active service his luck ran out. On 17th October 1915 Harry was killed in action at Hulluch, Northern France aged thirty-six, and is buried in Arras Road Cemetery, Roclincourt, Pas de Calais.

Although not one of the five England rugby captains to die in the Great War, it is appropriate to discuss the sporting career of John Edward Raphael, the England rugby international who captained an unofficial 'British Isles' Rugby team on a tour of Argentina in 1910 and who also captained Surrey County Cricket Club in the summer of 1904. John Raphael was one of the most talented sportsman of his generation and his story is worthy of a closer examination.

He was born on 30th April 1882 in Brussels, the son of Jewish parents, Albert and Harriet, whose permanent home was in Hendon. More commonly known as Jack, he was born into a very wealthy banking family, a dynasty that in the 1920s even rivalled the Rothschilds. Jack was educated at Merchant Taylors' School where he enjoyed great success, in and outside of the classroom. An outstanding scholar, Jack also played in the school cricket team for five years scoring runs and taking wickets. On attending St John's College, Oxford, where he read history, Jack gained his Blue in rugby, scoring a try in three of his four matches against Cambridge, cricket where he scored 130 in 1903 and 99 two years later, just failing to join the elite group of batsmen who have scored two centuries in the Varsity match, and water polo. A versatile rugby player who could play centre, wing, full back or 'rover', it was inevitable that Jack would one day play international rugby.

He made his debut for England as an Oxford student in January

1902 in the defeat to Wales, alongside both Harry Alexander and Percy Kendall, and kept his place for the subsequent victories over Ireland and Scotland. Jack was not selected again until 1905 but for the following two years he was more or less a regular member of the team. The press reported favourably on his performances, particularly when facing the All Blacks for both Surrey and England. The difficulty for the selectors was to decide where to use him to best effect. He was viewed as too unconventional to fit easily into a four man three-quarter line and decided that he was too much of an individualist. *The Times* had no doubts – he was a 'rover' or 'flying man' and, when Jack was dropped for the match against Ireland in 1906, they predicted that Basil Maclear playing in this role for the opposition would cause England problems. The newspaper even called for a new selection committee to be installed. Jack was back for the next match and played successfully on the wing in the victory over Scotland before winning his ninth and final cap in the 22-0 victory over France.

This was not, however, the end of his rugby career. In 1910, when Tommy Smyth was leading a British Lions team to South Africa, Jack led sixteen Englishmen and three Scots on a six match tour of Argentina in order to celebrate the centenary of the republic. The team was billed as the 'Combined British' by the hosts but in later years was given 'Lions' status. It should be pointed out that only four of the touring party had international experience and it was very much a 'second string XV'. All six matches were won, including the 'test' which was the first match for which Argentina awarded caps. Jack, playing full back, had an excellent tour and shone in the test match where he "made exceptional moves." The tour suited his unconventional style and he displayed his full range of skills, what *Wisden* described in his obituary as "a beautiful kick, a brilliant field and possessed of a good turn of speed."

In parallel to his successful rugby career Jack was also a first class cricketer. While at Oxford he scored four first class centuries which included, in 1904, a career best 201 against a Yorkshire attack that included the great Wilfred Rhodes. His runs were made out of an Oxford total of 374 and took only 270 minutes: an impressive strike rate. Later that summer he was made captain of Surrey and impressed his teammates when scoring 111 against Worcestershire. However his cricket career was, at best, inconsistent. His seventy-seventh and final first class match was in 1913 by which time Jack had compiled 3,717 runs.

Although clearly a natural sportsman, Jack went on to prove that he had other talents. In 1905, he entered Lincoln's Inn and was called to the Bar in 1908. He stood unsuccessfully as a Liberal Party candidate in a by election at Croydon in 1909 and continued to live a full and rounded existence. With the outbreak of war John overcame his pacifist tendencies and enlisted. By December 1914 was with the 18th Battalion King's Royal Rifle Corps. He was later appointed to the General Staff but in June 1917, Lieutenant John Raphael found himself at Messines Ridge. Tragically, on the 7th June, he was hit by shrapnel from a burst shell while leaving a dug out. At first it appeared that his injuries were not life threatening but, despite an operation, he died from his wounds at Remy four days later with the knowledge that the Allied attack had resulted in the capture of Messines Ridge.

There was, however, an interesting sequel to Jack's death that has only recently come to light. On March 27th 2014 the *Daily Express* printed a story that was both fascinating and very moving. As with all of our sporting heroes, the loss of a husband, son or brother hit their loved ones very hard. Jack's mother Harriet was certainly devastated by the loss of her talented son and she quickly went about ensuring that his memory would never be forgotten. A service was organised at St Jude-on-the-Hill Church in Hampstead Garden Suburb near the family home and the sculptor Charles Sykes, who had designed the famous Rolls-Royce mascot, the Spirit of Ecstasy, was invited to create a memorial to ensure that Jack would never be forgotten. The marble plaque with a bust of Jack was unveiled on the north wall of the church by the headmaster of Merchant Taylors', John Nairn. Underneath was an appropriate motto, "If character be destiny then his is assured." Harriet also ensured that the 296 page coaching manual which Jack had nearly completed, *Modern Rugby Football*, was published and that a scholarship was founded in his name at Oxford University.

By 1929 Harriet, who had lost her husband before she lost Jack, was in poor health herself. She journeyed to Jack's grave in Lijssen-thoek military cemetery in Flanders to make an unusual request of the Head groundsman, Walter Sutherland. Harriet's proposal was that, when the time came, her ashes would be buried with those of her beloved son. As she knew, this was contrary to military rules, hence her decision to go straight to the groundsman rather than follow official channels. Harriet was used to getting her own way and, on this occasion, she was not to be deterred. Risking his job in the process, on Harriet's death, Walter Sutherland dug a small hole next to the grave and buried the urn beside it. Mother and son were allowed to be at peace together. The story of Walter Sutherland's actions remained a closely guarded secret in the Sutherland family until Walter's 92 year old son George revealed the story close to one hundred years after Jack's death. It is a reminder that, with his death, England lost one of the finest all round sportsman of the Edwardian Age and a man who would have contributed much to the post-war world.

More Celtic Rugby Heroes of the Great War

Rugby Union footballers made a huge contribution to the war effort and, while it has been straightforward to categorise the players in previous chapters, there are numerous others whose sacrifice warrants examination. Some rugby clubs made almost unimaginable sacrifices to the Allied cause which it would be remiss not to acknowledge. It should be remembered that, while this book has concentrated on international rugby players, there were thousands of unsung heroes, both players and supporters who lost their lives in the conflict. In an amateur game it is much more difficult to obtain accurate statistics about the contribution of players. Records are either lost or variable in their accuracy whereas international careers are generally well documented. However, much good work has been done by historians to rectify this.

One recent example is Stephen Cooper's book *The Final Whistle: Rosslyn Park – A Rugby Club at War*. Rosslyn Park lost eighty-seven of the three hundred and fifty players and members who went to war. These men were lost in battles across the whole theatre of war, from all parts of the Western Front to Italy, Turkey, Mesopotamia through to Palestine and Egypt. A close examination of the Rosslyn Park XV of 1909/10 shows that six of the team died during the conflict. London Scottish too have a particular story to tell. According to the late poet Mick Imlah in his poem 'London Scottish 1914', four teams represented the club in the end of season fixtures against rivals Blackheath. Of the sixty London Scottish players taking part in these matches, forty-five were killed and, of the fifteen survivors, only one, a prop forward called Brodie, ever played rugby again. While it is difficult to confirm the accuracy of these figures, the scale of the tragedy is undeniable. What can be confirmed is that two hundred and five members of the club saw active service, around one hundred of whom were killed, possibly the greatest sacrifice made by one club. Glasgow Academicals might dispute this. The whole of their first XV joined up in 1914 and all saw active service. Eight died and six of the other seven were wounded. Another

Scottish club, Watsonians, saw eight of their 1913/14 team killed in action. Bristol Rugby Club named their ground the Memorial Ground in honour of those lost while Headingly Rugby Club saw its membership reduced by a quarter due to losses suffered in the war. As we have already seen, the names of eighty-six players and members of the Newport Club can be found on the recently restored memorial gates at Rodney Parade.

The first British rugby international fatality was a player with London Scottish and a Scottish international. Ronald Simson. A Lieutenant in the Royal Field Artillery, he died at the First Battle of the Aisne on 14th September 1914. A talented young centre capped in 1911, it was surprising to many rugby followers that he was overlooked after his debut. A good all round sportsman, Simson had scored a try and had been expected to win further caps. His death was followed only two days later in the same action by his clubmate and fellow Scottish international James Huggan. Huggan had also scored a try on his international debut, in the 1914 Calcutta Cup, his only game for Scotland and a match in which eleven of the participants were to die on the battlefield. Huggan's story is even more remarkable. This brave winger and surgeon from Jedburgh was recommended for the Victoria Cross as early as September 1914. That it wasn't awarded might be because the action involved saving the lives of sixty wounded Germans trapped in a barn. The barn was being shelled by German artillery but Huggan, with the aid of volunteers he enlisted, managed to rescue them from the burning building. Tragically, while moving some of his own injured men, he was killed by an exploding shell, a compassionate man, bound by his Hippocratic Oath.

The most celebrated Celtic rugby player sacrificed in the Great War was Basil Maclear, one of nine Irish internationals to die. The Irish contribution to the Allied cause is of particular interest. For a number of years interest in the Irish effort has tended to centre around the experience of the Ulster Volunteer Force, in particular the efforts of the 36th Division on the Somme. It is sometimes forgotten that the Great War predates the partition of Ireland. Plans to implement the 1914 Government of Ireland Act were postponed on the outbreak of war and, although many Irish still had Home

Rule on their agenda, and even though conscription was never enforced in Ireland, approximately 300,000 Irish volunteered to fight for the British Empire of whom 49,400 died. One of these was the greatest Irish rugby player of his generation, Basil Maclear.

Maclear was born on 7th April 1881 in Southsea, the youngest of five sons born to Captain (later Major) Henry Maclear, a doctor and an officer in the Buffs, and his wife Mary Casey. He was also the grandson of Sir Thomas Maclear, Her Majesty's Astronomer in Cape Town and a close friend of the explorer David Livingstone. Thomas was renowned in his field and has had a town in South Africa (Maclear) named after him, as well as a cape in Malawi (Cape Maclear) and Maclear's Beacon on Table Mountain. Most impressively Thomas even has a crater on the moon named after him. The Maclears were definitely a family of some importance. Basil was educated at Bedford Grammar School where he proved to be an excellent sportsman. In the school sports day of 1898 Basil won eight of the nine events that he entered: it was already clear that he was an exceptional talent. Basil won a place at the Royal Military College Sandhurst, excelling in rugby, cricket, athletics and shooting and winning the Sword of Honour in 1900. The future, both on the sports field and in the military, appeared to be full of promise.

By 1900 he was playing cricket for Bedfordshire in the Minor Counties Championship but it was rugby that really captured his interest. Not that Basil had much time to indulge his sporting interest. He joined the Royal Dublin Fusiliers on leaving Sandhurst, and was made a Captain in 1900 and a Brevet Major the following year. He was sent to fight in the Boer War and quickly saw action where he was mentioned in dispatches. By 1905 this striking looking man with his fair hair, neatly trimmed moustache and solid build, had command of his own unit. Standing at a shade under six feet tall and weighing around fourteen stones, in his early days Basil played in the pack. However by the time he returned home from his service overseas that year, Basil was a strong straight running centre with a powerful hand off and a deadly tackle. He was also a good goal kicker and once kicked twelve out of twelve kicks in a match, a much more significant achievement in the days before kickers were allowed to use a tee.

It was inevitable that Basil would make an impact on the international stage though not necessarily with Ireland, the land of his family. Basil was first given a trial with the country of his birth, England, but he was decreed "not good enough". He made his debut for Ireland in the centre, at Cork on February 11th 1905, when the English selectors were forced to regret the decision not to select him. Not only did Ireland win comfortably 17-3 but Basil scored one of Ireland's five tries and converted another. On 13th February, the *Standard* reported that,

> A finer first appearance in an International match… has probably never been seen…. His tackling was perfection, and several times, having spoiled the man who was passing, he followed up and collared the man who took the pass.

The *Western Mail* columnist, 'Forward', decided that Basil was "one of the greatest centre three quarters playing today – if not the greatest". The victory over England was not to be the last time that Basil would take revenge on the country of his birth. And two weeks later Basil kicked another conversion in the 11-5 victory over the Scots at Inverleith and even a 10-3 defeat to a strong Triple Crown winning Welsh team at Swansea could not disguise a very impressive first season of international rugby for Ireland's new centre.

The 1905 All Blacks tour saw Basil in the thick of the action, although like most other British players without much success. In total Basil faced the rampant New Zealanders on four occasions during the tour, all during November. The results are a good indicator of how the tour was progressing: Blackheath (lost 32-0); Bedford (lost 41-0); Ireland (lost 15-0); and Munster, where he was made captain, (lost 33-0). Basil didn't even have the satisfaction of seeing his sides score a single point against this relentless rugby machine. He was, however, the subject of some favourable press reports. Following the international match, which was incidentally the first 'all ticket' international, *The Times* reported that the white gloved, Cork County centre was Ireland's most effective player and said that,

> …no one was more zealous than, or so quick on the ball as B. Maclear and time after time he dashed in and spoiled the movements of the New Zealanders.

His display was certainly worth the cap that he did not receive. Due to a very strange ruling Irish players did not receive an Irish cap for games played against 'colonial' opposition, a precedent followed by the Scottish football authorities who only awarded a cap, (and only one at that), for games played against the other home countries until 1975. The Irish players did, however, receive their cap later whereas Scottish footballers had to wait until 2006 for their backdated awards.

The next match saw Basil win a fifth cap in a new role, a 'rover' or 'flying man' in the Dave Gallaher/Cliff Pritchard style, a selection decision that confirmed Basil's versatility. In a 16-6 victory over England Basil made his mark. *The Times* reported

> As for B. Maclear, he fulfilled the duties of flying man with a success which no one could have expected on such an afternoon. He was always on the ball, either making headway or executing fine tackling, and he was in the van of the terrific Irish rushes which yielded two tries for A. Telford in the second half.

Following Basil's vital contribution of a try and conversion to the Irish victory, *The Time*s concluded that,

> The Irish Union was very happy in its judgement when giving Maclear the independent position of flying man, for on the three-quarter line his restless energy and his enterprise were forever making him lose his position. So this roving commission was eminently suited to his game.

'Roving' did not always work for Basil however. Two weeks later he was 'roving' in the 13-6 defeat to Scotland and before the end of the game he had been moved into the pack in order to stifle the impressive Scottish forwards. One cannot help but feel that, in the modern game, Basil might have made a superb breakaway forward. For the final game, the championship decider against Wales in Belfast, he was moved to the wing, (his fourth position in seven international matches to date), where he scored a try in an 11-6 victory which allowed the two countries to share the title. *The Times* called the decision to play him on the wing "a distinct success."

But one match cemented the reputation of this Irish powerhouse.

It took place at the Balmoral Showgrounds, Belfast on 24th November 1906 where Ireland entertained the Springboks. In this game Basil, once again playing on the wing, scored a try that sixty years later was being described by the rugby writer J.B.G. Thomas as "as brilliant a try as has ever been scored for Ireland" and that Thomas included in his 1966 book *Fifty Two Famous Tries*. The context of the try was scored only added to the drama. Midway through the second half the Irish team were starring into the abyss, 12-3 down to dominant Springbok team when they won a scrum in their own twenty five. The ball was moved towards Basil's wing but went loose. Basil gathered the ball, beat John Hirsh and then, with a fierce hand off that was by now his trademark, he dispatched both Bob Loubser and Dirk Jackson, fended off the full back Stephen Joubert three times before breaking away twenty-five yards out and completing his sensational eighty yard run. The score inspired a determined Irish fight back and before very much longer Ireland scored their third try of the match and kicked a penalty to pull level at 12-12. In the end only a disputed try in the final minutes by Anton Stegmann allowed the South Africans to get away with a 15-12 victory. The *Globe* reported that,

> Basil Maclear's run will go down to posterity. It is not at all likely to be forgotten by those who were fortunate to be present. It was altogether out of the common in an international match for a man to score after running from his own '25' and the incident gathered particular force from the fact that Ireland then were apparently in a hopeless position. Maclear's try gave Ireland a new lease of life."

Making his contribution to the Springbok victory that afternoon was the South African forward Adam 'Barley' Burdett. Although a surprise selection for the tour, the twenty four year old Western Province player stood up well to 'Darkie' Bedell-Sivright in the defeat in Glasgow and did not appear out of place in Belfast. Surprisingly he never played for the Springboks in an international again. More tragically, he was killed at Robert's Heights, Pretoria, on 4th November 1918, one week before the Armistice.

Leading the heroic comeback against South Africa was the peak of Basil's rugby career. There was another victory over England (17-

9), where *The Times* described Basil, playing at centre, as "the outstanding figure among the three-quarters… making full use of his weight, strength and pace." But this was followed by defeats to both Scotland (15-3) and Wales. Against Scotland Basil defended well and prevented at least two further tries but he was starved of the ball. In the last match of the season, in Cardiff, Ireland crumbled to a 29-0 defeat. Basil never played for Ireland again, due to injury problems with his knees. After eleven consecutive caps in three seasons Basil had to call time on his short, yet brilliant, career.

Basil now gave his full attention to his increasingly successful military career. In 1912 he joined the staff of the Royal Military College, Sandhurst as an Inspector of Physical Training. He quickly won the affection of both cadets and officers but with the outbreak of war it was inevitable that he would find his way to the front line. Basil rejoined his regiment in February 1915 and a month later was in France. During April he was involved in the heavy fighting at Ypres where the British had taken over five miles of the front previously controlled by the French. They found the trenches in very poor condition but dug in. It was at this point, on the 22nd April, that the Germans used gas for the first time. The British had little or no protection as the cloud of greenish-yellow chlorine swept through the trenches. Men felt their eyes begin to sting and their throats tighten as they fought for breath, some coughing up blood. The Germans, however, could not capitalise on this success quickly enough and the front stabilized close to Ypres. On 8th May the Allies attack on Aubers Ridge failed, due to the strength of the German defences. The British lost 11,500 men in a battle where the German losses numbered fewer than 1,000.

At this point Basil was second in command of his regiment, the 2nd Battalion Royal Dublin Fusiliers, but on 8th May, he took over command. On the 24th May, a day after Basil had written what would be his last letter to his mother, the Germans launched a 3.00am gas attack north west of Wieltje near Ypres. It was followed by an infantry attack which the British tried hard to repel. Following the loss of the battalion commander, Basil rose to the challenge, encouraging all around him. During mid-morning Basil led a bombing party attempting to beat back the advancing enemy. In the ensuing action he was shot through the throat and died. The surviving officer, T.J. Leahy, led twenty men back from the trenches, all that was left of the seventeen officers and six hundred and fifty one men who had made up the 2nd Battalion of the Royal Dublin Fusiliers.

The death of this iconic sportsman did not go unnoticed and hardly a newspaper did not pay him a tribute. The *Morning Post* called him "one of the greatest three-quarter backs who ever played for Ireland, or any other National XV." They spoke of his fine physique and his ability to prove himself "accomplished in every sport that he took up." Seven months after his death, Basil was Mentioned in Despatches,

> Captain Basil Maclear, who showed great coolness in handling the Reserve Company of the Battalion, which he was able to bring up almost intact under very heavy fire; and also the great power of command which he showed himself to possess when suddenly called upon to command the Battalion… during a trying situation.

For the family it was another tragic loss. In the very early stages of the war, on 30th August 1914, his brother Lieutenant Colonel Percy Maclear, also of the Royal Dublin Fusiliers, was killed in the Cameroons in command of a battalion of the Nigeria Regiment. Another brother, Harry, also a Lieutenant Colonel, was lost on the Western Front on 15th March 1916. Thirteen years later, in 1928, the Irish Rugby Union presented Basil's mother with a rugby ball used in an international trial match containing the signatures of all those who took part. They urged her to accept the ball "in honour of the memory of her illustrious son."

Four tries and three conversions in his eleven games scarcely does Basil justice. Rhys Gabe, the famous Welsh centre who played against Basil a number of times, remembered him as "the Herculean Irish centre" who was "a charming personality and *persona grata* with all his opponents on and off the field." E.H.D. Sewell wrote in 1944 that, after watching 187 international matches, that "much of the best of the really fast wings was Basil Maclear; he would tackle anything and go down to any forward rush. His was THE hand off." As late as 1954 the programme notes for the England v Ireland encounter at Twickenham remembered him as

> ...a natural rugby player in any position on the field. Today he would have been a terror as a break-away forward. 'Darkie' Sivright himself once tried to crash-tackle Maclear and met a hand off that nearly dropped him unconscious.

That Basil was versatile is without question as he distinguished himself as a centre, wing and 'rover', even spending part of one international match in the pack. But it is as the forerunner to the great Irish centres Mike Gibson and Brian O'Driscoll that he will be remembered. They were both fortunate enough to enjoy careers that were both exceptionally long and overflowing with achievement which ensures that they are recognised as the greatest Irish backs in history. Yet Basil is not far behind them. His loss was one of the greatest losses to rugby during the war, possibly on a par with the deaths of Dave Gallaher and 'Darkie' Bedell-Sivright and ranks only behind the demise of Ronnie Poulton. Ronnie, with his renowned body swerve and pace, taking on the crash tackling Basil would have been a confrontation to relish. Ironically there is a connection between the two men. In his journal written on the Western Front, Ronnie records a match between two divisions played on 13th April 1915. Tragically it was the last game of rugby that Ronnie ever played and the referee on that occasion was the ex-Irish international Basil Maclear. Two of the greatest rugby players of their generation, destined to die within three weeks of each other, enjoying one final thrill in the game they both loved and so greatly enriched.

The man Basil Maclear directly opposed in his final international match, another 'Celtic Great', was also destined to die in the Great War. John Lewis Williams was a prolific Cardiff wing who scored seventeen tries in seventeen appearances, a record that he shared with his peer, Reggie Gibbs (who achieved it in one fewer appearance) and one which they later shared with Ken Jones until it was beaten by both Gareth Edwards and Gerald Davies in 1976 and 1977 respectively. Born in Whitchurch near Cardiff on 3rd March 1882 Johnnie, as he was known, attended Cowbridge Grammar School and, on leaving there, began his rugby career at Newport. He made his debut in 1899 as a raw seventeen year old and went on to make fifty appearances for this leading Welsh club, scoring nineteen tries and a dropped goal. During the 1903/4 season he moved back to his roots and joined Cardiff.

By the autumn of 1905 Johnnie was playing for Glamorgan against the All Blacks and a year later was winning his first cap against the touring Springboks. To break into the Welsh three-quarter line was no mean feat. Since the victory over New Zealand Willie Llewellyn had gone but the other three-quarters, Gwyn Nicholls, Rhys Gabe and Teddy Morgan, were still selected so the competition for places was stiff. Johnnie replaced Hopkin 'Hop' Maddock, the London Welsh winger who had won four caps following the departure of Willie Llewellyn from the international scene. Maddock had played with some success, scoring two tries in his first three internationals. He eventually won three further caps, two of which were gained with Johnnie playing on the opposite wing, and scored another four tries but his life was also to be cut short by the Great War. Despite serving throughout the war, the injuries that he sustained to his shoulder and chest, mainly on the Somme, eventually proved to be his undoing. Despite recovering well enough to win the Military Cross in April 1918 after he covered the retreat of his unit from Les Mesnil, 'Hop' Maddock died aged forty on 21st December 1921. The cause of death was given as tuberculosis so, controversially, he is not always listed as a war casualty. Gwyn Prescott writes about the thirteen Welsh rugby internationals who gave their lives, referring to 'Hop' Maddock only in a brief concluding chapter. On the other hand, Nigel McCrery, in his book, includes him among the fourteen international losses sustained by Welsh rugby. He is not listed by the Commonwealth War Graves Commission as being among the war dead.

Johnnie soon showed that he had all the skills required for a successful international career. *Dromio*, the New Zealand newspaper, said of him that "he learned to do all things well and with judgement; and his swerve inward from the touch-line was perfection." In fact, Johnnie was noted for both his swerve and side step. In Cardiff's clash with the touring Springboks he beat the great Arthur Marsbury all ends up before scoring. Marsbury shook his hand as Johnnie returned for the restart. Making their debut alongside Johnnie were three other players, all forwards. One of these was E.J.R. 'Dick' Thomas who was to serve in France with Johnnie in 1916.

Johnnie's first cap did not have the expected outcome. Wales, the favourites, were convincingly beaten by a Springbok team that had already lost to Scotland and struggled to beat Ireland. The media were surprised and reported that Johnnie did not receive enough ball to put his famous side step to any use. Both the Welsh backs and pack had an off day with only Charlie Pritchard living up to his reputation. Despite this setback Johnnie kept his place and, although Wales lost narrowly to Triple Crown winners Scotland, Johnnie showed his ability to score tries. Two in the 22-0 victory over England and a hat trick at Cardiff in the 29-0 demolition of Ireland served notice of things to come. The following season, 1907/8, Wales won the Triple Crown and defeated France in a friendly. Johnnie made his by now expected contribution with a vital try in the narrow 6-5 victory over Scotland and two more against Ireland. It was no surprise when at the end of the season he was invited to take part in the British Isles team to tour New Zealand and Australia that summer.

In fact to call it a 'British' team is not really an accurate description. The spectre of professionalism and concern over expenses was raising its head and both the Scottish and Irish rugby unions refused to give permission for their players to travel. The unions had difficulty in coming to terms with the large gate receipts taken on the All Black and Springbok tours and the use of the money thereafter. Even the small daily allowance received by the players on tour was a problem to these unions, especially to the Scots who were involved in a dispute with the RFU which threatened the 1909 Calcutta Cup. Neither the Scottish nor the Irish rugby unions were prepared to receive the Australian tourists in 1908/9. The tour, therefore, is remembered as an 'Anglo-Welsh' tour rather than a Lions tour although, as three tests were played, Lions historians now recognise it as an official Lions tour. Once again availability was a big factor in selection and only eleven of the selected twenty-eight had played international rugby.

The tour, under the leadership of Arthur Harding of London Welsh and Wales, was a success overall. In total sixteen of the twenty-six matches were won with one drawn. Seven of the nine matches played in Australia were won but no test matches were played there. In New Zealand three tests were played. The Anglo-Welsh team lost the first and last by substantial margins, but

Two faces of football on the Western Front. Top: Christmas Day relaxation, 1915 gave way to gas masks on the pitch in 1916 (bottom)

Manchester United's 1911 Championship team, including Billy Meredith (seated far right) Sandy Turnbull (seated third from left), Enoch West (to Turnbull's left) and Arthur Whalley, crossed legged, far left). Ernest Mangnall stands next to Meredith.

The Hearts team from which so many joined McCrae's Own

Football internationals. From top left: Evelyn Lintott (England); Jimmy Speirs (Scotland), Leigh Roose (Wales)

The First Football Battalion, 1914, including prolific striker Vivian Woodward, seated third from left

The legendary Wales side which beat the all-conquering 1905 All Blacks in Cardiff.

Left to right: Dave Gallaher (New Zealand), Ronald Poulton (England), David Bedell-Sivright (Scotland)

Blair Swannell (centre) at rest in the desert; Frederick Kelly, rower and composer, poised for the camera

Wimbledon champion Tony Wilding; Wyndham Haswelle, winner of the controversial 440 yards at the 1908 Olympics; Arthur 'Tibby' Cotter, mighty Australian bowler

Sportsmen still remembered: the memorials to Walter Tull (left) and Edgar Mobbs

managed to draw the second and Johnnie was selected for the first two. His try scoring rivalry with Reggie Gibbs really started on this tour and they were the top two scorers of the trip, with Johnnie touching down for twelve tries, one less than his Welsh teammate. Johnnie appears to have enjoyed the experience and put to good use the break from his job as a principal clerk (later partner) in a coal exporters based in the Cardiff Coal Exchange. On the lengthy voyage to the southern hemisphere Johnnie occupied himself by writing articles for the *South Wales Daily News* and the *South Wales Echo*, an interesting way of earning a supplement to the two shillings a day which he received as out of pocket expenses. What the Scottish Rugby Union thought one can only imagine.

On his return, Johnnie continued to represent Wales with distinction. He played in the victory over the touring Australians, the victory in the friendly against France and all three matches in a second consecutive Triple Crown. Tries against England and two against the French maintained his remarkable ratio of tries to games. In 1910 he missed the first three matches but returned against Ireland and scored his second international hat trick against them in a 19-3 victory, a performance which won the acclaim of *The Times* which called him "the best back on the field." In Johnnie's final season he played a significant role in Wales's first official Grand Slam (France was, since 1910, part of the Five Nations Championship when they first appeared in the championship table. However, historians do now recognise the Welsh wins of 1908 and 1909 as 'Grand Slams' as France played internationals against Wales but not against all the other home countries in those years.). Following Johnnie's two tries against Scotland, Billy Trew offered him the captaincy for the match in Paris. It is said that Trew did this because Johnnie could speak French, a skill that he had acquired through his work in the coal exporting business, and would make a good impression when speaking at the post match dinner. Whatever the reason it was an honour that Johnnie, by now one of the best Welsh players of the pre-war era, fully deserved. It ended well as Johnnie scored his record seventeenth international try in a 15-0 victory in front of the biggest crowd, 15,000, to watch a rugby match in France at this time. Trew reclaimed the captaincy and clinched the Grand Slam with a 16-0 win over Ireland two weeks later. Johnnie had played in his last international. He could look back with pride on an excellent international career which saw him not only share the Welsh try scoring record for the next sixty five years but also join Billy Trew, Dickie Owen and Jim Webb as the first players to win three Grand Slams. In his seventeen matches for Wales he was only on the losing side twice, a remarkable record at that level.

Winning Grand Slams was not Johnnie's only contribution to Welsh history. On the outbreak of war he joined the 16th Battalion of the Royal Welch Regiment, a Cardiff battalion, and was in the thick of the action on the Somme and in particular at Mametz Wood, a place synonymous with the Welsh losses in the Great War. The memorial, a red Welsh dragon which now marks the scene of the fighting, is a permanent link between the French wood and the people of Wales. The action, which took place at Mametz between 7th and 12th July 1916, saw the 16th Royal Welch and the 11th South Wales Borderers suffer the most appalling losses. Lack of artillery support meant that German defences were almost intact and, by allowing men to advance with their flanks gaping open, the Germans had the freedom to concentrate their machine guns to deadly effect. Johnnie's battalion was in trouble from the moment they went over the top on July 7th. Heavy machine gun fire cut them down and the attack had faltered before they reached the fringes of the wood. Not only did machine gun fire come from the wood itself, but also from the valley to the north east. Two more attempts were made but the soldiers got no closer than two hundred and fifty yards from the wood. Eventually the operation was abandoned for the day with the loss of four hundred men. One of the casualties was Company Sergeant Major Dick Thomas who had made his Welsh debut with Johnnie against the Springboks ten years earlier. Born in Ferndale and a policeman based in Mountain Ash, Dick had less success as a rugby player than Johnnie and had won only four caps. A tough, uncompromising forward who was also a Glamorgan Police heavyweight boxing champion, he had contributed to victories in each of the Grand Slam seasons of 1908 and 1909. Dick's body was never found and he is remembered on the Thiepval Memorial.

The extent of these casualties did not result in a change of tactics by the generals. At 4.15 on the morning of July 10th the remaining soldiers of the 16th heard an inspirational address from Lieutenant Colonel Ronald Carden. After tying a coloured handkerchief to his walking stick he addressed them

> Make your peace with God. You are going to take that position, and some of us won't come back – but we are going to take it. This will show you where I am.

As a very obvious target, Carden was hit several times and was killed as he reached the wood. The fighting carried on regardless with every man having to look after themselves. Obstructed by brambles and falling trees, men struggled to save themselves by throwing themselves into craters for protection. Finally the wood was captured on 12th July at the cost to the 38th Division of 190 officers and 3,803 other ranks. These casualties included thirty-four year old Captain Johnnie Williams who died of wounds on the 12th July, the most capped of the thirteen Wales rugby internationals to die in the war. Johnnie had been severely wounded by shrapnel on 7th July resulting in the amputation of his left leg. Despite this he managed to write to his wife, Mabel, telling her that he was in good spirits, but infection set in and his condition deteriorated. He is buried at Corbie Communal Cemetery leaving Mabel, only eighteen months after their wedding, alone in their Penarth home.

The taking of Mametz Wood achieved very little but the impact on the Welsh psyche has been marked. Some of this is partly due to the recollections of a remarkable collection of writers and poets who fought alongside Johnnie Williams. The result is that we know not only what happened to Johnnie and his men but also what they were feeling emotionally. Siegfried Sassoon and Robert Graves, both in the 2nd Battalion Royal Welch Fusiliers, fought at Mametz and wrote about it, Graves in at least three poems and in his hugely important memoir *Goodbye to All That*. In the same regiment, Frank Richards recorded the experiences of the ordinary soldier in his memoir *Old Soldiers Never Die*. From the 15th Battalion Royal Welch Fusiliers, the poet and artist David Jones and the novelist Llewellyn Wyn Griffith committed their experiences to paper. In his acclaimed masterpiece, *In Parenthesis*, Jones describes what happened to him in the 'Queen of the Woods', an experience which became something of an obsession for the rest of his life. Griffith wrote in his *Up to Mametz*

> I can only call it a kind of emotional explosion inside me, and under its impetus I wrote on and on until I came towards

> a kind of climax, the Battle of Mametz Wood in July 1916... there was no peace within me until I had faced and recorded this high point of the war where for me and so many other Welshmen the tragedy reached its culmination.

Clearly Griffith too, had the need write about his experiences. Just over seventy years after these writers and poets fought and Johnnie and Dick Thomas met a heroic and premature death, a memorial was erected at Mametz Wood. The red dragon stands proudly, a permanent reminder of those that gave their lives, a symbol of the Welsh contribution to the Great War.

Johnnie Williams and Dick Thomas were both significant losses but they weren't alone. Another member of the Wales Grand Slam team of 1909 became a victim of the fighting. Phil Waller played six consecutive internationals between December 1908 and January 1910, all of which Wales won. Phil was born in Bath on 28th January 1889 but was educated at Carmarthen Intermediate School. His father was employed by the Inland Revenue and this resulted in the family moving around the country. On leaving school Phil was apprenticed as an engineer to the Alexander Dock Railway Company, Newport where he was introduced to Newport Rugby Club. He joined Newport in 1907 and was described by club legend Tommy Vile as a "fine all round forward", although he was known to specialise in the line out and in the loose rather than as a powerful scrummager. The following year nineteen year old Phil was in the Wales team to play the touring Australians, a match that Wales won narrowly 9-6. A week later he impressed in Newport's narrow 5-3 defeat against the touring Australians, one of seventy-nine appearances that Phil made for Newport in his career. An ever present for the remainder of that Grand Slam season, impressing particularly in the 5-3 victory over Scotland where his defence was a key factor in the victory, Phil became one of the very few Welsh internationals to defeat a major southern hemisphere country and win a 'Grand Slam' in the same season.

Phil began the following season well. Following the opening match against France *The Times* reported that the Welsh forwards were "well up to international standard" and from this distance in time, one would not expect there to be significant changes to the Welsh pack. Nevertheless, for the first ever visit to Twickenham, three changes were made and Phil never played for Wales again. Not that his international career was over. In the summer of 1910 he was one of seven Newport players selected for the British Lions tour of South Africa, a tour that was to change his life.

Phil played in all three tests on the tour, a series which the Lions lost narrowly 2-1. Moreover, he proved his durability and importance to the party by playing in twenty three of the twenty four matches of a gruelling tour. A narrow defeat in the first test was followed by an equally narrow win in the second before the Springboks asserted their superiority with a 21-5 win in the final match at Cape Town. Despite the series defeat, Phil was clearly impressed with South Africa and at the end of the tour he decided to stay. For a Somerset born, West Wales educated, East Wales rugby player whose parents now lived in Alloa, Scotland, perhaps there was something of the nomad in him. Whatever the reason, Phil was still in South Africa when war broke out. Details about his life in South Africa, both before and during the war, are difficult to confirm, although we do know that he settled in Johannesburg and worked as an engineer with the local municipality. He captained the local Wanderers team for three years before enlisting as a gunner in the 71st Siege Battery South African Heavy Artillery in August 1915. Following involvement at Ypres, the Somme, Arras and Cambrai, Phil was killed near Bapaume on 14th December 1917, still only twenty-eight years old. He had just been granted well-deserved leave following the Battle of Cambrai. Rugby historian Gwyn Prescott has discovered that he and another officer were just leaving by car to drive to the nearest rail link when they were hit by stray shellfire. Both men were killed instantly. The other officer was the son of the South African statesman, Sir Percy Fitzpatrick, the man who initially proposed the observation of the two minutes silence on Armistice Day. Phil is buried in Red Cross Corner Cemetery, Beugny near Arras.

Phil was not the only British Lion to suffer in the war. Indeed the 1910 Lions were a remarkable collection of young men, nearly all of whom served in some part of the world during the war. Fortunately some of their stories have a happier end than that suffered by Phil Waller. Tales of their heroism make fascinating reading. Charles 'Cherry' Pillman and Arthur McClinton were both awarded the Military Cross and their colleague Stanley Williams, the Distinguished Service Order. Charles Timms, an Edinburgh University three-quarter went much further and won the Military Cross on four separate occasions, three bars given to denote the extra honours. William Tyrrell, a medical student, had similar recognition for his efforts. He won both the Military Cross and the Distinguished Service Order, the latter with bar, and after the war served on a committee investigating the effects of shell shock. He later joined the RAF, becoming an Air Commodore in 1935 and in 1939 was made Air-Vice Marshall. Between 1939 and 1943 William was Honorary Surgeon to King George VI and later created a knight for his services. Tom Richards was another remarkable 'Lion'. Tom was an Australian Olympic rugby gold medal winner who had toured with the 1908 Australian team, playing against both Wales (against whom he scored a try) and England. Due to his appearances for Bristol and Gloucestershire in 1909/10, he was considered eligible to be selected for the Lions tour that following summer and went on to play in two tests. On returning to Australia he became a travelling salesman and retired from rugby in 1914. Tom soon joined the Australian Imperial Force and became a stretcher bearer in Gallipoli before being sent to the Western Front by then a Second Lieutenant. He won the Military Cross after leading a bombing party of nineteen men on a raid in which they extended the line by two hundred and fifty yards. Tom's heroics came at a cost. In September 1935 Tom died from tuberculosis, a condition he blamed firmly on the gas inhaled during the war – an unrecognised, late casualty of the war.

Other stories, like that of Phil Waller, had a more immediate outcome. Another Celt, Eric Milroy, the Scottish scrum half, was one such casualty. Eric was a late arrival to the 1910 tour after completing his finals at Edinburgh University where he was studying Mathematics. On being given the number thirteen shirt, his luck deserted him and he contracted blood poisoning after playing in just four matches. He only fully recovered on the journey home during which he was treated by William Tyrrell. His rugby career did, however, get back on track, and he went on to captain Scotland in their last two games before the outbreak of war. He was one of the six Scottish players from the Calcutta Cup match of 1914 to be lost in the war. Eric's career away from the rugby field appeared to be equally successful. On leaving university Eric had worked as a chartered accountant in Edinburgh and the future looked promising for this bright, yet modest and popular Scottish captain with a boyish smile. On the outbreak of war Eric joined the 9th Royal Scots and by January 1915 he was made 2nd Lieutenant in the 11th Royal Highlanders. He was involved in the heavy fighting at Ypres during 1915 but by July 1916 he was promoted to Lieutenant in the Black Watch (8th Royal Highlanders) as a Lewis Gun Officer. Tragically Eric was lost at Delville Wood on the Somme on the 18th. He was twenty-eight years old.

Two years later, in the spring of 1918, his uncapped Welsh, Lions colleague, Noel Humphreys, was also lost. Born in Llangan near Cowbridge, the son of a vicar who had moved to Durham, he played at Tynedale in Northumberland which might explain his absence from the Welsh national team. During the war Noel more than made up for the honours denied him on the rugby field. He became a Captain in the Tank Corps (10th Battalion), was mentioned in dispatches and awarded the Military Cross, the citation reads

> …for conspicuous gallantry and devotion to duty. His tank becoming stranded, he commenced to dig it out, and though wounded, he completed his task and continued in action the whole day, finally bringing his tank out of action to the rallying point.

Noel was killed near Etaples in France on 27th March 1918, aged twenty-seven.

In the years before the Great War, the South African 'Springboks' were establishing an intense rivalry with rugby teams in the British Isles. Despite the failure of Wales to defeat the Springboks until 1998, Welsh clubs had more success. By the time war broke out in 1914, each of the three leading Welsh clubs had defeated the tourists on one of their two tours. Cardiff had, with Johnnie Williams scoring a try, defeated the Springboks on the 1906/7 tour while in 1912, although South Africa won all the international matches and lost only three of their twenty seven games, both Newport and Swansea gained hard fought victories. Playing for Newport, in a team that became known as 'the Immortals', was a young three-quarter who had the potential to enjoy a long and successful international career.

William Purdon Geen was born in Gold Tops, Newport on 14th March 1891 into a family with an impressive rugby pedigree. His uncle, Frank Purdon, had played in the first Wales international fixture in 1881 and won four caps. A close neighbour in Gold Tops must also have been an inspiration. Louis Phillips is remembered as one of the greatest all round sportsmen in Newport's history. He had already made his mark as a swimmer, cricketer and international standard water polo player but it is as a rugby player that he is best remembered. He won four caps for Wales playing at half back and was part of the Triple Crown winning team of 1900 but his rugby career was cruelly cut short by a serious knee injury at the age of twenty-two. This did not prevent Lou going on to represent Wales at golf, a game he continued to play for the rest of his life, a life that ended near Loos in March 1916 when he was shot in the chest.

Lou Phillips must have been an inspiration to many Newport schoolboys including William Geen. However Billy, as William was now known, developed his rugby skills away from any influence that Lou Phillips might have provided. In order to continue with his education, Billy left Newport and was educated at Haileybury College, a boarding school in Hertfordshire from where he progressed to Oxford University. At Haileybury Billy had been a noted cricketer both as a fine wicketkeeper and captain of the First XI and he went on to represent Monmouthshire in the Minor Counties Championship. But it was with the oval ball that he made his name and Billy made a sensational start to his university rugby career. Picked on three occasions to represent Oxford in the Varsity match, Billy made a huge contribution to a thrilling Oxford victory in his first in 1910. Playing on the wing, outside the dazzling Ronnie Poulton who scored two tries of his own, Billy scored three tries in a 23-18 victory. It would have been four but for Billy's failure to ground the ball properly after crossing the Cambridge line. *The*

Times was unimpressed with this carelessness as Billy had time to finish the job properly, but he learned his lesson. Later in the game when given another chance to score, it reported that Billy grounded the ball "as if it were made of Venetian glass". That carelessness apart, it was an impressive performance, one of only eleven occasions in Varsity match history where a player has scored a hat trick of tries. Among the Cambridge backs was another future Welsh international, Bryn Lewis. He scored two of Cambridge's four tries and his team might well have won had he not needed to leave the field with an injury thereby giving Ronnie Poulton the opportunity to win the match for Oxford. Bryn Lewis was to win two Welsh caps before losing his life at Boesinghe in April 1917.

When not playing on the left wing for Oxford, Billy was playing in the centre for Newport while periodically representing his county, Monmouthshire, and the Barbarians. Billy's trademark was what the *South Wales Argus* called "his dancing footwork" prior to a defence splitting side-step and, although "raw in the tackle", he learned to go low, a technique which resulted in him developing into a sound defender. Although, according to an old school friend, quoted by Nigel McCrery, Billy was sometimes considered to be a 'moody player' who rarely shone behind a beaten pack, he was also an instinctive player who was capable, like Poulton, of moments of sheer genius.

Many of these skills were displayed on 24th October 1912 when, in front of an impressive crowd of 18,300 at Rodney Parade, Newport defeated South Africa 9-3. Billy, playing on the wing as a late replacement for Welsh international George Hirst, tackled well and saved a number of certain tries. Fred Birt scored a try, conversion and drop goal ensuring that the Springboks suffered their first defeat of a tour in which all five internationals were won. Unsurprisingly, Billy was now selected to make his Wales debut against the same opposition, on the left wing. Making their debuts alongside him were an outside half from Monmouth School and Cambridge University, where he was a choral scholar, named Horace Wyndham Thomas and a tough forward from Briton Ferry now playing for Neath, Fred Perrett. Billy distinguished himself once again and, in the pouring rain, made several dangerous runs, one of which almost led to a try. Wyndham Thomas too made his mark and might have won the game for Wales when his attempted dropped goal was incorrectly disallowed by the referee. The crowd was convinced that the score, worth four points before 1948, should stand but to no avail. Wales lost 3-0.

All three debutants kept their places for the opening match of the 1913 Five Nations Championship against England. Although Billy once again played well showing his undoubted pace, it was not enough to prevent a 12-0 defeat. Billy was dropped following this defeat, although Fred Perrett kept his place for the remaining three matches, all of which were won. Perrett, now out of work, finally succumbed to the money offered by the 'Northern Code' and joined Leeds that summer, followed by a move to Hull where he was playing in the early part of the war. Wyndham Thomas too had played his last game for Wales. Cruelly denied his place in Welsh folklore, this supremely talented outside half secured a five-year appointment with a firm of shipping agents in Calcutta and sailed to India immediately after the England game. His departure was a great loss to Welsh rugby. A brilliant Cambridge Blue, Wyndham was seen as one of the potentially great Welsh players of the era. Billy, however, did win a recall to his country's colours when he was selected, this time in the centre, to play Ireland at St Helen's, Swansea in March 1913. Once again he did not let anybody down. *The Times* commented on his ability to run straight when playing in the centre as well as the timing of his pass and effective swerve. There were criticisms of his defence, in particular a surprising reluctance to fall on the ball when the Irish were driving forward. Wales won 16-13 but, although Billy might well have kept his place against England at the start of the following season's championship, he pulled out, "not well enough to play" according to *The Times*. His withdrawal probably cost Billy four more caps but other players came in and did well so at the age of twenty-two Billy's international career had ended.

With the outbreak of war it was inevitable that Billy would volunteer. He quickly joined the 60th King's Royal Rifle Corps and embarked on a period of training in Petworth, Sussex before arriving at the front near Ypres in May 1915. Billy, a Second Lieutenant in the 9th Battalion, was soon in action in the Second Battle of Ypres but his war was to be tragically short. Last seen engaged in hand to hand fighting, leading his men, Billy was killed on 31st July 1915 at Hooge. The official record records his last moments

> Geen fought gloriously, and was last seen alive leading his platoon in a charge after being for hours subjected to liquid fire and every device the Germans could bring to bear to break through. 17 officers and 333 other ranks of this battalion were killed in the engagement, in which officers and men showed themselves worthy of the best traditions of the Regiment.

His body was never found; Billy is remembered on the Menin Gate.

Sadly the war ended in a similar way for the two men who made their international debuts with Billy. Second Lieutenant Horace Wyndham Thomas died at Guillemont on the Somme on 3rd September 1916 and is remembered on the Thiepval Memorial while Second Lieutenant Fred Perrett of the 17th Battalion Royal Welsh Fusiliers died of his wounds in Boulogne on 1st December 1918, nearly three weeks after the Armistice. He was severely injured in his thigh and hand by machine gun fire on the same day, November 4th, the poet Wilfred Owen was killed. He is buried in Terlincthun British Cemetery, Wimille in northern France. Fred Perrett was, for a number of years, omitted from the lists of those Welsh players killed in the war due to his latter career in Rugby League, an omission indicative of the way in which players who 'went north' were regarded in the hierarchy of the amateur game.

With the death of Billy Geen there is no such ambiguity. Although his academic career at Oxford curtailed his availability to play for Newport, (he played only thirty-seven times for the club although he did score an impressive twenty tries and one dropped goal), the *South Wales Argus* remembered him fondly in its obituary on 6th August 1915. He was a "dazzling left wing" who played his best rugby outside Ronnie Poulton while at Oxford. "No wing," it was written, "was ever better matched in physique, in style, in skill and in 'colour' than were those brilliant sons of Oxford – Billy Geen and Ronnie Poulton." Although never attaining the spectacular heights on the rugby field as his Oxford colleague, Billy too epitomizes much that is best about our pre 1914 sportsmen. One of seven hundred and forty boys from his old school to be lost in the fighting, Billy Geen, twenty-four years old at the time of his death, represents yet another example of the 'lost generation'.

The Men of Kent

In comparison with rugby union, cricket appears to have suffered smaller losses. Very few of the big stars of the 'Golden Age' died in the fighting and it is easy to imagine that cricket escaped the worst of the tragedy. Closer examination of the statistics, however, tells a very different story. Christopher Sandford records in his book *The Final Over* that two hundred and ten professional first class cricketers out of a total of two hundred and seventy-eight registered players answered their country's call during the war of whom thirty-four were killed. However Andrew Renshaw, editor of *Wisden on the Great War: The Lives Of Cricket's Fallen*, has recently discovered that the true figure is much higher and that two hundred and eighty-nine cricketers with first class experience were killed. The definition of a first class cricketer can vary, although we can be sure that twelve test cricketers made the ultimate sacrifice. The proportion of those who died in the action is the highest of all the sports with one cricketer in six failing to return. There were relatively few county cricketers in England, while in the colonies there were fewer full-time cricketers than might be imagined. Viewed this way, cricket too should be seen as having responded to the call.

Reaction by the cricket authorities was swift. The County Championship was suspended for the duration, although by the declaration of war Surrey had already been crowned champions, and in South Africa season 1913/14 was the last for five years. In Australia the Sheffield Shield continued during 1914/15 but was suspended thereafter and did not resume until 1919. Lord's, the home of cricket, was swiftly requisitioned by the Army and county captains Sir Archibald White and Arthur Carr, of Yorkshire and Nottinghamshire respectively, each with military commitments, followed Middlesex and England captain Pelham Warner in reporting immediately to do their duty. As we have already noted, W.G. Grace was soon calling for cricketers of a suitable age to set a good example and come to the aid of their country "in its hour of need". In a letter to *The Sportsman* on 27th August he argued for the cessation of county cricket as it "is not fitting at a time like this that able-bodied men should be playing cricket by day and pleasure-seekers look on." Had Grace lived he would, no doubt, have been pleased to learn that by the end of the war four hundred and seven cricketers had been decorated for gallantry. Although the bible of cricket, *Wisden*, reporting on the 1914 season early the following year, had little to say as regards casualties, it was not long before it became an "almanac of obituaries". Not only players made a commitment. Committee members, ground staff, administrators, supporters, indeed everybody connected with cricket clubs all over the country, first class or otherwise, was affected. Cricket was 'to do its bit'.

Perhaps the best known loss to the sport was the Kent and England slow left arm bowler Colin Blythe. Surprisingly for such a good bowler, Colin was never an automatic choice for England and played only nineteen tests, six in his home country. Blythe's limited caps were due mainly to the presence of the remarkable talents of Yorkshire's Wilfred Rhodes who took more wickets in the first class game than anybody else in history (4,204) and worked his way up the England batting order from number eleven until he was opening with Jack Hobbs. Nevertheless, few cricket historians would argue with the view that Colin Blythe of Kent and England was one of the greatest bowlers ever to have graced the English game. In the 'Golden Age' of cricket when the sport was the national game and spectators filled the grounds to witness the fascinating battle between bat and ball, and when county cricket was deemed to be more important than test matches against 'colonials', Colin was one of a small group of players whose bowling could carry a side on its own. That this should be so is the result of one of the most unlikely journeys to stardom that can be imagined.

Colin, or Charlie as he became better known, was born on 30th May 1879, into a struggling family living in Deptford, to where the family had relocated from Kent in the 1840s. The oldest of twelve children, only one of which died in infancy, a remarkably low number for a family living in such a deprived location with over 30% unemployment, Charlie left Alverton Street School to begin work as an engineer/fitter at Woolwich Arsenal. This appears to have been a turning point for Charlie and not one for the better. It was around this time that Charlie began to suffer from ill health caused, according to one doctor, by a lack of fresh air. It was more likely that long hours of work followed by intense studying led to health issues. The truth was that Charlie had a much bigger health problem – he had been diagnosed as being epileptic. The stigma surrounding this condition in the early years of the twentieth century was far greater than today, and this poor health was to dog Charlie during his career, particularly in stressful situations. As well as this, Charlie had a sensitive and artistic nature – a very good violinist for whom music was as important as cricket – but was prone to bouts of melancholy. Added together he was not the stereotypical outstanding international sportsman.

Yet Charlie's prowess at cricket was soon evident. Denied the advantages provided by the English public schools, he had begun to play organised cricket locally around Blackheath. In July 1897 he was spotted after being asked to bowl at the Kent all-rounder Walter Wright during Kent's match against Somerset at the Rectory Field, Blackheath, a game at which Charlie was a keen spectator. His impressive bowling was not only seen by Wright but also by William McCanlis, an ex-captain and now a highly regarded Kent coach. Both men were impressed with Charlie's raw, but natural, ability. A trial was arranged and Charlie was soon heading to Tonbridge Nursery, possibly the best place in the country to develop his skills. The regime was strict and the hours of bowling and perfecting technique were long, but by the summer of 1899 Kent had available to them a slow left arm bowler with his own particular style, refined by numerous guest appearances for local clubs, who was now ready to make his mark. Showing all the determination and endeavour that would become his hallmark, Charlie forced his way into the Kent First XI and made his debut on 21st August 1899. His start was nothing short of sensational. With his first ball in first class cricket, playing against a very strong Yorkshire side, Charlie took the wicket of batsman Frank Mitchell who, uniquely, played cricket and rugby for England and cricket for South Africa. He had announced himself in as dramatic a way as he could have wished. After playing in three further matches that summer, Kent's new left arm spinner had taken 14 wickets. The following season, 1900, he became well established in the Kent side and rewarded their faith in him by taking 114 wickets at an average of 18 runs. He was on his way.

Charlie continued to work as an engineer fitter in the winter months but it was not long before cricket became an all the year round activity. Although the exceptionally dry summer of 1901 rendered Charlie less dangerous, with Rhodes unavailable he was selected to represent his country in Australia in the winter of 1901/2. On 13th December 1901, the highly-strung violinist made his England debut at the Sydney Cricket Ground. Also making his debut that day under the somewhat maverick captaincy of A.C. MacLaren was Sydney F. Barnes, an almost totally unknown bowler who many shrewd judges argue is the greatest bowler of all time. It began well for both men, with Barnes doing the damage in the first innings and another debutant, Len Braund, in the second, England won by an innings. Charlie supported both bowlers well and finished with match figures of 7 for 56, a very promising start for the debutant England bowlers. The eccentric MacLaren even gave Charlie a gold watch to mark the occasion. It was not to last. The experienced Aussie batsmen got to grips with England's raw attack and won the next four tests. Charlie took only 11 more wickets in the series and did not play for his country again for three years until he was selected to again replace the injured Rhodes at Headingly in the third test of England's series victory over Australia. Unfortunately for Charlie, the return of Wilfred Rhodes ensured that this was the only test that he played in England's 2-0 win.

In the winter of 1905/6 Charlie was back on tour, this time to South Africa where, although Warner's team were well beaten 4-1, Charlie was mainly responsible for England's victory at Cape Town with match figures of 11 for 118, his best test match return thus far. In the return series the following summer, won 1-0 by England, Charlie eclipsed even that tally. In a performance at Headingly that ultimately won the series for England Charlie took 8 for 59 and 7 for 40 giving him match figures of 15 for 99, the best by an England bowler at that time and only bettered by seven bowlers in the history of test cricket for any country. Surprisingly Charlie's test career rather faded away. He toured Australia again in 1907/8 but played in only one test. In the return series in the summer of 1909 Charlie was picked for the first test at Edgbaston and took 11 for 102 securing the match for England. But the effort proved to be so stressful and took so much out of him that he found it impossible to play in the next test at Lord's. He returned for the fourth test at Old

Trafford and took another seven wickets, (5 for 63 in the first innings), but missed the final test and played in just the final two tests on the tour to South Africa in 1909/10. In the last of these, at Cape Town, Charlie took 7 for 46 in the first innings and finished with 10 wickets in a match that England won, although the series was lost 3-2. This was the fourth time in nineteen tests that Charlie had taken more than ten wickets in the match, however his test career was over.

It is possible that the strain of playing test cricket affected, or at least was perceived to affect, his performance at international level. A doctor even recommended to the Kent committee, according to George Plumptre in his book *The Golden Age of Cricket*, that Charlie should not play test matches so great did he find the strain. A taxing spell of bowling could bring him close to a breakdown and that his sensitivity, coupled with ill health, seemingly made him unsuitable for international cricket. Yet some of his performances were quite exceptional. A test match record of 100 wickets in nineteen tests at 18.63 a wicket is a considerable achievement, especially given Charlie's epilepsy. Achieving a test match average of five wickets in a match for a left arm spinner? Most England captains would take that without hesitation.

There was far less debate regarding Charlie's performances for Kent. By 1904 *Wisden* had seen enough to make him one of their 'five cricketers of the year' and his form in the domestic game was remarkably consistent. Kent certainly reaped the rewards, winning the championship in 1906, 1909, 1910 and 1913. In each of these years Charlie made a significant contribution. In 1906 *The Times*, reflecting on Kent's title victory, concluded that the best batsmen found it hard to score runs even on perfect wickets when Charlie was bowling. This opinion was supported by Charlie's performance in the title-clinching match against Hampshire when he took twelve wickets to ensure victory. In their second triumph, in 1909, Charlie took 213 wickets followed by 175 in the victory a year later. Even as late as 1913, his test career now well behind him, Charlie was a match winner and he took 167 wickets as Kent stormed to another title. In the last three seasons before the war broke out, Charlie topped the national bowling averages and was still taking well over 100 wickets a season, a feat he achieved every summer except one, when he suffered particularly from his ailments. In seven seasons

Charlie took over 150 wickets in the season. During his career Charlie took eight wickets or more in an innings on fifteen occasions and thirteen wickets in a match also fifteen times. His career figures show that Charlie with 2509 first class wickets at an average of 16.80. Even in his final season Charlie took 170 wickets at a better than career average of 15.19. Hidden in these summative statistics there are some remarkable performances. In what *Wisden*, with great understatement, called a "good day's work", Charlie took 17 for 48 in a single day at Northampton in 1907, including a spell of 7 wickets for 1 run in 36 balls. This was not a one off. Two years later he took 14 for 56 in a day at Leicester and a further two years later took 14 for 84 at Cheltenham, once again in a single day.

What made Charlie so successful? This was an era when the ball moving away from the right-handed batsman was in its infancy as a tactic with which to trap a batsman. Bowlers relied on pace, in-swingers, off-breaks and googlies in order to take wickets. Slow left armers were the only bowlers who consistently got the ball to move away, hence in England the prominence of left arm spinners such as Ted Peate, Bobby Peel, Johnny Briggs, Wilfred Rhodes and Charlie Blythe, who all flighted the ball in such a way as to encourage the batsmen to play the classic shots. There was no attempt to fire the ball in at the leg stump – a very negative tactic used by Warwick Armstrong in Australia – but to play as the English spinners did required great skill. Charlie certainly possessed that. C.B. Fry said that Charlie had the ability to bowl the quicker ball which made him hard to score off, while H.S. Altham is quoted in Plumptre that "to watch his mastery of flight and spin was an aesthetic experience", no surprise perhaps given his musical sensitivities. He also spun the ball considerably. The doyen of cricket writers, Sir Neville Cardus, said that "Blythe was all nervous sensibility… and that his trick was sharp and sudden spin." On hard wickets, Cardus tells us, "he spun the ball with more alacrity, and with a sharper rise, than any other bowler I have seen" while on damp, uncovered wickets he could be unplayable. A wet, drying, crumbling wicket inevitably meant that Blythe would be given the ball, even on occasions to open the bowling. A master of flight, Ranji found Charlie more difficult to attack than Rhodes, particularly when an in-swinging 'arm' ball was delivered with no discernable change in action. By 1908 Charlie had subdued 'The

Master', Jack Hobbs, by dismissing him eight times in thirteen innings. In Porter's biography of Hobbs the author tells us that "Blythe was a great attacking bowler who had a swirling loop in his delivery. He gave the ball plenty of air and kept it up to the batsman even when he was being hit." If Ranji, Fry and Cardus are great admirers and Hobbs has become your 'rabbit', then you must be a player to reckon with.

With the sound of the guns drifting over the channel to the cricket fields of Kent, Charlie's career drew to a close. He had married Janet Brown (known as Gertrude) in 1907, an attractive woman, his junior by ten years, and they had settled in Tonbridge. With the security of a healthy benefit of £1,500 awarded in 1909 which was now safely invested and the prospect of a coaching job at Eton College available when he retired, the future looked bright. Even the onset of war need not have affected him directly. His ill health, in particular his epilepsy, meant that Charlie could easily have opted to carry out war work at home in the way his England colleagues Hobbs and Rhodes opted to do with much less reason. This, however, was not Charlie's way.

In late August 1914 Charlie joined No 1 Reserve Company of the Kent Fortress Royal Engineers and was stationed near home in the Tonbridge area. The Company specialised in bridge and light railway construction and initially was responsible for reinforcing defences and military infrastructure around the south coast. This work suited Charlie with his engineering skills but as the war dragged on it became inevitable that he would be posted overseas. In mid 1917, by now a Sergeant, he was attached to the King's Own Yorkshire Light Infantry, a battalion that had already seen action in Egypt, the Somme and the Battle of Arras around Oppy Wood. In August Charlie was in the Ypres Salient supervising night patrols and laying temporary railway lines between trenches and ammunition stores. By November the soldiers were reaching Passchendaele, after taking ninety-nine days to walk five miles. What the soldiers found was truly awful. Corporal Baker of the Canadian Expeditionary Force discovered on November 7th shook him to the core. In his attempt to deliver a wounded colleague to safety, Corporal Baker came across a trench packed with soldiers that he took to be asleep. On investigating further he later wrote,

> I shall never forget what I found. Down that stretch of trench the boys were sitting in grotesque positions and every one was dead.

What Baker took to be a trench was, in reality, a series of shell holes joined up and exposed to overhead shrapnel fire coming from both sides of No Man's Land.

The day after Baker's discovery, November 8th, Charlie was working on Wild Wood Spur where the soldiers were trying to improve the forward movement of munitions during the attack on Passchendaele. They were just south of the Ypres-Wieltje road when a random shell exploded above the heads of Charlie's working party. Charlie, along with three colleagues, was killed instantly, four of the three thousand fatalities lost at Passchendaele. They were buried nearby at Oxford Road Military Cemetery.

The loss of Charlie Blythe was felt throughout the world of cricket. The most popular of players, tributes were genuine and heartfelt. In 1918 *Wisden* acknowledged that his loss was "the most serious that cricket has sustained during the war." Writing mainly about his cricketing ability, *Wisden* published one of its most detailed and complimentary obituaries:

> Blythe had all the good gifts that pertain to the first rate slow bowler, and a certain imaginative quality that was peculiarly his own. Very rarely did he get to the end of his resources. To see him bowl to a brilliant hitter was a sheer delight. So far from being disturbed by a drive to the ring he would, instead of shortening his length to escape punishment, send up the next ball to be hit, striving of course to put on, if possible, a little extra spin.

The writer described his spin as "something out of the ordinary" and as particularly effective on a sticky wicket or a dry slightly crumbling surface. His ability to inject pace was recalled and that "the ball that went with his arm often approached the speed of a fast bowler with… the advantage of being unsuspected." Major H.S. Altham, once again in the pages of *Wisden*, remembered the character of the man present in his bowling.

> There can never have been a great cricketer less military in

> temper than Colin Blythe; the artistry of his bowling was but the expression of his sensitive and highly strung temperament, his physique was never strong, but when the call came, he never hesitated…

A monument was soon erected in his memory at the St Lawrence Ground in Canterbury, while at Lord's hangs a painting by Albert Chevallier Taylor entitled 'Kent v Lancashire at Canterbury in 1906' which clearly shows the bowling action of the great Kent left arm bowler. His memory continues. Ex-Prime Minister turned cricket historian, John Major, puts him in the line of great slow bowlers possessing "truly great left arm spin". In 2009 the England cricket team, led by Andrew Strauss, visited Oxford Road Military Cemetery in Flanders and laid a stone cricket ball on Charlie's grave. Strauss later expressed how moving an experience his team had found the occasion. Perhaps the last word should go to Sir Neville Cardus who, reflecting in 1949, wrote:

> A shell made by somebody who had never known cricket and directed by eyes that had never seen a Kent field, fell on Blythe and killed him. On any of those quiet, distant, delicious afternoons at Canterbury, when Blythe bowled his gentle spin and the summer blossomed all around, could even the ironic gods have discerned the course of events which was to take Blythe over the seas and leave him there part of the foreign dust?

Charlie Blythe was a professional cricketer but in those pre-war years it was vital that a successful county had at least a sprinkling of sparkling amateur players. The captain of every first class cricket team in England before the war was always an amateur and professionals were made very aware of their place in the scheme of things. The pre-war era was undoubtedly the Golden Age, not only of cricket, but of the gifted amateur. Although most amateur cricketers survived the war and retained the captaincy at both county and test level, they never made quite as significant a contribution to English cricket after 1914. Within the teams themselves the batsmen of the golden Edwardian Age tended to be amateur. Great batsmen of the time – MacLaren, Fry, Ranji, Jackson, Foster, Jessop, Woolley,

Spooner – were all amateurs, whereas the leading bowlers – Rhodes, Hirst, Barnes, Blythe – were professionals. There were exceptions, such as Johnny Tyldesley the great professional Lancashire and England batsman and Tom Haywood the Surrey opening bat, but it can be accepted an accurate generalisation. Amateurs tended to display a transient brilliance, contributing sparkle rather than stability, and consequently had a limited life in the first class game. For many it was difficult, due to work and family commitments, to tour. For others, such as Reginald Foster a brilliant batsman who scored 287 on his England debut in Sydney in 1903, it was difficult to play throughout an English summer. Foster played only eight test matches but remains the only man to have captained England at both cricket and football. The most gifted amateur player in the Kent XI in this period was another victim of the Great War, Kenneth Lotherington Hutchings, a batsman who was good enough to be capped seven times, all against Australia, in the face of stiff competition from some of the greatest batsmen ever to play for England.

Ken was born the youngest of three brothers, all of whom played for Kent, on 7th December 1882 at Southborough, Kent. He was educated at Tonbridge School and the dark haired, athletic young man played in a strong First XI with great success during his last four years at the school. By the summer of 1902, nineteen year old Ken was playing for Kent, showing himself to be a batsman in the true amateur traditions, thrilling the crowds with his hard hitting, free scoring style. He was a daring extrovert who relied on his natural fitness, nimble footwork and a keen eye in order to drive bowlers almost exclusively off the front foot. He hit the ball harder than anyone else according to the Yorkshire stalwarts David Denton and George Hirst, and reserved his back foot play almost entirely for defence. He was also able to bowl a fast right arm delivery when required and was as fine a fielder as he was batsman, making him a cricketer of the top rank.

Like his teammate Charlie Blythe, Ken played a crucial role in Kent's historic title victory in 1906. That summer was indeed his best season. Not only did he finish third in the national averages, but hit 1,454 runs for Kent in the championship at an average of 60.58, figures which included four centuries. The speed of his scoring was also an asset as it placed Kent in winning positions. *The Times* reported in 1906 that it was not just the volume of runs he scored but the fact that "he disheartens and upsets the best of bowlers and so makes the task of the later batsmen proportionately easier." The title race with the very strong Yorkshire team of Hirst and Rhodes went to the final game, the deciding match Kent against Hampshire. With Charlie Blythe taking twelve wickets the scene was set for the Kent batsman. Ken obliged with 124 exciting runs, reaching a century in 65 minutes. Once victory had been achieved and the title was secure, *The Times* expressed the opinion that:

> The dramatic figure, however, of the Kent eleven, is Mr Hutchings.... He had done nothing very extraordinary when he was pressed to become a regular member of what was even then a very strong side. On a fast wicket Mr Hutchings is the most dangerous batsman in England. He hits no ball which does not require a certain amount of stopping, and many balls to which he has only played back reach the boundary. His most forcible stroke is on the offside but his straight driving is also very powerful and, indeed, unless he strokes the ball straight to a fieldsman, four runs are generally a probability.

1906 proved to be the highlight of Ken's domestic career. Such was his reputation following that first title success that Ken was included in the England party, accompanied by Charlie Blythe, on the 1907/8 tour to Australia. Ken played in all five tests, a century in the victorious second test at Melbourne helping to cement his place for what proved to be an undistinguished series for both him and the English team. During the match, on 4th January 1908, *The Times* reported

> So far the feature of the match has been Hutching's innings. It is the general opinion that nothing finer has been done by a batsman from England since Ranjitsinghi was here ten years ago. His power of wrist and forearm is considered marvellous and the way in which he flicked the ball away on the leg side filled old test match players with amazement.

England won the test by one wicket in a thrilling finish and before he was bowled, yorked by Albert Cotter (of whom more later), Ken had raced to 126, doubling his score in three quarters of an hour.

Nothing comparable was to follow in the remainder of the series, and on his return Ken was ignored by the selectors for the first three tests of the return series with Australia in the summer of 1909. With England losing 2-1, Ken returned for the fourth test at Old Trafford and was retained for the final test at the Oval where, batting at number eight, he scored 59. Both tests were drawn and Ken's England career ended. Domestically, Ken still had achievements to savour with championship titles won with Kent in 1909 and 1910. But his career from here faded and in 1912 he retired from the first class game. His ability and charm were not, however, forgotten. H.S. Altham recalled that,

> In style he was a thorough individualist; in defence he was a good back-player; but he will be remembered best for his driving. Blessed with abnormally strong wrists and forearms, the power of his straight and on-driving was really alarming yet there was no spectacular effort on the stroke, only a lightening acceleration at the vital moment. As a fielder, whether in the slips or in the out-field, he was magnificent; with his crisp black hair, strong athletic body and sparkling methods, he was the idol of the Kent grounds.

His total number of first class runs, 8,003 in 161 matches at a career average of 34.94 and test average of 28.41, scarcely does him justice. Ken was clearly one of the most exciting batsmen in an age that was overloaded with gifted amateurs. He was also one of the best loved.

Ken's war experience is quickly related. He joined the King's Liverpool Regiment, which by the summer of 1916 had been attached to the Welsh Regiment to fight on the Somme. A Lieutenant, he was hit by an enemy shell on 3rd September 1916 and died immediately. His body was never found and he is remembered on the Thiepval Memorial. He is remembered as one of the most exciting amateur batsmen of the Edwardian Age, a status preserved by A.A. Thompson in *Cricketers of My Times*, who lamented:

> Though a crabbed unemotional Northerner, I sometimes think that if one last fragment of cricket had to be preserved, as though in amber, it should be a glimpse of K.L. Hutchings, cover-driving under a summer heaven.

Cricket Losses in the Colonies

It was not only on the lush grounds of England where cricket felt the loss of much loved and admired players. The sacrifice made by the colonies throughout the war is well documented and any visit to the battlefields of the Western Front or the Dardanelles will quickly confirm this. Niall Ferguson, in his brilliant and ground breaking history *The Pity of War*, using statistics obtained from the War Office, has quoted a total of 646,850 casualties suffered by the countries of the British Empire excluding Britain itself. Of these 198,000 were fatalities, 427,587 wounded and 21,263 held as prisoner when the hostilities finally ceased. When examining the military deaths as percentages of manpower, Ferguson turns to J.M. Winter and quotes a figure of 8.8% of those mobilized as the percentage of British Empire (excluding Great Britain) killed. Australia suffered most with 14.5% of their soldiers killed, followed by New Zealand with 12.5%, Canada 9.7%, India 5.7% and South Africa 5.1%. In comparison, Ferguson tells us that Britain and Ireland lost 11.8% of their soldiers. As a good Scot, he also points out that Scotland suffered the death of 26.4% of their soldiers, a higher percentage than any country in the Great War with the exception of Serbia (37.1%) and Turkey (26.8%). There can be no doubt that the soldiers of the far flung parts of the British Empire were in the thick of the battle, with many making the greatest sacrifice of all. Colonial cricketers in this category, although not great in number and little remembered today, nevertheless are a significant part of the story.

The first and best known Australian cricketer to be killed in the war was a fast bowler, Albert 'Tibby' Cotter. Tibby was born in Sydney, the son of an English-born butcher and a Scottish mother, on 3rd December 1883, and is generally considered to be the fastest bowler of the first decade of the twentieth century. Between the years 1904 and 1912 he was the spearhead of the Australian attack and often known in England, a country where his reputation was particularly high, as 'Terror Cotter'. He was playing Sheffield Shield cricket for New South Wales at the age of eighteen and, by the time he was twenty, Tibby Cotter was opening the bowling for Australia. In 1903/4, the season he made his test debut, Tibby topped the first class averages and, on the strength of his performances, the tall, well built, young tearaway forced his way into the Australian side that was in the process of losing the Ashes to 'Plum' Warner's England team. Tibby was picked for the fourth test played at Sydney Cricket Ground but his selection could not prevent an English victory which gave the tourists an unassailable 3-1 lead, enough to regain the Ashes. Tibby made an undistinguished start to his test career and took only three wickets in the match, a game settled by the then unique, baffling, googly bowling of Bernard Bosanquet who took 6/51 in Australia's second innings including a spell of 5/12. The fifth and final test played at Melbourne was, however, a very different matter and England faced for the first, but not the last time, the full ferocity of Australia's quickest bowler. In their first innings England crumbled in the face of 'Terror Cotter' and collapsed to a score of 61, Tibby taking 6/40. Hugh Trumble finished the job in the second innings when he completed the second hat-trick of his distinguished test career with his last ball in first class cricket. Australia won by 218 runs and Tibby had topped the Australian bowling averages for the series. Albert 'Tibby' Cotter had arrived.

It was fifteen months before Australia played another test match, an almost inconceivably long time in today's year round cricket. Tibby was, as expected, selected for Joe Darling's team to tour England in 1905, a series eagerly anticipated on both sides of the world following the remarkable Ashes summer of 1902, a year fit to compare with the modern classics of 1981 and 2005. But what sort of bowler was Australia's new tearaway fast bowler? That he was quick is not in dispute. Porter tells us that:

> ...he was the fastest and most frightening bowler of his day. Never afraid to pitch the ball short and bounce it at the batsman's head, he was capable of making all but the bravest a trifle apprehensive.

Some claim that he was the first bowler to use a bouncer regularly as a form of intimidation (although there had been quicker bowlers such as fellow Australian Ernest Jones who is reputed to have bowled a ball through W.G. Grace's beard), and possibly the first bowler to use a slip cordon. He was a little erratic in his early days, an observation made by *The Times* when covering Warner's tour, but this did improve with experience. *Wisden*, reflecting on the 1905 tour, was of the opinion that

> up to a certain point of the tour he had so little command over his length that his bowling was a quaint mixture of long hops and full pitches.

But his extreme pace made him dangerous and, once he gained command of his length by shortening his run up, "on his day he was deadly."

> His action is a bit low, but he has plenty of pace, a sure foothold on any wicket, and can generally make the ball get up in a disconcerting fashion.

By "a disconcerting fashion" *Wisden* meant a ball that was generally chest high but sometimes flying dangerously over the helmetless batsman's head. On the 1905 tour, bowling at a now past his prime W.G., Tibby hit the great man with a full toss. W.G. gave a catch next ball and walked. Nobody, not even W.G., enjoys facing real pace. It is just that some play it better than others.

The England captain in 1905, F.S. Jackson, the hero of the series, reflected in the 1943 *Wisden* that Tibby was even faster than Ernest Jones for a couple of overs. The Australian wicketkeeper, Sammy Carter, is quoted by Alan Gibson in his book *Jackson's Year*, the story of the 1905 series, as saying "You could put Gregory on top of McDonald, and the pair of them wouldn't be as fast as Cotter." Jack Gregory and Ted McDonald were the Australian fast bowlers who destroyed England in 1921 when batsmen were reputed to have shaken with fear before facing them. Carter should know – he kept wicket to all of them. Given this reputation, it is surprising that Tibby isn't remembered as one of the most feared Aussie bowlers. Perhaps the really memorable fast bowlers hunt in pairs – Lillee and Thompson; Lindwall and Miller; Roberts and Holding; Gregory and McDonald; Trueman and Statham; Larwood and Voce; Wasim and Waqar – or even the quartets favoured by the West Indies in the 1980s and, to a lesser extent, England in the mid and late 2000s. What is noticeable about the 1905 touring party is that Tibby was the only true fast bowler in the party. This was not unusual in pre war years. Indeed it was not unusual on the uncovered wickets to see slow bowlers open the bowling, Charlie Blythe being an example. Australia, with the exception of Ernest Jones and Fred 'The Demon' Spofforth, had not really produced fast bowlers at this stage. Even Spofforth relied on movement more than pace in all but his early years.

The 1905 tour is well-documented and we have a picture Edwardian England getting to grips with the steady growth of international sport. Big crowds, enthusiastic supporters of all ages and class, gathering to watch home grown players remind the 'upstart' colonials of the natural order of things; subjects of the British Empire determined to prove their right to be at least the equals of teams from the mother country. There was certainly no lack of spice in these encounters. It was expected that much of the spice in the forthcoming series would be supplied by Tibby Cotter. Alan Gibson has pointed out that Tibby's performance in the final test at Melbourne had sent shock waves through the England camp and, although senior batsmen like MacLaren, Fry and Jackson had not toured in 1904, news of Australia's new fast bowler travelled quickly. One description written by Robert Lynch following a match between The Gentlemen of England and Australia described Tibby as "a compact, hard man, with jutting hips and a strong neck… who before he bowls takes a long race up towards the wicket, ducking like a water hen as he runs, and juggling his wrist in the oddest way." The account, to be found in Christopher Martin-Jenkins' *Cricketers Companion*, goes on to describe how Tibby released the ball in a "violent hurl" so that the wicket-keeper, standing a long way back, was as a "shivering schoolboy, determined to be plucky, and standing with his mouth open and groaning inwardly as he saw the little dark devil of a ball speeding towards him." The wicket-keeper, Lynch tells us, considered running for his life.

The 1905 series was a moderate success for Tibby but much more so for Stanley Jackson's England team, and the captain in particular, which prevailed 2-0 in a series where they won the toss in every test and rarely let Australia an opportunity to dominate. Tibby took 124 wickets on the tour, a fine performance which included 12/34 in one day at Worcester after which the press began to refer to him as the 'Sydney Express.' The series began well for him as he and Frank Laver bowled England out for 196 at Trent Bridge on the first day. Laver took seven wickets to Tibby's three, but there was no doubt in the minds of the England batsmen as to which bowler was causing the psychological damage. One correspondent wrote after this bowling performance,

> I hope we shall see no more of the monstrous style of bowling adopted by Cotter. Deliberately to pitch halfway down the wicket, with no other object than to frighten the batsmen by making the ball go over their heads, is emphatically not cricket.

Clearly the bodyline controversy of the 1930s was not the first time that fast bowling showed its capacity to anger and frustrate.

Before he went out to face him in the second innings MacLaren paced around the pavilion making it clear to everybody present his intentions towards the 'Sydney Express'. "I'll Cotter him, I'll ... Cotter him" were the words recounted by Cardus later, but it would be no surprise to learn that further expletives were used. MacLaren had played in the Gentleman of England fixture referred to above and watched Cotter, according to Lynch, "with something of the fascinated amazement with which they say a rabbit watches a stoat." He was determined that on this occasion Tibby would be put to the sword. In one of the great test innings, MacLaren scored 140 of the 222 scored when he was at the wicket and forced Tibby out of the attack, tipping the balance firmly in England's favour. It takes a great batsman to do this and MacLaren could be very special indeed, and he had great support from his captain, Jackson, who scored an undefeated 82, and when the captain tossed the ball to Bosanquet in the second innings, England's mystery bowler took 8/107 and the test match was won. Tibby missed the following two tests, both drawn, through injury, and did little in the fourth, a match convincingly won by England. Although Tibby took 7/148 and 2/73 at the Oval the match was drawn and the series was over.

England, however, had not seen the last of Tibby Cotter. When they next toured Australia in 1907/8, with Charlie Blythe and Ken Hutchings on board, Tibby was waiting. Although he was only able to play in the first two tests in his country's 4-1 win, Tibby made his mark taking 6/101 in the first innings at Sydney and 5/142 in the first innings at Melbourne, where the centurion Ken Hutchings was one of his victims. Eighteen months later he was back in England with an Australian side led by Monty Noble. He played in all five tests and took 17 wickets, 15 of which were taken in just three innings, a statistic that implies that he was more of an intermittent threat by this time. His performances were, however, good enough to help Australia to retain the Ashes with a 2-1 series victory. His next series, against South Africa and the only one in which Tibby played that was not against England, took place in 1910/11. In a 4-1 series win Tibby took 22 wickets including 6/69 in the first South African innings of the series at Sydney. When England arrived a year later under the leadership of J.W.H.T. Douglas they surprised their hosts in winning 4-1 after losing the first test at Sydney. Tibby played in the first four tests but had moderate success with 12 wickets. The England openers, Jack Hobbs and the remarkable Wilfred Rhodes, saw him off with an opening stand of 147 at Adelaide and a record breaking 323 at Melbourne, a test match that proved to be Tibby's last.

That this was the end of Tibby's test career was not entirely due to a perceived loss of effectiveness. In 1912, when the next series was due, Tibby would still be six months short of his 29th birthday, hardly a great age even for a fast bowler. Instead his career ended as the result of a battle between some of Australia's senior players, including Tibby, and the Australian Board of Control. The problem was a combination of money and power. It is worth remembering that Australia had only won a form of independence since in 1901 and many of the new institutions now emerging in Australian sport were very much feeling their way. Cricket tours were a minefield when the issue of expenses and payment were discussed and in 1909 the Board set out its terms and conditions. In the past players had been given shares in the profits of a tour once all costs had been taken care of. Senior players, such as Victor Trumper were given special rates befitting their status. Players were also able to select the tour manager, usually a member of the team who could 'double up'. On both tours to England in 1905 and 1909, Frank Laver was chosen. In 1909, although the selection of the tour manager remained with the players, the financial arrangements changed. Expenses were cut and no special terms were allowed. The players reluctantly accepted the new arrangements. This proved to be only the start. On New Year's Eve 1911 the Board met to discuss arrangements for the 1912 Triangular Tournament, (including South Africa), to be held in England. The players wanted Laver to manage the tour once again but on this occasion the Board refused to back down. The six leading players, Tibby, joined by Warwick Armstrong, Sammy Carter, Clem Hill, Vernon Ransford, and Victor Trumper, all stood their ground. None of the rebels were picked for the tour, a tournament unsurprisingly won by England, and only Armstrong, who later captained Australia, and Carter represented their country again.

Tibby could, however look back on a successful career. His test record of taking 89 wickets in 21 tests (4.24 wickets per test) at an average of 28.64 per wicket shows a strike rate not too far behind that of Glenn McGrath (4.54 per test) and Dennis Lillee (5.07 per test), although nobody would pretend that he was in their league as a bowler – he was far too erratic. The top fast bowler who his statistics mirror is the great England 'bodyline' bowler, Harold Larwood who also played in 21 tests taking 78 wickets, 11 fewer than the Australian. Tibby would have to concede that wickets were generally more helpful to bowlers in his day and, unlike Larwood, he did not have to face the genius of Don Bradman. He did, however, have some superb days when he was almost unplayable, such as his four wickets in four balls for Glebe against Sydney in 1911. He was, without doubt, the best Australian fast bowler of his era and, although not an era remembered for great Australian fast bowling, Tibby deserves his place in cricket history. Tibby could also bat when the mood took him and he once scored 68 in 20 minutes for New South Wales against Victoria and 121 in 64 minutes for Glebe in a Grade match. But, with the outbreak of war, his career was over. It was time to do his duty.

In April 1915 Tibby joined the Australian Imperial Force and his participation was immediately seen as a recruitment opportunity. Tibby became part of a powerful publicity campaign aimed at recruiting as many healthy young Aussies as possible. He was soon accepted into the 1st Australian Light Horse Regiment, although his riding experience was somewhat limited, and landed in Gallipoli on the 25th April 1915, part of the initial force. Now part of the 12th Battalion, he took part in the fighting at the second battle of Gaza and was commended for his 'fine work under fire.' The official history recorded that Tibby Cotter "behaved in action as a man without fear."

Following Gallipoli, Tibby was sent to Egypt to prepare for the campaign against the Turks in Palestine. Harold Larwood, much too young to have taken part in the war, recounts an amusing tale told a few years later. In March 1916 a cluster of troops on leave gathered at Gazireh Sports Club, in Cairo to watch a cricket match between the English troops and the AIF forces. The Australian soldiers were a mixture of light-horseman and headquarters staff recovering from the evacuation from Gallipoli. The English troops contained some good players and included the recent England captain J.W.H.T. Douglas. But they were not prepared for the powerfully built light horseman who arrived from duty in Suez, discarded his hat, shirt and leggings and proceeded, after apologising for his lack of practice, to deliver a succession of bouncers, yorkers and typically erratic full tosses, which the stunned English troops, including Douglas, found difficult to counter. This, of course, was Tibby Cotter returning to ruffle English feathers. Bats were knocked out of hands and stumps were broken, and most men were out without scoring, recalled Larwood. Tibby then picked up his bat, pasted the ball all over the field before retiring to catch a train back to Suez, the end of a day where he must have remembered fondly his encounters with England in the heat of a test match rather than a much needed break from the heat of war.

Recreation was deemed to be necessary in wartime and this was probably not the first occasion that Tibby had witnessed, or even participated in, a cricket match during the campaign. The poet, Robert Graves, recounts a game between officers and sergeants at Versailles in 1915 when a bird cage with a dead parrot inside was used as a wicket. There is evidence that the Australians played cricket during the evacuation of Gallipoli in order, it is said, to give the Turks the impression of normality. There is no record of the Turkish reaction.

By 1917 Tibby was working as a stretcher-bearer. This work, as well as being crucial to success in battle, was difficult emotionally.

Sergeant Frank Kennedy of the 3rd Australian Battalion described his experience as a stretcher bearer in Gallipoli.

> The first order I had was to try and get the bodies carried under cover. But carrying the stretchers down those slopes was about the most difficult thing a stretcher-bearer could do. We were constantly stepping down, stepping down – perhaps stumbling over some bushes – while all the time trying to ease the pain of the chap on the stretcher.

The task must have seemed endless as the battle continued to rage all around. Kennedy continues,

> But we carried on right until the evening, doing our best to get all those that were wounded. You might be coming down from the front line and suddenly you'd hear a mournful cry from a bush perhaps twenty yards away, 'stretcher-bearers, stretcher-bearers', and all you could do was to ease your stretcher down on the ground for a moment, go over and see to the case, give him an injection if necessary or some tablets to ease the pain, and tell him you'd come back for him.

This experience was typical for stretcher-bearers throughout the war and Tibby must have been able to recount similar tales of suffering.

Not for much longer though. In October 1917 Tibby was involved in the attack on Beersheba, the last great mounted cavalry charge in history. Sometimes referred to as the Third Battle of Gaza, this action involved the capture of a garrison at Beersheba and resulted in the beginning of the Southern Palestine Offensive of the Sinai and the Palestine campaign. Following a series of attacks against strong defences, the Australian 4th Light Horse Brigade, with bayonets in their hands and rifles slung over their backs charged into the town and captured it just as the garrison was withdrawing. It was an important victory and with 171 killed, far from a disastrous day for the Allied Forces. They had seen much worse. But for the thirty three year old Tibby Cotter it was the end of the road. According to both John Major and Harris and Whippy, Tibby had a premonition that "something is going to happen" and, tragically, he was proved to be right. What actually happened is something of a mystery but what we do know is that he was shot at close range by a Turkish soldier. A recent article by Andrew Sprowl has suggested that he was shot by a soldier who had been captured but not yet checked for weapons. If true this would explain why his death was never fully explained, not even to his family. Sprowl also argues that his death was given so little publicity because of the forthcoming referendum on the introduction of conscription due to be held in Australia very soon. The Government had no wish at this time to highlight the dangers that were ever present and that could affect everybody, even Australia's well built, strong, healthy and finest fast bowler.

Whatever the circumstances, Tibby's death was another tragedy for the Cotter family. Four weeks earlier, on 4th October, Tibby's brother, John, had been killed at Ypres. Serving as a private in the A.I.F. the body of the forty one year old was never recovered and he is remembered with so many others on the Menin Gate Memorial. John is forgotten to history, his sacrifice being one of the many thousands of sacrifices made by Australian soldiers. Tibby, however, warrants his place in cricket history as one of the most significant losses of the Great War, one of the first in a line of Australian fast bowlers who were to bring excitement to cricket lovers for the rest of the century.

As we have already seen, Tibby Cotter played the vast majority of his test cricket against England. Test cricket before 1914 was understood and recognised to consist only of fixtures between the two enemies, England and Australia. It was true that international fixtures with South Africa had taken place in Port Elizabeth as early as March 1889 when C.A. Smith (later Sir Aubrey Smith of Hollywood fame) captained England to victory in his only appearance for his country but at the time neither this fixture or the second match at Cape Town were recognised as true international matches. These fixtures were given retrospective test match status in 1914, helped no doubt by the success of the 1912 Tri-angular tournament. It wasn't until 1914 that 'Plum' Warner's century in 1899 at Johannesburg was recognised and allowed the England captain to join the relatively few players to achieve the feat of scoring a century on his test debut. That South Africa was able to persuade the cricket establishment to include them is due in no small part to a quartet of bowlers who raised the status of South African cricket to new, previously unattained heights, in the years immediately prior to the outbreak of war. We have already seen how Bernard Bosanquet has been credited with the invention of the 'googly', a form of spin bowling that enabled him to win at least two test matches against Australia almost on his own. Bosanquet is rightly credited with inventing the googly and even today in Australia it is often referred to as the 'Bosie'. However it was a small group of South African bowlers who ensured that this form of bowling would cement its place as an invaluable weapon for the slow bowler. Tragically two of their numbers were to die as a result the South African involvement in the Great War.

Reginald Oscar Schwarz was born on 4th May 1875 in Lee, south London, the son of Robert Schwarz, a merchant from Surrey. He was given a very 'English' public school education at St Paul's School, London followed by a university experience at Cambridge. On leaving Cambridge Reggie joined the London stock exchange and stayed there for three years. In 1902 he emigrated to South Africa and worked for the South African Railways until 1904 when he joined the South African stock exchange. Through all of these career moves, Reggie was developing an outstanding sporting reputation. By the time that his cricket career took off with his test debut in January 1906, Reggie was already an international sportsman – an England rugby international. In 1893 he had won his rugby Blue when selected in the Cambridge team to play Oxford and the Richmond player, who had already represented the Barbarians, finally made his debut playing at half back against Scotland in 1899. It looked as if this might be Reggie's only cap but two years later he was back in the England side to play both Wales and Ireland. His international rugby career, however, was not littered with success. England lost all three games in which Reggie played and collected the wooden spoon in each of the two seasons in which he was involved.

Reggie's cricket career was more successful. Despite his failure to win a cricket 'Blue', Reggie had played briefly for Middlesex in 1901 and 1902 and, when he made the decision to emigrate to South Africa, he joined Transvaal. By the time England, led by Warner, toured South Africa in 1905/6, Reggie had mastered the art of bowling the googly and was, uniquely, using it as his stock delivery.

Reggie had first displayed his newly found prowess with the ball on the South African tour of England in the summer of 1904. This was a tour of 22 matches of which 10 were won and 2 lost but, although there was a match against an England XI it was never given test match status. Reggie topped the first class averages on the tour with 65 wickets at an average of 18.26, so it was no surprise when he was selected for his first test at Johannesburg in January 1906. Making his debut alongside Aubrey Faulkner, Bert Vogler and Gordon White, the match saw the coming together of the four googly bowlers who were to raise the status of South African cricket The opposition included, of course, Charlie Blythe but on this occasion it was the South Africans who held the upper hand. As we already know, Blythe won the fourth test for England with his 11 wickets but the rest of the series belonged to South Africa who won the other four tests, the first being South Africa's first test victory. Rugby international defeats now pushed well to the back of his mind, Reggie made a solid contribution during the series with 18 wickets in the five tests. Opposing him in four of those tests was his ex-Middlesex colleague Leonard Moon. A product of Westminster School and Pembroke College, Cambridge, Moon had a moderate cricket career, although he did score seven centuries for his university between1897 and 1900. A schoolmaster, he joined the Devon Regiment during the war and was killed in Salonika in November 1916.

Although South Africa had produced four notable googly bowlers, and although it is true to say that he was less successful in tests than Faulkner and Vogler, there is no doubt that Reggie was the pioneer. A quiet and rather retiring, modest man, he had been the student of Bosanquet and had greatly influenced his teammates. Once the top order batsmen had gone, the remainder found Reggie very difficult to deal with. Porter, in his biography of Jack Hobbs, tells us that

> He was an able student and acquired many of Bosanquet skills. Slow in flight, Schwarz was deceptively quick off the wicket. He also achieved great break, mainly from the off. As he tended to break just one way, he should have been easy to play, but his pace negated any advantage the batsman might hope to seize by uninhibited attack.

Returning to England with the South African team in the summer of 1907, this time for a three test series, England were bent on gaining revenge. This they did, by winning at Leeds, with Charlie Blythe's 26 wickets in the series being the major factor in the victory. The four South African googly bowlers did make their mark by taking 41 of the 50 England wickets to fall in the series. Once again while on a tour of England, Reggie topped the English bowling averages for the season with an impressive 137 dismissals at the cost of 11.79. He had made a great impression on the English batsmen, so much so that R.E. Foster offered advice in the 1908 *Wisden* as to how to play him. Foster ventured that it was best to go for ones and twos' as Reggie was very difficult to hit despite his slow and predictable delivery, due to his quick pace off the pitch. With six men placed on the leg side and a sometimes awkwardly lifting ball, it was difficult to find gaps in the field placing. Foster, quoted in Porter, is quite definite when advising fellow cricketers,

> Play him with your legs – old pavilion critics forgive me, but we have to deal with bowling you never had to trouble about – don't hit him until the bad ball comes.

You can sense the frustration felt by one of England's leading amateur batsmen, the player who at the time held the highest score in a test match innings (287 at Sydney in December 1903, a record he held for the next twenty six years).

Some batsmen must have taken notice as Reggie's next series, the 1909/10 clash with England, proved to be his least successful. South Africa won 3-2, but Reggie only bowled a total of eight overs in the four tests in which he played and failed to take a wicket. When batting, not usually his strongest suit, he did make some runs in the final two tests when they were badly needed but with a top score of 44 his performances were not memorable. Reggie's next series in Australia a year later was much more successful. Despite a 4-1 defeat, Reggie took 25 wickets at 26.04 in the series including 5/102 in Australia's only innings in the first test at Sydney and 6/47 in the first innings when the teams returned to Sydney for the final test. Playing for Australia of course was Tibby Cotter, the only series where they faced each other in the test match arena. As we know, Tibby was not allowed to represent Australia in the Triangular

Tournament of 1912 but Reggie was there. His career, however, was running down. South Africa lost five and drew one of their six matches and Reggie played in only three, achieving little of note in any of them. His test career was over but he could look back with satisfaction at figures which recorded 55 test wickets at an average of 25.76. In first class cricket overall the figures are even better, 398 wickets at 17.58. Add to this his influence in South African cricket overall and we can see that Reggie Schwarz was a cricketer of some significance.

To a lesser extent, so was Gordon White. Gordon was another of the quartet of South African googly bowlers, although it should be said that he was the least successful of the four with the ball. He was, however, a good batsman and therefore, like Aubrey Faulkner, qualifies more as an all rounder. (It should be noted that all four players were capable batsmen but Gordon and Aubrey were definitely the best). He was born in Port St John's, Cape Province on 5th February 1882 and first came to the attention of the cricket world on the 1904 tour to England. As we know, no tests were played on this tour but Gordon scored 937 runs at a respectable average of 29.73 and took 56 wickets at 14.73. the highlight of which was probably the hat trick that he took against Kent. By the time that he made his debut for South Africa alongside the others who made up this unique quartet, great things were expected of Gordon. He did not disappoint. In that 1905/6 series against England he topped the South African batting averages with 437 runs at 54.62, helped by a score of 147 in the third test victory at Johannesburg. On the tour of England in 1907, he did little of note in the tests but did score 162 not out at Bristol against Gloucestershire. This was a tour where away from the tests Gordon had more success with the ball and he took 72 wickets on the tour at an average of just under 13 runs per wicket. R.E. Foster gave *Wisden* his opinion of Gordon the bowler, informing contemporaries that he was liable to be given a high number of lbw decisions. Although not deceptive in flight Gordon, says Foster, was able to gain these decisions with the ball that broke very little and carried straight on. This was his top spinner and Foster was right, it did gain him numerous lbw decisions.

Once again in the 1909/10 series against England, it was Gordon's batting which caught the eye, particularly when he scored 118 in the victory at Durban, and he finished with an average of

35.5 in the series. By now Gordon was considered to be the best right handed batsman in South Africa, with the ability to play crisp, late cuts and a mixture of clean drives both sides of the wicket as well as possessing a sound defence. Those who saw him described him as a free and attractive batsman and, although he did not find the soft English wickets to his liking, he did leave a favourable impression. Gordon missed the series against Australia in 1910/11 but was back for the Triangular Tournament. Along with Reggie Schwartz and the rest of the team, Gordon had a tournament to forget. Although he played in five of the six tests Gordon achieved nothing better than 59 not out against Australia at Trent Bridge. Like Reggie, Gordon's test career was now over. His test match figures of 872 runs at an average of 30.06 and 9 wickets at 33.44 along with career statistics of 3740 runs at 27.70 and 155 wickets at 20.05, may seem modest today but Gordon had played his part in the rise of South African cricket.

When war broke out both Reggie and Gordon prepared to come to Britain's aid. Gordon joined the 1st Battalion, Cape Corps, South African Forces in the early months of the war and during the war reached the rank of Lieutenant. Reggie, by now settled back in England and working once again on the London Stock Exchange, became a Major in the 6th Battalion of the King's Royal Rifle Corps, this after surviving a very eventful start to his war service. Reggie first saw action in German South-West Africa in 1914 where he was Mentioned in Despatches. By the end of 1916 he had won the Military Cross for 'exemplary gallantry during active operations against the enemy'. This honour had first been introduced earlier in the year so Reggie was an early recipient and it ranks below only the Victoria Cross and the Conspicuous Gallantry Cross. Reggie carried on throughout the war in the same vein and was also Mentioned in Despatches for a second time as well as being wounded on two occasions. He later became Deputy Assistant Quartermaster and was Assistant Controller of salvage. Despite this remarkable record of front line action, Reggie survived the war and must have greeted the signing of the armistice with some relief. Gordon, unfortunately, did not live to see the end of hostilities. On the 17th October 1918, the 36 year old South African all rounder died of wounds in Gaza and is buried in Gaza War Cemetery.

Reggie's joy at the signing of the armistice was, however, short lived. On the very same day that the terms of the cease fire were being signed in the railway carriage in the forest of Compiegne, he was admitted to hospital suffering from bronco-pneumonia. The tragic reality was that Reggie had contacted the deadly 'Spanish flu' which had first emerged in Spain in the Spring of 1918.The first wave of this terrifying disease peaked in the early summer of 1918 when many people believed that the horrendous conditions of war – the food shortages, rationing, conditions in the trenches - were helping the rapid spread of the disease. Some felt that a plague had descended upon them and that its occurrence was some kind of divine punishment issued from on high. These rather far fetched opinions gathered strength when a more deadly wave peaked in the autumn, just in time for the armistice, and which did not begin to subside until the spring of 1919. The truth was that this deadly flu had a viral cause and it left the populations of some countries devastated. In France 166,000 died but elsewhere the figures were even worse – Germany 225,330; Britain 228,900; United States 550,000; It was estimated that in India 16,000,000 died giving total losses of around 20,000,000, more than those lost in the war itself. The heaviest impact was on children and young adults. It was calculated that 25% of victims were 15 years old or less, while a further 45% were between 16 years and 35 years . The viral cause was not confirmed until 1933 by which time the mutant virus had largely disappeared.

Not soon enough for Reggie alas. Seven days after the signing of the Armistice he died. His obituary in *The Times* talked of his "absolute modesty and self-effacement…. without a trace of side." It referred to his sporting success and his "attractive voice and way of speaking" which commanded the affection of all who knew him. *The Times* recognised his enthusiasm to be involved from the beginning of the war and his many gifts which "were bound to ensure his success as an officer …in the service of his country." He was clearly a man who earned the respect and affection of those that knew him both on the sports field and when leading his troops. One of the best all round sportsmen to die in the Great War, Reggie's passing, along with that of Tibby Cotter, is a reminder of the great sacrifice made by the British colonies in that 'war to end all wars'. His death also reminds us that it is not only brutal battles in the theatre of war that can lead to tragic loss. Reggie was buried in Etaples-sur-Mer on the North West coast of France. He was 43 years old.

Booth, Jeeves and Burns – All-Round Cricketers on the Somme

English cricket in the early years of the century benefitted greatly from exceptionally talented all-round cricketers. While it would be true to say that many cricket historians immediately think of the great batsmen – MacLaren, Fry, Ranji and Foster – when discussing Edwardian players, (or 'gentlemen' in the case of most batsmen), it is the all-rounders who have made the greatest mark in the record books. The career figures of Wilfred Rhodes and George Hirst are beyond our wildest imagination today. Rhodes with 4,187 wickets and 39,802 runs in 1,107 matches leads the way when compared to all cricketers but Hirst with 2,727 wickets and 36,203 runs in 826 matches was not far behind. Their status in Yorkshire is legendary even today and when the batting and bowling talents of Stanley Jackson, England captain and hero of the 1905 Ashes series, are added it is clear to see that the county and England benefitted hugely from Yorkshire all-rounders. Although the remarkable Rhodes continued his test career until April 1930, (it lasted 31 years and 315 days), in the years immediately before 1914 the England selectors were looking for the successors to the great Yorkshire men of the Golden Age. It was to Yorkshire they turned.

Major William Booth was born the son of a successful grocer in the Yorkshire town of Pudsey on 10th December 1886. 'Major' was his Christian name and not a rank in the British army. Coming from his comfortable yet ordinary working background, he would not have entertained the idea of being a high ranking officer in the army, although, ironically, he became a Second Lieutenant. Famous in the seventeenth and eighteenth centuries for the manufacture of wool, in the nineteenth century it was cricket in Pudsey that captured the public imagination. Yorkshire's first great opening batsman, John Tunnicliffe, was born nearby and in the future Pudsey Borough was to be the birthplace of two of England's greatest captains, Len Hutton and Raymond Illingworth, as well as the recent England fast bowler Matthew Hoggard. These players, as well as that other great Yorkshire and England opener Herbert Sutcliffe, played their early cricket for the Pudsey club. Major attended Fulneck School, a school managed by the Moravian religious sect, before joining the Pudsey St Lawrence club where, as Sutcliffe was to do ten years later, he played his early cricket. Indeed in 1908 he played with the exceptional thirteen-year-old Sutcliffe as well as Henry Hutton, father of the great Sir Leonard. By now Major was playing in the Mexborough League as captain of Wath Athletic Club, an experience which would have helped this talented bowler who was also looking to develop his batting. It should be remembered that League cricket was, and still is, important in the north of England. Gary Sobers and Basil D'Oliveira, two all round cricketers of particular fame, both had their first experience of English cricket in the northern leagues.

1908 was a year of great significance for the twenty-one year old Yorkshire prospect. By now Major was playing regularly for Yorkshire 2nd XI and that year he made his County debut at Dewsbury. With Yorkshire claiming the championship that summer, it was very difficult for Major to claim a regular starting place and his debut performance of one run and no wicket in six overs did nothing to persuade the selectors of his worth. Nevertheless he was on his way. Playing with him in his early appearances was Jimmy Rothery, a talented batsman who played 150 matches for Yorkshire between 1903 and 1910 winning two championships in the process. An attractive, rather artistic looking, right hand batsman, Jimmy Rothery suffered from a poor temperament and frequently failed to conquer his nerves while batting. It made him inconsistent and despite his achievements (which included making 161 against Charlie Blythe at Dover in 1908, a significant innings against one of Yorkshire's main rivals for the title) he retired in 1910 with a batting average of 21. During the war Jimmy served with the Royal Fusiliers Sportsman's Battalion and then the East Kent Regiment ('The Buffs'). He was to serve only three months at the front before being seriously wounded and transferred home. Tragically, after being moved to several hospitals and care homes, he died in Beckett's Park Hospital, Leeds after failing to recover from an operation. This was just weeks before the signing of the Treaty of Versailles in June 1919 so Jimmy became one of the thousands who died after the guns had fallen silent.

As Jimmy Rothery's career came to a rather disappointing conclusion, Major Booth was going from strength to strength. He had qualified as an electrician and obtained regular work at a large colliery at Wath-on-Dearne and was now financially secure, and could look to improve his cricket each summer. In 1910 he played in sixteen of Yorkshire's twenty-eight championship games and took 49 wickets at an average cost of 21 runs. His batting, still inferior to his bowling, nevertheless, achieved an average of 17. Yorkshire officials and supporters began to talk of him as a dashing middle order batsman and a medium paced bowler with the ability to swerve the ball late and possessing a vicious off break which came off the pitch at pace, not unlike the great Hirst himself. By the end of the year, when he reached his twenty-fourth birthday, Major could look forward to becoming a regular member of the county team. This optimism could only have been confirmed when Major read a report recorded in the Yorkshire County Cricket Club Selection Committee minute book in 1910. G.J.V. Weigall, who completed the report, enthused about young Major even if less impressed with the other young Yorkshire bowlers. According to Mick Pope in his *Headingly Ghosts*, Weigall wrote,

> I must give M.W. Booth the place of honour as a grand all round cricketer. I go as far as to say there is no better bowler in Yorkshire on a fast wicket, except Hirst. He is very fast off the pitch and the ball always comes at a nasty height to play. His batting too is really good and he has a thorough knowledge of the game. He is also an excellent field."

The popular, tall and handsome Pudsey cricketer was now seen as a player who could spearhead Yorkshire cricket into a new era.

The following summer, 1911, Major did indeed establish himself in the First XI, playing in every championship match, and ended the season with 82 wickets at 26.37 and a much improved 1,239 runs at an average of 25.81. Highlights included a hat trick against Worcestershire at Bradford and a score of 210 in just four hours also against Worcestershire but this time on the picturesque ground at New Road. But when he came up against Plum Warner it was still Major's medium fast bowling with his high action, late swing and nip off the pitch which caught the eye. In the 1911 *Wisden*

Warner wrote an article entitled 'Our Young Cricketers' and in it he said of Major:

> The only time I played against him, I thought Booth of Yorkshire a good bowler. He has a very high action, and makes the ball swerve away at the last moment. There is too, something puzzling about his flight, and if the wicket is doing anything he can make the ball pop up nastily. In some ways he reminds me a little of Barnes. Booth is not very strong physically and requires careful nursing, but I think in his first six or seven overs he is likely to get anyone out…

To be compared to George Hirst was compliment enough but to be spoken of by an England captain in the same breath as Sydney Barnes was quite another. Barnes had an intermittent England career due largely to his preference for playing league, as opposed to county, cricket, but in 1911 he was at the height of a career that saw him take 189 wickets in 27 tests at an average of 16.43. He too was a fast medium bowler who could swing the ball very late. In fact it is unlikely that anybody has ever done it better. That Major never did, or would have, attained the heights of Barnes as a bowler is beyond dispute but he was a better bat. This ability to contribute in both batting and bowling resulted in Major being invited to play in Jessop's XI to play Warner's XI in what amounted to a test trial. In a steady performance Major dismissed both Jack Hobbs and Phillip Mead, two notable scalps, but in 1911 he was still not quite ready for test match cricket.

The following year, 1912, Yorkshire regained the championship title and Major made a significant contribution. His batting form dipped a little with 709 runs at 18.65, but for the first time he took 100 wickets in a season: 104 at 19.17. A career best 8/45 against Middlesex at Leeds, 8/52 against Leicestershire at Sheffield and a hat trick against Essex at Leyton were the highlights. By the following year Warner's concerns about Major's physical strength were emphatically laid to rest. He ended the season as the highest wicket taker, with 181 wickets at 18.46 which, put alongside his 1,228 runs at an average of 27.28, made him one of the hardest working cricketers in the country. Major also picked his matches well when making eye-catching contributions. The Roses match, always a Bank

Holiday attraction, saw him achieve match figures of 11/156 at Leeds while he continued to excel in front of Warner and his Middlesex colleagues. At Lord's he scored 107 not out in under two hours and took 9/136 in the match. In the return game at Sheffield he once again drew attention to the recent England captain by taking 6/20. The year was capped when he was selected for the Players to play the Gentlemen in what was then one of the highlights of the cricket calendar, *Wisden* made him one of their five cricketers of the year and he was picked to tour South Africa under the captaincy of J.W.H.T. Douglas. The year could not have been much better and Pudsey showed its pride in their new international cricketer. A dinner was held in his honour attended by the great and the good of Yorkshire cricket – David Denton, Wilfred Rhodes, Roy Kilner and George Hirst among them. A silver cup was presented which contained an inscription which read,

> Presented to Major W. Booth by the members of the Pudsey St Lawrence Cricket Club and friends in appreciation of the eminent position attained by him in the world of cricket.

In presenting the cup, the ever supportive Hirst said to his audience, "If your Major is successful in South Africa you should be pleased; if not, then make excuses for him."

Unfortunately excuses were necessary and Major had them. A couple of days before the first test in Durban he was thrown out of a car as it hit a bank. Although shaken up, Major was not badly injured and, despite a back injury, made his test debut. Although he opened the bowling and took 2/38, Major made little impact on a match dominated by Barnes. He was left out of the next three tests but did returned for the final test at Port Elizabeth where, batting at number ten he made 32 and took 4/49 in the South African second innings, in a match which England won by ten wickets. Making their debuts in the fifth test were two talented South Africans, the opening bowler Bill Lundie and the batsman Reginald Hands. Reg Hands was a particularly interesting player. Not only was he making his debut alongside his brother, Philip, the first time brothers had played together in a test match, but, like Reggie Schwarz, Reg had played international rugby for England. An Oxford Blue and barrister who had played in the Varsity match of 1910 when Ronnie Poulton scored five tries, he had played in the England pack against both France and Scotland in 1910, enjoying victories in both, the first under the captaincy of Edgar Mobbs. Playing alongside the debutants was Claude Newberry, a quick, right arm, leg break bowler who bowled with some success in the last four matches of the series. This was the last time that these three South Africans would represent their country: by the Armistice all three were dead. Twenty-seven year old Private Claude Newberry was killed along with 576 of his countrymen at Delville Wood on the Somme in 1916; Second Lieutenant Bill Lundie at Passchendaele in September 1917; Captain Reginald Hands who, on 20th April 1918 at Boulogne, finally succumbed to the effects of gas poisoning.

All this was in the unknowable future. Major returned to the home near the Britannia Inn that he shared with his brother James and devoted sister, Anne Louise, with seven test wickets at the cost of 18.57 and a batting average of 23.00 – a modest performance but with the expectation that more opportunities for international cricket would follow. There were no test matches played during the summer of 1914 but Major enjoyed the season nonetheless. He finished with 158 wickets at a cost of 17.85 and 731 runs with an average of 19.17, another very successful season especially with the ball. By now Major had struck up a very effective bowling partnership with Alonzo Drake, a footballer who had played professionally for a number of clubs including Doncaster Rovers, Sheffield United, Birmingham City and Huddersfield Town. Drake joined Major as a regular in the Yorkshire side in 1911 and in the years immediately before the war they achieved some remarkable success together. On a number of occasions they bowled unchanged throughout an entire innings, most famously in August 1914, when, with war already declared, they did this in consecutive matches against Gloucestershire and Somerset. In Somerset's second innings Drake took all 10 wickets while Major, surprisingly, failed to take one. When war broke out Drake, a heavy smoker, was deemed unfit to serve and subsequently lapsed into ill health. He later suffered from cancer of the throat and died in February 1919.

Major had no problems in joining up and in September 1914 he enlisted in the 15th (Service) Battalion (1st Leeds) The Prince of Wales's Own West Yorkshire Regiment – 'The Leeds Pals'. With Stanley Jackson serving on the recruiting committee there was little doubt that Major, along with teammates Roy Kilner and Arthur Dolphin, would be accepted. The footballer, Evelyn Lintott was also present. Major had no doubt that he was doing the right thing. "It is our duty Mr Pullin. We cannot do anything else" he told the Yorkshire cricket journalist, A.W. Pullin. Enlisting as a private, Major completed his initial training at Colsterdale in the Yorkshire Dales and then Ripon. By the following year he had been promoted to Second Lieutenant and was heading to Egypt to meet the threat posed to the Suez Canal. By June 1916 it had receded so Major was posted to France and the Western Front in time for the big push on the Somme where 'the Leeds Pals' would be involved in the thick of the action.

The plan was that the 'Leeds Pals', supported by the 'Bradford Pals' and the 18th Durham Light Infantry, would create a defensive line north of the village of Serre before advancing. On 30th June, before the manoeuvre began, Major's biggest 'pal', Roy Kilner, was injured by German shelling and taken back to England. He was lucky. As dawn broke on the bright, clear morning of the 1st July, men prepared for the onslaught. Private Arthur Pearson, a member of Major's regiment, described the experience, quoted by historian Peter Hart:

> Every man climbed out of the trenches at the whistle of the officers and not a man hesitated.... When I ran up the rise out of the trench I was under the hail of bullets which were whizzing over my head. Most of our fellows were killed kneeling on the parapet.

As the officer in charge of the No 10 Machine Gun team, Major was one of the first men out of the trenches at 7.30 that morning. Pope tells the story:

> Men were cut down quickly all around him from the machine-guns 15 yards or so away. Booth stopped to move forward Private Morrison Fleming, who had knelt down to help an injured comrade. Ahead were two shell holes, and Booth told the private to make for one. Morrison Fleming dropped into the relative safety of a shell hole, but Booth did not make it. After only a few yards a shell burst caught him, and amidst the mass of bodies a shell fragment

> penetrated the shoulder, and must have touched the heart. Still Lieutenant Booth tried his utmost to go forward, but he was fatally wounded.

Another colleague, Private Abe Waddington, injured in both legs and hand, crawled into the same shell hole. Surrounded by the dead and dying he recognised Major from when they were opponents in the Bradford League. Major passed away in Waddington's arms. They had to leave the body which was not recovered for another nine months when it was only identified by an MCC cigarette case in his pocket.

All the battalion officers who went into that futile attack were either killed or injured, 24 in all, and they included Evelyn Lintott. The oral historian, Lyn MacDonald, using her interviews with survivors, described the scene witnessed by the West Yorkshire Relief as they ventured into Thiepval Wood that evening:

> As they neared the wood, between the roar of explosions behind the sickening gas soaked mist, in the forefront of the noise that raged at them from every horizon, the small party of West Yorkshires became aware of another sound. It was like nothing they had ever heard before… a sound that chilled the blood; a nerve-scraping noise like enormous wet fingers screeching across an enormous pane of glass. It was coming from the wounded, lying out in No Man's Land. Some screaming, some weeping with fear, some calling for help, shouting in delirium, groaning with pain, the sounds of their distress had synthesized into one unearthly wail.

Perhaps it was a relief that Major died relatively quickly. He was buried in Serre Road Cemetery No 1, one of 2,412 graves of which 1,728 (71.6%) contained unidentified soldiers, one of the highest percentages in all cemeteries on the Somme.

At home Major's death was a tragic loss to all who knew him. Nowhere was this seen more clearly than by the reaction of cricketers. Major's great mentor, George Hirst, said that he was "one of the grandest lads who ever lived, and could not express how deeply his cricket comrades felt his loss", while Lord Hawke, the former Yorkshire captain and the voice of Yorkshire cricket, described Major as "one of the most promising and charming young cricketers it was ever my lot to meet". His most recent captain, Sir Archibald White, described him as "a splendid fellow", and while it is easy to pay extravagant compliments to those who gave their lives in the service of their country, there is no doubt that Major was highly regarded both as a cricketer and as a man. His career figures, 4,753 runs at 23.29 and 603 wickets at 19.82, are impressive but only tell part of the story. There is no doubt that, had they lived, he and Drake would have spearheaded Yorkshire's bowling attack into the 1920s.

But it was as a man and valued colleague that he was most missed. Roy Kilner, whose best man Major had been, named his youngest son after his friend, and even today there is a small side street in Pudsey called Booth's Yard. In September 1920, at the Church of St Lawrence, Pudsey, a memorial tablet was unveiled on the wall, a permanent reminder of Pudsey's first international cricketer. Yet the greatest loss was felt by his family. The War Office telegram telling the news of his brother's death was received by James Booth. In it Second Major John C. Hartley wrote,

> I am deeply sorry to inform you of the death of your brother, while gallantly assisting in a battalion attack. He was killed instantaneously.... Your brother was loved by officers and men, and had earned his commission through real merit. His place will be indeed hard to fill.

The family found it difficult to accept their loss. Some time later Private Abe Waddington, soon to be an England test cricketer himself, visited the family home and told James and his sister Anne that he had held Major as he died. Anne never accepted the loss of her beloved brother. Major's bedroom remained exactly as he had left it, a light burning in the window each evening in the hope that he would return. This she did for the remainder of her life. Anne died in 1956.

Major Booth was certainly not the only cricketer to lose his life on the Western Front with his best years as a player ahead of him. He was not even the only potentially great all round cricketer to die on the Somme battlefield. A second all-rounder of note was not yet a test cricketer but, after W.G. Grace, possessed possibly the best known name of any cricketer: Percy Jeeves. It is generally accepted that the Warwickshire all-rounder was the inspiration, at least in name, of the P.G. Wodehouse 'gentleman's gentleman' in his very popular short stories. Even today Percy Jeeves is known to many people through the search engine Ask.com. This service was originally called 'Ask Jeeves', deriving from the ability of 'the gentleman's personal gentleman' or valet being able to answer any question posed to him. It has been said recently that Woodhouse saw Percy Jeeves playing for Warwickshire against Gloucestershire at Cheltenham in 1913 and he made such an impression, more with his personality, immaculate appearance and quiet confidence than his playing ability on this occasion, that the author recalled him a few years later when he was looking to name Bertie Wooster's valet. Others have claimed that Woodhouse saw Percy play at Hawes in the early years of his career, but this is unlikely. Research has led me to another Private Percy Jeeves killed in the Great War, a young nineteen year old soldier from Cambridge who served with the 2nd Battalion, London Regiment of the Royal Fusiliers and who was killed on 19th September 1918 near Rouen, but it is inconceivable that Woodhouse knew him. Whatever the truth, Jeeves was introduced in the first of the Jeeves and Wooster short stories written in New York in 1916. He featured in thirty-five short stories and eleven novels and became one of the most famous names in twentieth century literature. However, with the publication in 2013 of Brian Halford's biography, it is the real Percy Jeeves, the cricketer, who is now making a belated return to the limelight.

Percy was born on 5th March 1888 in Earlsheaton, Dewsbury in Yorkshire, the third of four sons. Earlsheaton was a busy town with a population of about 5,000, many of whom worked in its three woollen mills, producing blankets and rugs. Despite being born in the heart of Yorkshire, Percy was the only one of the boys to show a lasting interest in cricket and great natural ability. While at school in Earlsheaton, Percy proved to be a hard hitting batsman and a fast/medium bowler with the ability to make the ball swerve. On moving to Goole on Humberside at thirteen, Percy's bowling in particular made an immediate impression. Within a year he was a regular in Goole's 2nd XI and took 6/25 on his debut, surprising his adult opponents with his smooth approach to the wicket, his fluid bowling action and his ability to move the ball both ways, an unusual skill in a young bowler. A few years later Hawes Cricket Club made Percy its professional. In between his responsibilities for the upkeep of the ground and wicket, Percy took 65 wickets at a cost of 7.5 runs per wicket, hugely successful figures for a teenager. It was inevitable that Yorkshire would show an interest and he was soon invited for a trial. It had recently become the dominant force in English cricket, winning their first championship in 1893 and a further seven by 1908. With such a strong team, Yorkshire saw no need to pursue Percy's services and nothing came of his trial. However the captain at Hawes, Mr Arden-Crallon, did not give up. According to Brian Halford, he met the secretary of Warwickshire, a Mr Ryder, while on holiday in Wensleydale and, largely as a result of their numerous conversations, Percy joined this up and coming county in 1910.

Up and coming Warwickshire certainly were. Finishing a modest 14th in 1910, they pipped the reigning champions Kent to the title the following year. Percy did not contribute to this unexpected triumph as he had to qualify for the county before he could play in the championship. He was dispatched to the Birmingham League where he would be 'toughened up' for the challenges ahead. An all round sportsman, Percy also found the time to play football for Stirchley Co-operations in the Birmingham Wednesday League and attracted the attention of the mighty Aston Villa. He wasn't tempted as cricket remained his passion and Percy was unlikely to do anything which might jeopardise his chances of a successful career in his favourite sport. His qualification period was not due to end until 1913 but in 1912 he was allowed to play against both touring parties, Australia and South Africa. Even more encouragingly, there was a vacancy for an all-rounder in the Warwickshire team and Percy was quick to seize his opportunity. In his first full season, 1913, he took 15 wickets in his two matches against Hampshire and helped dismiss a strong Kent side for 132 by taking 4/32. He hit his first 50 against Leicestershire in July and followed this up with 86 not out against Yorkshire. What pleasure it would have given Percy to have made those extra 14 runs against the home county that had rejected him. By the end of the summer he had taken 106 wickets at 20.88 and scored 765 runs at an average of 20.13.

He had made the transition to three day cricket without problem but, like Major Booth, Percy had impressed the critics more with the ball than with the bat. This continued the following year when

Percy was only able to collect 403 runs, but took another 90 wickets which got him noticed. With no test matches scheduled for the summer of 1914, the highest profile matches were the annual Gentlemen v Players matches. In 1914 three fixtures were arranged, at The Oval, Lord's and Scarborough, although the final match, due to be played between 7th and 9th September, was cancelled due to the outbreak of war. Percy played in the first fixture at the Oval between 9th and 11th July and took 4/44 in the Gentlemen's second innings to help the Players to a victory by 241 runs, one of their best victories in a series of 274 matches. In taking the wickets of Reggie Spooner and C.B. Fry, Percy showed that he could compete at the top level. He did not play in the return match at Lord's when the Gentlemen gained revenge with a convincing victory of their own, but he had made his mark. Plum Warner, an opponent in that game, predicted a test career for the popular Warwickshire all-rounder but, unforeseeably, and after only 50 matches, Percy was about to complete his second and final season in first class cricket. With career figures of 1,204 runs at 16.05 and 199 wickets at 20.03, we can only speculate at what might have been.

Like the player who could have been his rival for a place in the England test team in the coming years, Major Booth, Percy was quick to respond to the outbreak of war. He joined the 2nd Birmingham Battalion, the 15th Royal Warwickshire Regiment – 'The Birmingham Pals' – almost immediately and undertook a six month period of training at Wensleydale. In late 1915, Percy embarked for France. By July 1916 he was in the thick of the Battle of the Somme. The Royal Warwickshire Regiment had been given the task of attacking the village of Poetise on the Albert-Bapaume road, a strongly defended village which the Germans saw as crucial to their stranglehold on the fortress of the Thiepval Spur, control of which barred the way to any advance in the northern section of the Somme battlefield. Both the Devons and the Gordon Highlanders had suffered heavy losses in this area on the nights of July 19th/20th, but it was seen as so crucial to British success that a further heavy artillery barrage was begun on the night of 22nd July with the intention destroying German defences, leaving British soldiers to advance unopposed the following morning. The barrage failed. German machine guns remained, perfectly positioned and undamaged, ready to inflict maximum casualties as the British, and an even larger number of Australians, approached. The first assaults took place earlier than planned, at 22.00 hours on the night of July 22nd, and consisted of attacks on Wood Trench situated between Delville Wood and High Wood. Percy and his colleagues were moved up to join what was already a disastrous offensive, at 23.50 hours. What had begun as a warm, sunny, July summer's day with temperatures reaching 77 degrees, ended in confusion and horror. Peter Hart quotes Private Francis Fields, also in the 15th Battalion, Warwickshire Regiment, describing what he saw:

> It was a night of such kaleidoscopic effects that I can still see them vividly. It must have been terrifying in its utter inhumanity to the men of the new drafts from England. Every variety of sound, colour and odour assailed and overwhelmed our senses, so that we felt immune to the perpetual threat of death or mutilation – until it came.... The wood was alive with points of light from machine guns, vivid with shell flashes and coloured by the urgent signal flares of Bengal lights; patches of black smoke and flickering red came from the burning debris. From Longueval, almost behind me came the reflected flashes of an exploding dump.

Perhaps this was Percy's last sight. He was killed on the night of 22nd/23rd July 1916 and no trace of him was ever found, his bones still resting beneath the French countryside.

During the years 1908 to 1911, when both Major Booth and Percy Jeeves were striving to establish themselves in the upper echelons of English cricket, another all-rounder was experiencing the best seasons of a ten year career which took him almost, but not quite, to the top of the English game. William Beaumont Burns played 217 games of first class cricket, making 9,479 runs at an average of 27 and which included 12 centuries. Less successful with the ball, he still took 214 wickets at an average cost of 29.59 and had a reputation of being very quick, if a little suspect in his action. William was born on 29th August 1883 in Rugeley, Staffordshire, one of three brothers, all of whom played cricket. After attending Kings School, Ely where he played in the 1st XI, William played for Staffordshire in the Minor Counties Championship, his first appearance coming when he was only sixteen. Before long he was scoring centuries and heading the Staffordshire batting averages. A career in county cricket clearly beckoned.

In May 1903 William made his debut for Worcestershire against Oxford University at The Parks and other non county championship appearances followed. William qualified to play in the 1904 championship and wasted no time making his mark. In 19 matches he scored 834 runs, the highlight a memorable 165 scored in 180 minutes against Oxford University. He finished the season with a batting average of 26.The following season was less successful but in 1906 William reached 1,000 runs in a season for the first time, including another 165 against Oxford University, by now his favourite opponents, and further centuries against Warwickshire and Hampshire. The result was an invitation to tour New Zealand with the MCC at the end of the year under the captaincy of E.G. Wynyard. This was far from a full strength MCC team containing only amateur players and which was well short of test status, but his invitation to tour confirmed that William was attracting attention.

Although contributing little of significance, William gave good service on the tour during which, rather surprisingly given the strength of New Zealand cricket, only two matches were lost, including one of the two 'unofficial tests'. (The other 'test' was won.) The tour was really an attempt to further cultural links between the two countries as well as to help the development of New Zealand cricket, "an Imperial adventure" as it was described by Owen Mann in an essay reflecting on the impact of the tour. It was also seen by the young team as an opportunity to have some fun. The loss of the forty-five year old Wynyard to a tendon injury during the tour possibly gave the younger players more freedom. Certainly the feeling was that it was unreasonable to expect amateur players to be away for six months and not enjoy themselves. One account of the tour, written by fast bowler Percy May, suggested that the tour was an opportunity to meet "the right type of woman". Some players took this to great lengths and three of them became engaged to New Zealand women before the end of the tour. Presumably they were of the 'right type'.

On his return William, possibly recovering from the social and cricketing effects of the New Zealand tour, failed to reach his expected 1,000 runs. However between 1908 and 1911 he achieved this every season. During these years William had some excellent performances, the best being 196 against Warwickshire when he and Ted Arnold put on 393 runs for the fifth wicket, still a county record, and helping his team to their biggest winning margin, an innings and 223 runs, which remained unchallenged until 2002. Playing for the Gentlemen of Worcestershire against the Gentlemen of Staffordshire, admittedly not a first class match, William plundered a magnificent 334 in four and a half hours. In 1911 he achieved his largest aggregate with 1,438 runs at an average of 31.95. These successes led to further representative honours. In September 1910 he played for a Lord Londesborough XI against the MCC team that had recently toured South Africa and he became a regular participant in the Gentlemen v Players series. In 1910 he achieved his best performance in this fixture when he took 7 for 58, including 3 wickets in 4 balls. By now William was developing into something of an all-rounder as his bowling progressed. He began bowling seriously, and very quickly, in 1908 and had his most successful seasons in 1909 and 1910 when he captured 44 and 58 wickets. So quick was he that it is said that batsmen would instinctively back away to leg as he was bowling in fear that he would 'pin them to the sightscreen.' In the obituary of Plum Warner written years later, *Wisden* contends that he had objected to 'bodyline bowling' for years, ever since 1910 "when W.B. Burns bowled it for a few overs for Worcestershire against Middlesex at Lord's." Warner was at the time trying hard to distance himself from the 'bodyline' tactics of Larwood and Voce during a tour of which he was the manager – a manager, it must be said, who voiced no objections to the tactics until the series had been won 4-1. It is interesting that William, rather than a well remembered test match 'quickie', is the bowler to whom he refers when expressing his supposedly long held concerns. Frank Chester, later to become the most respected of cricket umpires and a teammate of William's, wrote in 1956 that William was the fastest he had seen for a few overs but that he was too erratic. He concluded that

> With such speed, Burns could not develop accuracy and usually batsmen had to pay more attention to protecting their skins than their wickets. A wild fast bowler is much more dangerous in a physical sense than one who bowls consistently down the line.

It may also be relevant that William was deemed to have a questionable bowling action. In his obituary *Wisden* says that he could bowl at great pace but that "the fairness of his delivery was often questioned – and not without good reason". Nevertheless, William's success with the ball, unfair or not, allows us to class him as a genuine all-rounder in the latter years of his cricket career.

The summer of 1911, however, was William's last successful season. He retired in 1913 and moved to Canada. On the outbreak of war William returned and joined the Worcestershire Regiment. On July 7th 1916, and now a Second Lieutenant, William found himself at the Battle of the Somme. On a warm, yet overcast day with drizzle in the air, he confronted the Germans at Contalmaison, three miles north-east of Albert and not far from where Percy Jeeves was to die two weeks later, and where three members of the Hearts Football team were killed just one week earlier. The story of exactly what happened to William is best told by Captain H. Fitz M. Stacke in his history of the Regiment written in 1928.

> On the 7th and 8th July the drizzle developed into heavy rain, converting the trenches into troughs of knee-deep mud. At about 2.00pm the enemy were heavily reinforced and commenced a powerful attack. The German artillery pounded the ruins held by the Worcestershire's and strong bombing parties of the enemy worked down from the higher ground. A desperate struggle raged around the ruins of the Church where a party of the Worcestershire's, inspired by two brave subalterns, 2nd Lieutenant AW Isaac and 2nd Lieutenant WB Burns, fought on until all were overwhelmed.

William's body was never found and, like Percy Jeeves, his name appears on the Thiepval Memorial. *Wisden*, in a detailed obituary, remembered William as "A dashing, hard hitting batsman, a useful fast bowler and a brilliant field." Worcestershire County Cricket Club remember him as one of the seventeen members of the club to perish in the Great War, all of whom are named in the memorial placed in the Members Pavilion, and the last of the three exciting English all-round cricketers to perish on the Somme battlefield.

Tony Wilding – 'Tennis's first matinee idol'

Of all the famous sportsmen covered in this book, one name stands out as a true international star. If he had been playing today it is likely that he would have been as familiar on the front pages of newspapers as on the back, possessing a 'Twitter' account with thousands of followers and a 'brand' that would rival that of David Beckham. A celebrity film star girlfriend, dashingly handsome good looks and an adventurous spirit that charmed all that met him, he had all the equipment to ensure lasting fame and stardom. He was the New Zealand four time Wimbledon tennis champion Anthony Frederick Wilding. Even on his death his contribution to New Zealand in general and his sport in particular were recognised. In the recently published *Dictionary of New Zealand Biography*, Helen Walter has quoted from his obituary in *The Press*,

> Even more than the All Blacks, he had carried the name of the Dominion into the regions of the earth where it was probably unknown until it became associated with his fame.

For much of the first seventy years of the twentieth century neighbouring Australia dominated the world's tennis courts but it was this New Zealand lawyer and adventurer who led the way. There is no doubt that if any tennis player could have adapted from the world of long trousers, wooden racquets and formal manners to the many demands of tennis in the modern era it would have been Tony Wilding. He would have been a gift to the twenty-first century world of promoters, agents and marketing men.

Who exactly was Tony Wilding? He was born on 31st October 1883 in Christchurch, the son of a barrister, Frederick, who had emigrated to New Zealand from Hertfordshire in 1879. His mother, Julia Anthony, was the daughter of a former Mayor of Hereford and she bore Frederick five children of which Tony was the second, the oldest son. Having a wealthy, sports-mad father gave Tony plenty of opportunity to indulge his own interest in outdoor sports. Frederick had represented New Zealand in the cricket field and he was also recognised as being a good rider, rower, footballer and a very good shot. The family lived in a beautiful, large home, befitting the family's position in society, which included stunning gardens, a swimming pool, cricket wicket, croquet green and a tennis court, all ideal for a family with sports-mad children to improve their skills. Tony was a natural but he was not the only sporting talent in the family. As well as his father, his sister Cora, five years younger, also had success when she captained the school hockey team and won the school tennis championship. When he wasn't indulging his interest in sport, Tony was attending William Wilson's private school for boys, where he excelled at football and cricket, followed by a short period of study at Canterbury University College. After six months, and having secured a place to read Law at Trinity College Cambridge, Tony set sail for England where his sporting interest would take a new turn.

It was while studying at Cambridge that Tony began to realise his potential on the tennis court. He had already won the Canterbury Championship as a seventeen year old in 1901, but while at Cambridge he first entered Wimbledon in 1904 and followed up his limited success there by capturing the Scottish national championship a few weeks later. The following year Tony was part of the Australasia Davis Cup team which reached the final of this already popular and prestigious competition. Known as the International Lawn Tennis Challenge, the Davis Cup was introduced in 1900 and in 1905 became truly international as it expanded outside the USA and UK for the first time. Although decisively beaten by the USA, Tony and his teammates had made a mark. Armed with his Law degree, Tony returned to New Zealand in late 1905 and joined his father's practice but soon returned to England on being called to the Inner Temple where he began qualifying as a barrister. He still found the time to travel around Europe, often on his motorcycle, and played in a succession of successful tournaments, some with his father.

In late 1906 he returned to the Southern Hemisphere and won his first major (what is now called Grand Slam) title that December. This was the Australasian Championship, the forerunner of the Australian Championship so coveted by today's top players, where he convincingly defeated Francis Fisher, another New Zealander who later became a notorious MP, in the final. For good measure, Tony also secured the Men's Doubles title with fellow countryman,

Rodney Heath. A week later, Tony added the New Zealand Championship title to his fast growing collection of trophies.

Tony was now a force in the world of tennis. But what propelled him to success so quickly? Despite his playboy image and his love of mixing with world figures – he often played tennis with ex-British Prime Minister and current leader of the Conservative Party, Arthur Balfour, as well as King Gustav of Sweden – Tony took his game very seriously. He practised hard to eradicate his weaknesses, particularly his backhand, which he attempted to master on the long voyages from New Zealand to Europe. He became something of a baseline player who made effective use of top spin, indulging in long rallies and dictating the pace of the game. This required exceptional fitness so Tony cut out alcohol and smoking as well as adopting a strict training regime of walking, skipping and the use of punch bags. He took advice from the former world heavyweight boxing champion Bob Fitzsimmons on matters of fitness while he learned from watching other successful tennis stars, in particular the British Doherty brothers, Laurence and Reggie, who had won nine of the ten Wimbledon Men's Singles titles between 1897 and 1906. By then Tony was the fittest player on the circuit and, while not as natural a player as his great Australian rival Norman Brookes, he also possessed the best temperament. Some said that playing the best of seven sets, rather than five or three, would suit Tony more, such was his staying power. At six feet two inches and weighing one hundred and eighty five pounds, Tony confirmed Brookes' opinion that he was "without doubt one of the finest specimens of manhood physically".

The years between 1906 and 1909 saw Tony gain his greatest successes in the Davis Cup. Playing with Norman Brookes, they won the trophy in three consecutive years from 1907 while Tony also won the Wimbledon Doubles title with Brookes in 1907 and with Josiah Ritchie in 1908 and 1910. The Australasian singles title was regained in 1909. Wimbledon, however, proved a tougher nut to crack. Played at Worple Road until 1922, Tony quickly became the tournament's first heartthrob. Those who remember the excitement caused by Bjorn Borg in the 1970s can imagine a similar, if rather less hysterical display, by spectators on the arrival of the handsome, debonair New Zealander. But it took time for Tony to dominate the tournament. Until 1922 the tournament was literally a challenge cup. Once won, the holder of the title did not play again in the tournament until the final the following year. The tournament was competition to decide which 'challenger' would earn the right to play for the title. This format meant that it was far easier to retain the trophy than it is today – only eleven men have successfully defended the singles title since 1922, although Perry, Laver, Borg, Sampras and Federer have done so on more than one occasion. In winning four years running, as Tony did between 1910 and1913, he played far fewer matches than Borg, Sampras and Federer did in achieving the same feat or better. Nevertheless, Tony became a legend of the sport by winning these titles and the scale of his achievement is not to be under-estimated.

He won his first title in 1910 when he defeated three times winner Arthur Gore in four sets. Tony served and volleyed his way to victory, a tactic he did not usually employ but was extremely effective on a grass court which had survived a wet tournament. The following year might have only involved his playing one match but it was a much more difficult experience. In the heat of a glorious summer day his opponent, Herbert Roper-Barrett, was forced to retire with the match level at two sets all. Despite not being at his best Tony's fitness was the decisive factor. In 1912 Arthur Gore was beaten, once again in four sets, but it is noticeable that the British press was less than fulsome in its praise. *The Times* acknowledged that Tony possessed few, if any, weaknesses and commented on his tactical ability. There was, however a reluctance to praise his ability and even criticism of "a lack of personality", although this might be due to Tony suffering a lack of confidence in this particular match. Was the criticism founded on Tony being seen as an athlete rather than an artistic tennis player, or was it due to his colonial upbringing or even his popularity with the ladies? It is impossible to tell but what is certain is that his fourth Wimbledon victory was his best and hardest fought. Starting the match as the underdog against the equally fit and extremely talented American Maurice McLaughlin, Tony prevailed in three close, hard won sets. Even *The Times* acknowledged his tenacity in never giving up or allowing his opponent to relax. In fact 1913 proved to be his best year as he also won the World Hard Court title in Paris and the Covered Court Championship in Stockholm, three major titles on three different surfaces. On July 4th 1914, just one week after the assassination of the Archduke Ferdinand, Tony prepared to defend his Wimbledon title for the fourth time, against his old rival Norman Brookes. On this occasion, despite playing well, Tony was defeated in straight sets. *The Times* appeared to like him more in defeat reporting that "he done his darndest; angels can do no more". The disappointment felt by his female admirers was graphically and dramatically described by the newspaper when they reported that "there was a ripple of white throughout the stands as women took out their handkerchiefs and cried". There was some consolation when he and Brookes won the Men's Doubles but the war would bring down the curtain on the tennis career of Tony Wilding.

A life without tennis should not have held too many terrors for Tony. By 1909 he had qualified both as a barrister and as a solicitor of the Supreme Court of New Zealand. Not that the law took up too much of his time. Tony had developed an interest in motorcycles and fast cars and particularly enjoyed making motorcycle trips with a sidecar. In 1908 he had driven from John o'Groats to Lands End and two years later drove from London to Lake Geneva and back, a distance of some 3,000 miles. Tony invariably headed to where the roads were toughest such as Serbia and Hungary and in the New Zealand summer of 1909/10 drove from Christchurch to Auckland in five days. With his tennis winnings (or, more properly, expenses) Tony was able to book flying lessons and before long he had taken to this newest form of travel. Through following the example of many of his fellow countrymen and dividing his time between the UK and New Zealand, Tony was being seen as a combination of the perfect English gentleman and the perfect example of colonial manhood.

The idea of settling down and marrying does not appear to have taken hold in these tennis playing years, but Tony enjoyed female company. In 1913 he began a relationship with the beautiful American actress Maxine Elliott, the daughter of a New England sea captain and one of most famous women in America. Fifteen years older than Tony, Maxine Elliott had a colourful past. She had married at the age of fifteen, fell pregnant and lost the baby before obtaining a divorce. She then took to the stage under name Maxine Elliott (she was born Jessie McDermott) and made her stage debut in 1890. Five years later Maxine had her first big break when she was hired by the theatrical manager and playwright Augustin Daly, and built on this success when she married the comedian Nat C. Goodwin in 1898 with whom she worked at home and abroad. In 1905 Maxine was presented to King Edward VII who must, given his reputation as an admirer of beautiful women, have been impressed by her charms. She was described by a contemporary as having "brilliant black hair, ivory skin, enormous midnight eyes and features of even proportion. Following her second divorce in 1908, Maxine became close to the financier J.P. Morgan, although it is doubtful if she ever had a sexual relationship with the seventy year old banker. Whatever the exact nature of their relationship, Maxine took his advice in financial matters and the result was that she became an extremely wealthy woman, owning homes in the USA and Europe as well as being the only woman to own her own theatre, 'The Maxine Elliott' situated on 39th Street, just off Broadway. Her acting ability was often questioned and reviewers sometimes debated as to whether her success was due more to her looks than an ability to act, an allegation faced by many female film stars in subsequent years. It is generally accepted that Maxine was not really in love with the stage but was very glad of the rewards it gave her, insecurity over her finances being a legacy of her early years. In 1913 Maxine took the plunge into the world of silent films and footage survives from 1918 of her cavorting with Charlie Chaplin and his entourage in the great man's studios.

This was the woman who had finally succeeded in encouraging Tony to consider commitment to a relationship. They appear to have been genuinely in love and marriage was certainly a possibility. Following the successes of 1913 Tony was beginning to lose interest in his tennis career and his mind was definitely turning towards a career after his sporting days were over, possibly with marriage in mind. Despite his family's legal background and his own success in this field, the law had never held that much interest for him. In 1911 Tony had worked for a British wood pulp firm, Henderson Craig and Company and two years later became a director of the Victor Tyre Company – successful tennis player or not Tony still needed to earn a living. His tennis career extended into 1914 and once the Wimbledon Championships were over Tony headed for the USA. His last competitive match was a Davis Cup doubles played with Norman Brookes against the German pair Otto Froitzheim and Oskar Kreuzer in Pittsburgh on August 1st, the day that Germany declared war on Russia. In an attempt to save the tie, the organisers cut lines of communication so that the players knew nothing of the crisis in Europe. Following the match the German pair, finally aware of the developing situation, rushed to return to Germany. On their voyage home they were intercepted by a Royal Navy ship and were interned for the duration of the war. Tony and Norman Brookes withdrew from the forthcoming USA Championship and quickly returned home to join the war effort.

On arriving in Britain Tony used his contacts in order to obtain a commission in an area where his expertise and interests could be put to best use. Tony was personally acquainted with the First Lord of the Admiralty, Winston Churchill, and had no difficulty in being accepted into the Royal Marines. He was there for only a few days before being transferred to the Intelligence Corps where it was hoped he would put his knowledge of the roads of Europe to good use. By the end of October, however, Tony was part of the Royal Navy Armoured Car Section as a Second Lieutenant. His love of cars and bikes made this an obvious posting and he envisaged being involved in something adventurous, thereby missing the boring training suffered by other recruits. He began by designing a two-wheeled trailer with a gun which could be towed behind an armoured car. By March 1915 Tony had been promoted to Lieutenant and was working with the first armoured cars based on the Rolls Royce Silver Ghost which could travel at 45mph and had a machine gun fitted in a revolving turret. He quickly realised the significance of his work and wrote home that "this is a motor war. Horses are more or less useless". Tony appears to have reached this conclusion before many of the generals. In May he was promoted to Captain, and placed in command of the 'Seabrook Armoured Lorry'. Frustrated by a lack of action, Tony led two of these vehicles and his thirty men in an attack on German gun crews. Although Tony wrote that he hated war and the abominable slaughter that came with it, he was always looking for adventure.

Tony did not have much longer to wait. The Allies had planned a surprise attack on Aubers Ridge by attacking either side of a village called Neuve Chapelle. The plan was to use artillery bombardment to begin on 8th May in order to cut the barbed wire and to destroy German defences before making an advance. Tony was expected to be involved in both the bombardment and the advance. He wrote optimistically to his mother in a letter quoted by Harris and Whippy on the eve of the attack:

> I think my guns will do great work and help the Infantry a good deal.... The General is most helpful with our task.

But when writing to his old commander Chilcott, Tony revealed his true feelings regarding the position. Writing the day before his death Tony considered his prospects:

> For really the first time in seven and a half months I have a job in hand which is likely to end in gun, I and the whole outfit being blown to hell.

Tony knew what was expected of him and that, if successful, the action would help the infantry enormously. He continued:

> I know the job exactly, and the objects in view from my study of them – it is the only way to play in business or war.

The Allied attack was meant to be a surprise but the Germans were waiting expectantly. The British had received poor intelligence and there was a flawed battle plan. German trenches were in a much better condition than those of the British and were well prepared for attack. Worse still, the tactical bombardment had been ineffective with too few shells and those that were available lacking the necessary explosive power. There was no hope of reinforcements being sent to this part of the front. With action taking place both at Ypres and Gallipoli, Allied Forces were stretched to breaking point.

The Second Battle of Artois, better known as the Battle of Aubers Ridge, began on the 9th May. Tony and his men began shelling at 5.00am and the action continued nearly all day. At 4.30pm, along with three colleagues, Tony took a well-earned break and headed for a dug out. What happened next is detailed by *Daily Telegraph* journalist Andrew Wallis Myers who published a biography of Tony in 1916. He wrote that Tony had observed and directed the fire from the gun platform and the trench at the same time as "being under the hottest counter-shelling". Acknowledging that it was a miracle that Tony had not been hit he tells us,

> When his gun crew came down into the trench, Wilding sought out a place to lie down, cracking a joke with his chief petty officer. More than one officer warned him not to go into the dugout. It was located directly in the danger zone and more exposed to the fire of the enemy. But Anthony, acting always on his own judgement crawled in…. Shells came hurtling near. It was one of the greatest trench bombardments of the war. At 4.45 there came a hearty burst of laughter from the dugout. Immediately afterwards a heavy shell exploded on its roof.

Tony and three comrades were killed instantly. Lying in the wreckage with Tony's body, blown from his pocket, was a gold cigarette case, a souvenir of a recent tennis triumph in the Riviera.

At about the same time on 9th May a second international sportsman was also making the ultimate sacrifice. Harry Berry, an English rugby international from Gloucester, had been born in the same year as Tony Wilding, on 8th January. The ninth child of the family, Harry was orphaned by the age of fourteen. He left school and two years later joined the 4th Battalion of the Gloucestershire Regiment. Too young to see active service in the Boer War, Harry was given the task of overseeing Boer prisoners of war, and it was during this period that he began playing rugby. So successful was he that he captained the Gloucester's for five seasons, a very rare achievement for any soldier from 'the other ranks'. Regular bouts of malaria led to Harry leaving the army in 1909 but within a year, running a pub with his recently married wife Beatrice, he was in the England rugby team where he made his mark as a good lineout forward who also excelled in the loose. Harry's first cap came against Wales in the new Twickenham stadium and he played well in a 6-3 victory. By the end of the season England had won three of their four games, the only blemish being a 0-0 draw with Ireland. Nevertheless the English team were crowned champions and Harry had scored tries in two of his four games. Surprisingly, although winning the county championship with Gloucestershire and playing for Gloucester until 1913, Harry was never picked for England again.

As a reservist Harry was called up to serve on August 4th 1914 and reported to Woolwich Arsenal. By February 1915 Corporal Berry was in France constructing a trench system that would reinforce the existing line. The biggest danger was falling victim to enemy snipers but in March Harry arrived in the vicinity of Neuve Chapelle. In early May Harry marched the eleven miles to the support trenches, arriving on the 8th just in time for the action. The Gloucester's were not involved in the first advance but at 4.00pm, on hearing of French success at Vimy Ridge, the generals ordered a second attack and Harry and his colleagues went over the top. As Tony Wilding had suspected, it was a futile act. Men were killed as they emerged from the trenches and those that made it across No Man's Land found the wire uncut. In the general confusion men were just mown down, some being killed as they retreated. In all 262 men of the Gloucester battalion were killed. One of them was Harry Berry. His body was never recovered and he is commemorated on the Le Touret Memorial to the missing, a much-loved husband and father to three year old Harry George and a newly born daughter, Phyllis Irene, who he had never seen.

Harry has been largely lost to history except, of course, to those in his family and community. Tony, however, has been remembered as an international sportsman of true significance. His commander, the Duke of Westminster, wrote immediately to his mother saying, "He was one of my finest officers and had done very good work", a sentiment repeated by his father when he wrote to a friend that it was "better for Anthony to have fallen in the manful discharge of his clear duty than to have remained in safety in England… done very good work." In New Zealand the Canterbury Lawn Tennis Association bought land in Woodham Road to be used as tennis courts. The area was to be known as 'Wilding Park' and it became the principal venue for tennis in New Zealand and ensured that his name would be remembered. In 1978 he was inducted into the International Tennis Hall of Fame, an honour well deserved. In 1950 Norman Brookes, who had survived the war and was later knighted "in recognition of service to public service", ranked him as the fourth best player of all time after Bill Tilden and the Doherty brothers. Although over sixty years have passed since this assessment and many other great players have come and gone, this still places him above Donald Budge, Fred Perry, Jack Kramer and also above the 'Four Musketeers' of France, Rene Lacoste, Jean Borota, Jacques Brugon and Henri Cochet who dominated tennis in the 1920s and early 1930s. Tony left a clear memory with all who saw him play.

What of the women closest to him? His sister Cora went on to become a well known figure in her own right. A successful artist, Cora set up health camps for children and then the Youth Hostel Association of New Zealand in 1932. She was awarded the MBE in 1952 and died thirty years later. Maxine Elliott, the woman he surely would have married, made her own contribution to the war effort. From very early in the war Maxine gave money and time to the cause of Belgian relief, even to the extent of moving there. For this she was awarded the Order of the Crown (Belgium). In 1917 she signed for Goldwyn Pictures and made several films. Her last stage performance came in 1920, going out on a high with a favourable review from the critic Alexander Woollcott who wrote that, "Besides her lustrous beauty, she has a dignity, a pleasing and thoroughly mastered voice, taste, humour and intelligence." After retiring in order to "grow old gracefully", Maxine died in 1942, a very wealthy resident of Cannes in France. She never married again. Perhaps the glamour and sheer star quality of Tony Wilding, New Zealand's premier sports star, adventurer and war hero was just too difficult to follow.

Olympic Heroes

The Olympic Games developed in the modern era following the foundation of the International Olympic Committee prior to the 1896 Games in Athens. By the time of the 1908 Games in London their popularity and, consequently future, seemed assured. Although the Games were relatively modest by today's standard, the four year cycle was becoming established and athletes began to set their sights on Olympic glory. The first modern Olympic heroes emerged in the years before the Great War and it was no surprise that some of the leading figures would be among the casualties. One, Wyndham Halswelle, was to make his name as an athlete in the 1908 Games, in a hugely controversial race which had long term significance for athletics, or track and field as it is often referred to today.

Wyndham Halswelle was born on in London on 30th May 1882, the son of an Edinburgh trained artist, Keeley Halswelle and his wife, Helen Gordon. Wyndham is usually referred to as being Scottish but only his maternal grandfather, General Nathaniel J. Gordon, had a truly Scottish background. Wyndham first served notice of his talent as an athlete as a pupil at Charterhouse School and then he attended the Royal Military Academy, Sandhurst. On completing his training at Sandhurst in 1901, he was commissioned into the Highland Light Infantry, which cemented his Scottish connections as he was based in Edinburgh. During the Second Boer War the regiment were in South Africa and, by 1902, Wyndham was serving there. It was at this time that his running ability attracted wider attention. Returning to Edinburgh in 1904, he paid serious attention to athletics, especially after being crowned Army Champion for 880 yards earlier that year.

The following year, Wyndham made a great impact on the British athletics scene. He won both the Scottish and AAA titles, then in 1906 achieved the remarkable feat of winning the Scottish titles in four events – the 100, 220, 440 and 880 yards – in a single afternoon. Not surprisingly the Scottish crowds were quick to adopt

Wyndham as one of their own. Earlier in 1906, Wyndham had run in the Intercalated Games in Athens where he won a silver medal in the 400 metres and a bronze in the 800 metres. Although these Games are not recognised by the IOC as bona fide Olympic Games they proved and invaluable experience for him as he built up to the London Olympics held two years later.

Olympic year started well for Wyndham. Early in the season he broke the British record for 440 yards, his new record standing for twenty-five years until beaten by Godfrey Rampling (father of the actress Charlotte Rampling) in 1933. Godfrey Rampling was a considerable athlete who won silver in the 4x400 metre relay team in the Los Angeles Olympics of 1932 and improved on this result four years later in the Berlin Olympics of 1936 when he and his teammates secured the gold medal. In between times he also took the gold medal in the 400 metre individual and relay events in the 1934 Empire Games. It took an athlete of such quality to better Wyndham's record. Wyndham's Scottish record stood even longer. It was not until 1961 that a young Glasgow University student, Menzies Campbell, beat Wyndham's Scottish record for the 300 yards. Campbell went on to race in the 1964 Tokyo Olympics and to captain the British Athletics Team in 1965 and 1966. He is better known today as a senior Liberal Democrat, having led the party between March 2006 and October 2007.

The 1908 Olympic Games were intended to be held in Rome but the eruption of Mount Vesuvius in 1906, led to an economic crisis in Italy which resulted in Rome abandoning its plan to host the event. London, as it was to do in 1948, stepped into the breach. The Games lasted an unequalled six months with the opening ceremony taking place on April 27th, and the closing ceremony on the last day of October. The Games was given the royal seal of approval when King Edward VII opened them, at the new state of the art White City Stadium.

But the IV Olympiad got off to a difficult start. The initial difficulty concerned the use of national flags in the opening ceremony. In the 1906 Intercalated Games teams marched behind their national flags for the first time at the opening ceremony. This practice was repeated in London but caused numerous problems. The USA refused to dip their flag in front of the Royal Box, a response to the failure of their flag to be displayed above the stadium before the opening. Although the flag was eventually dipped in front of a collective group of the Royal family, the incident caused a good deal of controversy. There was even a suggestion later that the gesture was connected to American support for Ireland in its struggle for Home Rule, but this is unproven. Further problems resulted when Finnish athletes refused to march under the Russian banner and Swedish athletes refused to march at all due to the failure of their flag to be displayed above the stadium. Politics and the Olympic Games have a history, it would seem, as long as the Games itself.

Nevertheless, with more athletes than ever before competing in 22 sports and 110 events in a brand new purpose built stadium holding a record 68,000 spectators (the first to be built specifically for the Games) London had done remarkably well at very short notice. The hosts were rewarded with a total of 50 gold medals, more than twice the number gained by the USA. Wyndham Haswelle's gold was to prove one of the most significant and certainly one of the most controversial. Entered, along with the future double VC winner Noel Chavasse and his twin brother Christopher, for the 400 metres, Wyndham qualified for the final in an Olympic record time. In the final Wyndham, racing against three Americans in a four man field, might have expected trouble from the beginning. The race was not run in lanes, as it is today, so barging and blocking were not uncommon. On this occasion, the race was to be run under the stricter British rules rather than the more relaxed American race etiquette and, as Wyndham's fellow competitors were all USA athletes there was potential for trouble. Indeed the starter warned all four runners about jostling before the race. Coming off the final bend William Robbins was leading and about to be overtaken by John Carpenter. Wyndham was well placed just behind both of his rivals and ready to pass them on the final straight, a tactic that he had used successfully in earlier rounds. As he made his move Carpenter forced Wyndham very wide and blocked him using an elbow. The umpire signalled for the tape to be broken, in effect halting the race, and after an hour of deliberation it was decided that Carpenter should be disqualified and the race re-run two days later. Wyndham was certain that the decision was the correct one and stated:

> Carpenter's elbow undoubtedly touched my chest, for as I moved outwards to pass him he did likewise, keeping his right arm in front of me. In this manner he bored me across quite two thirds of the track, and eventually stopped my running.

Not that the USA team saw these events in quite the same way and they were quick to complain. They complained that they were "rooked, bilked, cheated, swindled and robbed", while the USA media had no doubt as to why Wyndham had been favoured. The British runner was described as "the idol of the British aristocracy" and the "favourite toff of the cockney crowd". *The Times*, on the other hand, felt the American actions to have been far more questionable stating that it was "a definite and carefully thought out plan... contrary alike to the rules that govern sport and to our notions of what is fair play." Perhaps the incident reflected a mutual distrust between the nations, one trying to hold on to a vast and influential Empire and displaying an associated degree of arrogance, the other showing the hunger and confidence of a nation building towards its position as the superpower of the twentieth century. Or was it just the competitive nature of four athletes trying to win a gold medal?

The re-run took place with only one athlete – Wyndham Halswelle. In a show of unity and support for John Carpenter, William Robbins and the third American, John Taylor, refused to re-run the race. A reluctant Wyndham, who had to be persuaded by AAA officials to take part, won in a 'walkover' completing the distance in a time of 50.2 seconds, nearly two seconds slower than his time in the semi-final race. He became the only athlete to win an Olympic title as the result of a walkover. More pleasing to him, he became the first Scottish athlete to win Olympic gold, the forerunner of the much more celebrated Eric Liddell, 400 metre gold medallist in the 1924 Games, whose story in told in the Oscar winning film *Chariots of Fire*, and Alan Wells, the 1980 Moscow 100 metres champion. Wyndham, however, was not the only Scottish athlete to win gold in 1908. Archie Robertson had played his part in securing a British victory in the three mile team race but, unlike Wyndham, Eric Liddell and Alan Wells, his was not an individual gold medal. Wyndham can also lay claim to being the first and, as far as I can ascertain, only British athlete to win Olympic gold, silver and bronze medals in an individual event – David Hemery and Mary Rand also possess all three medals but won one of their medals as part of a relay team. Wyndham, it can be argued, won his silver and bronze medals at the unofficial Intercalated Games but at the time the Games were considered official. It was a great achievement whichever way one looks at it.

The consequences of the 1908 400 metres final were far reaching. In future, international 400 metre races would be run in lanes and, even more significantly, the International Amateur Athletic Federation was founded to establish uniform, worldwide rules for all events. This didn't console Wyndham who was soured by the experience. He quickly lost interest in athletics and ran his last race at the 1908 Glasgow Rangers Sports. John Taylor gained some consolation by becoming the first African American to win an Olympic gold medal as a member of the medley relay team. Unfortunately, shortly after his return to USA, the very popular and highly respected Taylor contracted typhoid fever and died aged 26. William Robbins went on to become a relay world record holder in 1909 and lived to the age of 76, dying in 1962, while John Carpenter, the villain of the piece, disappeared from athletics and died in 1933. Wyndham Halswelle went to war.

As a regular in the Highland Light Infantry and having the rank of Captain, it was inevitable that Wyndham would be involved in the war from the beginning. His contribution, however, was all too short. By March 1915 he was in the thick of the action in France and had already contributed a revealing account for a regimental magazine which tells graphically of the trench experience.

> I called on men to get over the parapet. There is great difficulty in getting out of a trench, especially for small men laden with a pack, rifle and perhaps 50 rounds in the pouch, and a bandolier of 50 rounds hung around them, and perhaps four feet of slippery clay perpendicular wall with sandbags on the top. I got about three men hit actually on top of the parapet. I made a dash at the parapet and fell back. The Jocks then heaved me up and I jumped into a ditch – an old trench filled with liquid mud – which took me some time to get out of.

He reports that the men gained a total distance of fifteen yards, dug in for three hours the retreated to their starting position. In the process 79 men were killed. A few days after, on the 31st March, Wyndham was at the heart of the Battle of Neuve Chapelle, organising the defence of a sector near Laventie in France. He was wounded by rifle fire, given immediate medical attention and returned promptly to his position. Tragically, Wyndham was struck by a sniper's bullet and died instantly. He was thirty-two years old. Wyndham's remains were buried in the graveyard of the Royal Irish Rifles at Laventie, near Armentieres. In 2003 Wyndham was inducted into the Scottish Sports Hall of Fame, and his three Olympic medals can now be viewed in this Edinburgh museum.

Wyndham was not the only Olympic athlete killed in the first year of the war. Gerard Anderson, the world record holder over the 440 yard hurdles, was fully expected to win a medal at the 1912 Stockholm Olympics. An ex-Eton and Oxford scholar, Gerard had become a manager at the Cammell Laird shipyard in Birkenhead. But it was athletics that had brought his name to the attention of the public. In 1910 and 1912 he was the AAA champion over the 120 yards hurdles and, following his world record set at Crystal Palace in July 1910, he travelled to Stockholm as one of the favourites to win a gold medal. The 440 yard hurdles was not included in the programme but Gerard was selected to compete in the 110 yard hurdles. Unfortunately a freak accident led to his disqualification, and Gerard returned home empty handed.

On the outbreak of war, Gerard joined the Cheshire Regiment as a Second Lieutenant. The 25 year old was quickly involved in the action at the 1st Ypres and was recognised for his bravery when Mentioned in Despatches. However the 1st Ypres was costly for both sides and a horrible sign of things to come. There were more than 80,000 German casualties, many of them students, "the intellectual flower of Germany", according to Holmes. The BEF lost over 58,000 men in halting the German advance and saving Ypres. Holmes records that after a month of heavy fighting, the town was blackened by fire, battered by shelling and crumbling into ruins, it was still in Allied hands. The armies dug in and the Ypres Salient was quickly reduced to a wasteland of rubble and mud. It became a symbol of the soldiers' suffering and struggle over the following four years. It was here, at Hooge, that Gerard was killed sometime between the 7th and 11th November 1914, one of the first celebrated British sportsmen, to die on the battlefield.

One athlete who did gain Olympic success in 1912 was the Scot Henry McIntosh. Educated at Glenalmond College and Corpus Christie College, Cambridge he was a renowned 100 and 200 metre specialist, who was disappointed with his performances in these individual events when he failed to emulate Wyndham's success of 1908, but had the compensation of running the second leg in the British 4x100 metre relay team which won the gold medal. Post-Olympics, McIntosh continued his career and won an international event in Budapest in the summer of 1914, after which he was presented with a giant Italian marble statue. On the outbreak of war McIntosh joined the Argyll and Sutherland Highlanders but was tragically killed at the second Battle of the Somme on 26th July 1918, with the end of the war only four months away.

Another Olympic gold medallist and hero was a very different character from many of the sportsmen in this book. Frederick Septimus Kelly was a man whose social circle consisted of poets, politicians, scholars and composers, a far cry from the stereotypical image of a successful sportsmen today. A gifted musician and composer, better remembered today for his music, Frederick Kelly was nevertheless a very accomplished sportsman good enough to have won an Olympic rowing gold medal in 1908.

Frederick was born on 29th May 1881, in Sydney, Australia the fourth son of an Irish father, Thomas Herbert who had married an Australian, Mary Ann Dick. Thomas was a wealthy wool trader who provided a very comfortable, even privileged, existence for his family. Initially Frederick began his secondary education at Sydney Grammar School but it was felt he would gain more by attending Eton. The family believed, just as Tony Wilding's father had, that the opportunities provided by the top English public schools and universities would help a wealthy young man from the colonies to achieve his potential. While at Eton, Frederick first became interested in rowing, and with immediate success. In 1899, he stroked the school eight to success, and pursued his new interest at Balliol College, Oxford where he took up sculling. He read for a History degree, although it is clear that this was not his main interest as he gained only a fourth class honours in 1903. By now music had become Frederick's first love and he was president of the university music club, but he was also creating a serious reputation on the water. He won the Diamond Challenge Sculls at Henley in 1902 and 1903, the Wingfield Sculls in 1903 and the Grand Challenge Cup while rowing with the Leander Club, also in 1903. He had, of course, also rowed in the Varsity Boat Race, losing to Cambridge in 1903. Even more significantly regarding his future security, Frederick's father had died in 1901 leaving his son a wealthy man. His inheritance allowed Frederick and his sister to purchase a very comfortable home, Bisham Grange, in Marlow, Buckinghamshire (ironically the town that these days is now home to Sir Steve Redgrave) and enabled him to contemplate a future free from financial constraints. Wealth also drew Frederick into circles that he could never have expected at quite so young an age. He mixed in the very 'best' London society and spent time with Arthur Asquith, son of the Prime Minister, and the poet Rupert Brooke. Relaxed no doubt by his newly acquired wealth, Frederick had further success on the river with victories in The Grand Challenge Cup (1904 and 1905), the Diamond Challenge Sculls in 1905 and the Stewards Challenge Cup in 1906. Frederick's time of 8 minutes and 10 seconds in the 1905 Challenge Skulls was the record for 30 years.

Yet Frederick had no intention of blowing his good fortune and he looked to music for a career, one that might even make him some money. He became a protégé of Ernest Walker, the Indian-born English composer and, after leaving Oxford, attended a music school in Frankfurt in 1906, where he concentrated on the piano. During this period he gave private music recitals for friends and began to compose. Although it didn't give him the income that he would have liked, Frederick was by now seen as a musician of some note, particularly among his social circle.

However, with the 1908 Olympics approaching, an unsettled Frederick decided to return to rowing. Clearly Frederick felt that he had some unfinished business on the river. He was invited to be part of the Leander crew that was due to compete in the 'eights' held at Henley at the end of July. Rowing was a popular sport and although there were only four events, all for men, in the 1908 Games, eight nations participated. All four gold medals were won by Great Britain, not entirely unexpected as the country was clearly the world's leading nation in rowing and Frederick was one of the leading figures. Harris and Whippy quote him as being a rower of whom it was said " had a natural sense of poise and rhythm that made his boat a living thing under him", and many contemporaries said that he was the "greatest amateur stylist of all time". How Frederick would compare with the modern greats of British rowing is impossible to say but there is no doubt that Frederick was one of the leading rowers of his time. In the 1908 Olympics, as Britain pushed Belgium and Canada into silver and bronze positions respectively, Frederick cemented this reputation. It was a reputation that continued into the 1912 Stockholm Olympics where the Men's Eight, led by Eton and Oxford-educated Alister Kirby captained his team to a gold medal, one of the two won by the British rowers that summer. Tragically, the thirty-year-old Captain Kirby died as a result of a tumour on the knee while serving as a member of the Rifle Brigade in France and is buried in a cemetery in Marseilles. Frederick, meanwhile, was long finished with rowing: after the completion of the 1908 Olympic Games he never rowed competitively again.

Following his 1908 victory, Frederick decided to return to music but, as he was now known as an Olympic champion, he decided to make a fresh start elsewhere. For this reason, and thinking that he might be taken more seriously, Frederick returned to his homeland, Australia. After a few years working and studying Frederick made his debut as a pianist at Sydney Town Hall on 17th June 1911. Although he was not the main attraction, Frederick received good reviews for his performance which was entitled the 'First Musical Festival of the Empire'. His reputation as a musician now considerably enhanced, Frederick returned to Britain where he acted as a patron to groups of musicians such as the London Classical Concert Society during the years 1912 and 1913. As he moved among some of the most influential musicians and poets, the critic and composer William Denis Browne and the poet Rupert Brooke in particular, Frederick became aware of the international situation. His particular group of friends, 'The Latin Club', had contacts with Asquith, Lord Kitchener and Haldane so current affairs would have been a subject within this group of bright young men. Frederick himself could see the possibility of war but was very unsure as to where he, as a 'British Australian', should enlist when the time came. In the event, on the outbreak of war, Frederick obtained a commission to join the Royal Navy Volunteer Reserve for service with the Royal Naval Division. Here the newly created Sub Lieutenant joined Arthur Asquith, Charles Lister the diplomat, the financier Patrick Shaw-Stuart, Bernard Freyburg (later a VC and Governor General of New Zealand), Denis Browne and, of course, Rupert Brooke. This unique group, 'The Latin Club', would serve together.

Frederick and the others did their training along the south coast where they concentrated on rifle practice, drill and physical training but, by early 1915, were on the way to the Dardanelles. During the journey, Frederick became even closer to Rupert Brooke as they talked about music, literature and poetry. Harris and Whippy tell us that Frederick saw Brooke as "being made of really fine stuff, both physically and mentally" and he particularly enjoyed listening to Brooke reading his poetry. But it was not to last. Only three days before the landings the enthusiastic Brooke, hungry to make his mark on the battlefield, was bitten on the lip by a mosquito, developed blood poisoning and was transferred to a French hospital ship anchored in Skyros harbour. Here he died on the 23rd April, Shakespeare's birthday and St George's Day. Brooke was buried on the island in the presence of the other members of 'The Latin Club'. As Brooke lay dying, Frederick began work composing his tribute, 'Elegy for String Orchestra, In Memoriam Rupert Brooke'. Frederick now began to see his friend as following the line of Keats, Shelley and Schubert, all of whom died young. Following the poet's passing, it was Frederick who arranged his belongings for the journey back to England. A mere thirty-six hours after Brooke's burial in "some corner of a foreign field that is forever England" the Gallipoli landings began.

A few days later Frederick, with the Hood Battalion, landed on the Helles Peninsula at the foothills of Achi Baba. The battalion was used, in the main, to support attacks made by other units and therefore turned up whenever and wherever needed. The conditions were dreadful and the men suffered from the heat, dysentery and disease in addition to the usual dangers of warfare. Frederick fought at the Battle of Krithia on 6th May, and a month later he was fighting alongside the French, again in an assault of Krithia. On the 7th June, the same day as he was promoted to the rank of Lieutenant, Frederick was wounded by enemy shellfire. He recovered and quickly returned to action, experiencing the worsening weather conditions during the evacuation of the peninsula in November and December, but by January 1916, nearly all the men, including Frederick, were away. It was announced that Frederick had been awarded the Distinguished Service Cross "in recognition of services with the Royal Naval Division in the Gallipoli peninsula". He was also Mentioned in Despatches a few weeks later by General Sir Ian Hamilton "for distinguished service in 1915".

By the summer of 1916 Frederick was in France, an Acting Lieutenant-Commander, though he was spared the Battle of the Somme, at least for the time being. Instead he spent a relatively quiet period in Arras before being sent to the Somme in November to support yet another attempt to capture Serre, Beaumont Hamel and Beaucourt. In an action that became known as the Battle of Ancre, Frederick led an attack on a machine gun that was providing covering fire. In the darkness and thick mist that prevailed on that Monday evening, 13th November, Frederick was killed. His body was recovered and buried at Martinsart British Cemetery. His is among the 482 headstones that lie in this particularly attractive resting place, situated on the edge of the village, surrounded by working farms and meadows, with a wood nearby.

In death Frederick left a legacy, although unlike many sportsmen it was in the field of music rather than sport. The elegy that he composed for Rupert Brooke at Gallipoli was played at a memorial for the poet in London during 1919, while his musical compositions, along with his extensive diaries, now reside in the National Library in Australia where they are studied by researchers and scholars. Perhaps, after all, Frederick belongs more to the world of the lost poets like Wilfred Owen, Isaac Rosenburg, Charles Hamilton Sorley and Edward Thomas than the sporting theatre occupied by Sandy Turnbull and Dave Gallaher. Nevertheless his place in our roll of honour is well deserved. As the United Kingdom continues to lead the world in Olympic rowing it is only proper to recognise the contribution and the sacrifice made by one of Britain's first great oarsmen.

"Most conspicuous bravery"
Winners of the Victoria Cross

All the sportsmen in this book are heroes. Each made the greatest sacrifice by laying down their lives for King and Country and many were recognised for their efforts and decorated accordingly. There are a small number who achieved the highest honour of all and were awarded the Victoria Cross. A total of 628 VCs were awarded for acts of bravery in the Great War, more than for any conflict since the introduction of this medal by Queen Victoria in 1856 during the Crimean War. A total of 1,357 medals have been awarded since then with only three men having won VC and Bar, one of whom was Noel Chavasse who ran in the Olympic 400 metres in 1908. The award is given in the rarest of circumstances and only for "…most conspicuous bravery, or some daring or pre-eminent act of valour or self-sacrifice, or extreme devotion to duty in the presence of the enemy." Few sportsmen were awarded this honour but there were some whose stories should be recorded.

The first is the footballer Donald Simpson Bell who, on 5th July 1916, committed one of the bravest acts of a war which is littered with deeds of bravery and self-sacrifice. Although not the most successful of the footballers, on the battlefield Donald Bell possibly holds pride of place. Don or Donny, as he was commonly known, was born on 3rd December 1890, into the comfortable surroundings Harrogate, Yorkshire. He was one of seven children and began what would be a successful education at St Peter's Church of England School, Harrogate. Don was awarded a scholarship to Knaresborough Grammar School where, he succeeded academically and further developed his interest in sport, which had begun while at St Peter's. Don won his school colours in football, rugby, cricket, hockey and swimming, but football quickly became his first love. Already a well built young man by the time that he left Knaresborough, Don was a natural sportsman. Harris and Whippy quote an old school friend, another sporting schoolboy named Archie White, as saying that the six foot tall Don had "the build of a hammer thrower" but who also possessed the "gift of acceleration" and the "speed of a sprinter" over 30-50 yards. An article from the *Harrogate Herald* published in July 1916 tells us that his time for the 100 yard sprint "from a scratch start" was 10.6 seconds, a very impressive time for the early years of the twentieth century.

At the age of eighteen Don was offered a place at Westminster College in London where he trained to be a teacher. While a student, Don made his mark on the rugby field, but by turning out as an amateur in the Southern League with Crystal Palace, Don took his first step into the world of football. Playing in front of crowds that regularly topped 15,000, Don was exposed to the demands of professional sport although he remained an amateur still with an eye on the classroom as his career. In 1911, Don returned north to a teaching job in Starbeck Council School in Harrogate. He was signed by Newcastle United, then one of England's premier clubs, as an amateur player and given his opportunity as a member of their forward line. Despite showing plenty of pace, Don was soon moved back to defence where he played full back. A year later, he was spotted by Bradford Park Avenue and the offer of a little more 'boot money' to supplement his income of £2.50 a week from teaching, and the attraction of playing for a club based much nearer his school, was enough to swing it. Don was back playing his football in Yorkshire. He made his debut for Bradford Park Avenue as a full back in 1913, and was deemed good enough to be offered professional terms for the forthcoming season 1913/14. At twenty-two Don decided to leave teaching, at least for the time being, as a full time footballer. With the maximum wage now £4.00 a week, compared with the £2.50 a week he received as a teacher, it was not a difficult decision to make. Besides, he had all the equipment needed to succeed in the professional game. In addition to his pace and height, Don had filled out to thirteen and a half stone, a good build for a solid defensive player. In early November 1913, Don forced his way into the first team but unfortunately picked up an injury in January 1914, which kept him out for the rest of the season. Consequently he missed the excitement of taking part in his club's promotion to the first division that spring when they finished second to Notts County but ahead of Woolwich Arsenal in the race for the

Second Division title. Not that his contribution was forgotten by the local press who, according to Harris and Whippy, reported that "Bell is one of the best types of professional footballer, broadminded in outlook and scrupulously fair in his play".

Don must have anticipated the 1914/15 season with great optimism. Now committed to his football career, he had much to look forward to and there was every chance that his best years as a player were still in front of him. His personal life was also looking promising. During the summer of 1914 he met, and fell in love with, Rhoda Bonson, who was to become his wife. But they met in the same month that the Archduke Ferdinand was assassinated, an event that was to ensure that theirs would be the briefest of marriages. With war declared, Don immediately asked Bradford Park Avenue whether he could be released so he could volunteer. They agreed and Don became one of the first, perhaps even the very first, professional footballer to join up. On the 24th October 1914 he joined A Company of the 9th Battalion, West Yorkshire Regiment but at first he was forced, like many others, to spend a frustrating period of training at his unit's base in Surrey. A chance meeting with Archie White was to change this. White soon let it be known to his commanding officer that his friend was 'officer material' so in June 1915, Don received his commission and joined the Green Howards, another part of the Yorkshire Regiment. After arranging to marry Rhoda on his first leave, Don was at last on his way to France.

In late September 1915 Don found himself at Loos playing a supporting role at Rue du Bois, although he saw some action. On New Years Eve 1915, he was facing counter bombardment as his battalion supported a raid led by the Northumberland Fusiliers but in the early months of 1916, he had a relatively quiet time, which he passed by excitedly reading the copies of the *Harrogate Herald*. Regular access to this newspaper resulted in men writing to the editor, establishing close links to the community. Don took part and succeeded in keeping strong links with his friends and family. As he had promised, when leave was granted Don came home to marry his fiancée and on 5th June 1916, at the Wesleyan Church, Kirby Stephen in the Lake District, the young couple were wed. Even at a distance of almost 100 years it is very poignant to read the account in the *Harrogate Herald* two days later with the writer of the 'Wednesday Gossip Column' sending the newly weds his best wishes. In the same edition there is a letter from Billy Bell, Don's older brother and a member of the same regiment, telling of a recent meeting with his brother and expressing his regret at not being able to obtain leave for the wedding. He also gives details of his own rather hairy experiences in the trenches and expresses sadness at the recent loss of his cousin Jimmy who he didn't even know was in France. Even in the midst of happy occasions, thoughts of loss and tragedy were never far away. Two days after his wedding, with no time for a proper honeymoon, Don was on his way back to France. He would never see Rhoda again.

When Don returned to the front line preparations for the 'big push' on the Somme were well underway. As we know the battle began on July 1st, and Don was soon in action. On the opening day his division was held in reserve but on the 3rd he was moved up to the firing line to a position overlooking La Boisselle. Two days later, July 5th, Don took part in the action that won him the VC. On reaching a position between La Boisselle and Mametz Wood called Horseshoe Trench he, with his men, were consolidating their position and collecting wounded colleagues when they were fired on by enemy machine guns. Don, with two colleagues Corporal Colwell and Private Batey in hot pursuit, rushed the gun and shot the gunner. Don then threw a grenade at the gun thereby ensuring that it was put out of action. The men, inspired by Don's actions and their success in potentially saving the lives of many of their colleagues, now had the taste for more dramatic deeds. Archie White, quoted in Harris and Whippy, tells what happened next.

> Probably no one else on the front could have done what Bell did. Laden by steel helmet, haversack, revolver, ammunition and Mills bomb in their pouches, he was yet able to hurl himself at the German trench at such speed that the enemy would hardly believe what their eyes saw.

The mission was accomplished successfully and Don was an instant hero with honours sure to follow. Not that he saw it in those terms and he was very keen to give credit to his colleagues, especially the nineteen-year-old Batey. He modestly wrote to his mother,

> I must confess that it was the biggest fluke alive and I did

> nothing. I only chucked the bomb and it did the trick...

To a friend and former colleague he was equally modest writing,

> There is talk of me getting a military cross or something of the sort, talk about luck! Fancy, just chucking one's bomb, even if it was a bull's eye.

Luck or not, Don's good fortune was about to run out. Five days after his attack on German lines, Don was defending the recently captured village of Contalmaison. Sent to assist the 8th Yorkshires he led another counter attack on German lines, once again throwing bombs as he charged at the enemy in an attempt to drive them back. Giving no thought to his own safety, Don reached a position very close to the German line and, after taking careful aim, had some success in 'taking out' some of their guns. Tragically, he was hit and, although he made attempts to continue, he became weaker, collapsed and died.

The loss of such a popular soldier was felt both in the battalion and at home. The Revd. Doctor H.B. Workman, Principle of Westminster College, said of his old student that "Don was surely one of the finest representatives of Westminster." Private John Byers wrote to a devastated Rhoda that "The men worshipped him.... We have lost the best officer and gentleman that ever was with this battalion" while Don's commanding officer Lieutenant Colonel H.G. Holmes wrote to his parents,

> He was a great example, given at a time it was most needed, and in his honour, the spot where he lies and which is now a redoubt, has been officially named: Bell's Redoubt. He is a great loss to the Battalion and also to me personally, and I consider him one of the finest officers I have ever seen.

The naming of the redoubt so promptly was particularly revealing and its significance remains. On July 9th 2000 a memorial was updated and made secure when it was sponsored by the Professional Footballers Association. Inscriptions in both English and French draw attention to the high regard in which Don is held on the continent as well as in England.

There remained the question of military recognition and

honours. There was a precedent for a footballer receiving the Victoria Cross as a year earlier Willie Angus, a Lance Corporal in the Highland Light Infantry and Celtic footballer, had been recognised in this way. Twenty-seven year old Angus had won his honour at Givenchy, France on 12th June 1915, when he left his trench and rescued a wounded officer, Lieutenant James Martin, lying within yards of the enemy. Martin had been leading a covert bombing raid on an embankment in front of the German trenches. A large mine was detonated by the Germans as the raiding party attacked and Martin was badly injured in the explosion. At first it was thought that Martin was dead but, when it was realised that he was alive, Willie offered to rescue him. Eventually he was given permission to embark on what must have appeared to be a suicide mission. A rope was tied to Willie so that he could be pulled to safety if injured, so he set off with no chance of escaping enemy fire and with no thought for his own safety. He managed to carry Martin part of the way back before the Germans spotted them and opened fire. Willie protected his colleague with his own body before tying him to the rope, thereby enabling Martin to be pulled to safety. Willie then proceeded to distract the Germans by moving away from Martin so as to take the full force of enemy fire himself. Eventually he managed to crawl back to safety having received forty injuries in the process. These injuries resulted in the loss of his right eye as well as a foot. His commanding officer, Lieutenant Colonel Gemmill, later wrote that "no braver deed was ever done in the history of the British Army". Happily this ex-miner survived the war and lived a full life, dying in 1959 at the age of seventy-one.

Willie Angus, however, does not feature strongly in the history of football. As far as can be ascertained he played in only one game for the Celtic first team and records of his career are difficult to find. Bernard Vann, a Cambridge graduate who had played briefly for Northampton Town, Burton United and Derby County, was another winner of the VC. He had an even more outstanding military record having won the Military Cross on two occasions by 1916. Six weeks before the armistice, on 29th September, Vann, a thirty-one year old Sherwood Forester, won the VC when he charged German trenches, in a manner similar to Don's action two years earlier, killing three enemy soldiers in the process. Tragically just days later, on 3rd October, Vann was killed by a sniper. This remarkable man is not, however, remembered as a footballer but as the only ordained clergyman of the Church of England to win the VC as a combatant.

To all intents and purposes, Don is the only full time professional footballer to have won the Victoria Cross. The *London Gazette* reported his death and citation on 8th September 1916:

> ...for most conspicuous bravery. During an attack a very heavy enfilade fire was opened on the attacking company by a hostile machine gun. 2nd Lieutenant Bell immediately, and on his own initiative, crept up a communication trench and then, followed by Corporal Colwell and Private Batey rushed across the open under very heavy fire and attacked the machine gun, shooting the firer with his revolver, and destroying gun and personnel with bombs. This very brave act saved many lives and ensured the success of the attack.

Persuaded by her father-in-law, Rhoda was presented with Don's VC by King George V at a private ceremony on 13th December. In the meantime Don was buried at Gordon Dump Cemetery, one of 1,641 graves, 1,052 of which are unidentified. Don now lies in a section of the cemetery devoted to a small group of decorated heroes with three winners of the Military Medal lying alongside him. For many years his VC was displayed at the Green Howard Museum in Richmond, Yorkshire, but in November 2010 was bought by the PFA for a figure in excess of £200,000. It is intended to be prominently displayed in the new National Football Museum in Manchester. Rhoda, who had lost her beloved husband after thirty-five days of marriage, only three of which were spent in Don's company, received the annual widow's pension of £100. She never remarried.

Football was not the only sport to boast a VC. Given the number of internationals lost in the Great War it is inevitable that rugby union would be able to produce its own hero. Only four rugby international footballers have ever won the VC and three of them are Irish. Robert Johnson and Thomas Crean were awarded theirs in the Second Boer War while Frederick Harvey won his in the Great

War. Frederick Harvey, who was awarded the VC in 1917, had the good fortune to survive the war. The twice-capped Irishman, a teammate of Basil Maclear, had worked as a surveyor in Canada and was a member of the Canadian Army during the conflict. He served in the Canadian Mounted Rifles and, later, as part of the Canadian Cavalry Brigade. He won his VC during action at Guyencourt where he dashed at a German trench, jumped the wire, shot a machine gunner and captured the gun. He later won the Military Cross and the Croix du Guerre, in 1918, completing an outstanding military record. When he left the army he was a Brigadier General, and became commander of the 13th Alberta Military District in 1945 before enjoying a well-earned retirement. He died aged 91 in August 1980 in Alberta.

The story of English rugby's only VC does not take place in the trenches, for Arthur Leyland Harrison VC was an officer in the Royal Navy. Born on 3rd February 1886, to Lieutenant Colonel A.J. Harrison of the Royal Fusiliers and his wife Adelaide in Torquay, Arthur was educated at Brockhurst Preparatory School and Dover College. Like many of the sportsmen in this book, the first signs of raw sporting talent were visible in his early years. Arthur quickly showed himself to be an all round games player with the ability to succeed in most sports, but it was rugby union that captured his attention. Given the military background of Arthur's family it is not surprising that at the age of sixteen he began to train as a military cadet and embarked on a naval career. He was posted to Britannia Royal Naval College, Dartmouth as a cadet officer in May 1901. Arthur's naval career and his interest in pursuing a rugby career became entwined and before long he was playing a good standard of rugby in the Navy. As a member of the Hampshire branch of the United Services, Arthur's career was also progressing well and in 1906, he was commissioned as a Sub Lieutenant. Two years later the twenty-two year old Arthur was made a full Lieutenant.

Despite his interest in the game, Arthur's rugby career was progressing more slowly and he was something of a 'slow burner'. A bustling, enthusiastic forward who proved to be very effective in the scrummage, Arthur was a versatile member of the pack, although today we would probably class him as a back row forward doing much of the unseen, but necessary, grafting. In 1912 Arthur was selected for the Hampshire County XV and this advancement brought him to the attention of the England selectors. England were particularly strong in the two years preceding the war, winning consecutive Grand Slams and possessing, in Ronnie Poulton, Britain's finest rugby player. Nevertheless, even good teams can be improved and 1914 proved to be an excellent year for Arthur's rugby. On New Years Day he played for the Navy against Ronnie Poulton and a strong Harlequins team; and six weeks later Arthur was in the England team. Despite a 10-9 victory against a strong Welsh team in their opening game, the England selectors needed to 'stiffen' the pack for the Ireland game so on February 14th Arthur ran out in front of King George V, Prime Minister H.H. Asquith and 40,000 excited supporters at Twickenham intent on seizing his opportunity. At twenty-eight years of age, Arthur was not considered to be young and it was hoped that his experience and durability would improve the England team. The ploy appears to have worked. England ran in five tries in a 17-12 victory after falling 7-0 behind early on. Superior skill and fitness took its toll on the Irish and Arthur played his part. *The Times* reported that "the English forwards, stiffened in the scrummage by the two Harrisons, did better than against Wales." The second Harrison was Harold G. Harrison who played for the Army and who kept his place for the remainder of the season. Arthur, however, was surprisingly absent from the Scottish match where England clinched the Triple Crown with a 16-15 victory – the match where eleven of the participants went on to lose their life in the following four and a half years. It is worth noting that nearly a quarter of the 116 players who took part in the 1914 Five Nations championship in 1914 were killed either during the war or died of wounds just after it. Once again Arthur played in front of the King, who was accompanied by Prince Albert, the future King George VI, when he represented the Royal Navy in their 26-14 defeat against the Army on March 7th. A month later on 13th April, Arthur was back in the England side in the memorable 39-13 Grand Slam win against the French, the game where Ronnie Poulton scored four of England's nine tries. A second Grand Slam had been completed but, unknown to him, Arthur's international rugby career was over.

On the outbreak of war, Arthur as a serving officer with *HMS Lion* and, later, *HMS Vindictive*, was involved from the start. Indeed, he saw action immediately at Heligoland Bight in 1914 and Dogger

Bank a year later. At the infamous Battle of Jutland in September1916, Arthur was mentioned in dispatches and a month later he was promoted to the rank of Lieutenant Commander. However it was during the action at Zeebrugge that Arthur was awarded the highest honour of all. The Zeebrugge Raid was originally proposed by Sir John Jellicoe but was not officially approved until February 1918, when Sir Roger Keyes created a plan that would block the port of Zeebrugge and the Bruges canal preventing the Germans to using the port for their submarines, which had been causing immense problems to Allied shipping, particularly in the English Channel.

The raid began on the night of 22nd/23rd April 1018, and was led by *HMS Vindictive*. The plan was to scuttle three ships, *Thetis, Intrepid* and *Iphigenia*, in the port thereby creating the block. Meanwhile, the Allies created a diversionary attack involving 70 vessels and 1,700 men, with Arthur in immediate charge of the raiding party leading an attack against the enemy in an attempt to keep the diversion going. The raid started badly. Unexpected winds meant that a planned smoke screen was ineffective and, under heavy fire, the *Vindictive* was forced to moor in the wrong position, depriving the raiding parties of their artillery support. Arthur, hit by a shell fragment, was knocked unconscious and had his jaw broken before he had even disembarked. Nevertheless, when he regained consciousness he proceeded to lead his men ashore. Despite his injuries, Arthur pressed forward, leading his men despite the obvious dangers and inevitable losses. A total of 240 British seamen were killed and every other member of the party received some form of injury. Arthur, in great pain but showing resolution and courage of the highest order, led his men in an attempt to attack the guns on the 'Mole Head', realising that for the plan to succeed the enemy machine guns had to be silenced without delay. He was killed at the head of his men. His body was never found.

The attack was proclaimed as a success by the Allies. The *Thetis, Intrepid* and *Iphigenia* were scuttled, but not exactly where planned and this limited the effectiveness of the plan. However the raid had trapped 30 German U boats and dozens of destroyers and the action prevented Bruges being used as a submarine base for the rest of the war. Quite properly the Zeebrugge Memorial in West-Vlaanderen, Belgium records the bravery of the officers and their sacrifice.

TO THE GLORY OF GOD AND IN MEMORY OF
THESE THREE OFFICERS AND ONE MECHANIC
OF THE ROYAL NAVY WHO FELL ON THE MOLE
AT ZEEBRUGGE ON ST GEORGE'S DAY 1918 AND
HAVE NO KNOWN GRAVE

WING COMMANDER BROCK FA OBE
LIEUTENANT COMMANDER HARRISON AL VC
LIEUTENANT HAWKINS CEV
MECHANIC SECOND CLASS F/50269 ROUSE J

Arthur was awarded his VC posthumously, one of eight given to those participating in the Zeebrugge Raid soon afterwards, and a limestone and granite monument paid for by the Torbay branch of the Royal Naval Association was erected in Paignton. Arthur's VC is now on display at the Britannia Royal Naval College, Dartmouth where his naval career had begun, a permanent reminder of the great sacrifice made by this often overlooked yet most courageous of men.

Our final VC was another rugby player named Harrison, but this recipient was Jack Harrison and played the professional game of Rugby League rather than the strictly amateur Rugby Union. Jack was born on 12th November 1890 in Hull, the son of a plater and boilermaker employed in Earle's Shipyard. It was a tough, rather austere background in which young Jack soon learned how to look after himself. His parents, however, were ambitious for their son and were prepared to make sacrifices for him, and in 1910 Jack was accepted at St John's College, York where he enrolled on a Teacher Training course. On gaining his teaching qualification, Jack found employment in a York school before moving to Lime Street School in Hull. This move fitted in perfectly with his plans for Jack was, by now, also a professional Rugby League player with Hull, an established club and a founding member of the Rugby League Northern Union when it broke free from the Rugby Football Union. Jack had moved to the club 1912 after playing five games for York, and soon proved to be an outstanding winger with the ability to 'finish off' a try scoring movement. Playing outside the famous centre and record signing Billy Batten, the five foot eight inch tall winger scored 52 tries in season 1913/14, still a club record. An excellent team player, he finished with a career record of 106 tries in 116 appearances by 1916 which included six tries in one match against Wakefield, a record which stood until 1968. The highlight of Jack's club career came in 1914 in the Challenge Cup Final against Wakefield. Played at Halifax and won 6-0 by Hull, Jack scored one of the two tries that clinched the Cup. International honours must surely follow and, in 1914, Jack was selected to tour Australia with the British team.

Domestically too, Jack's life appeared to be going well. In September 1912, shortly after moving to Hull, he had met Lillian. Two years later, on the 1st September 1914, they were married. However, by now war had been declared and life was about to change for the young newly weds. The tour to Australia was cancelled and, although a son, Jackie, was born the following year, with the war by now well underway, Jack volunteered for the army. He began his training on 4th November 1915 but still found time to play some rugby for Hull. This wasn't to last and by August 1916, he had been commissioned as a probationary temporary Second Lieutenant in the East Yorks Regiment. This promotion meant that he now had no time for rugby, although he did see something of his many friends and colleagues. Hull had responded well to the 'call to arms' and the many volunteers were quickly organised into groups relating to their jobs or professions, 'commercials', 'tradesmen' and other more mixed groups. Jack joined the 11th Battalion and was stationed in the Somme area, a part of the Western Front that was experiencing the loss of 300 men on a daily basis. In February 1917, it was Jack's turn to experience the horrors of the front line.

It didn't take Jack long to make his mark. On 25th March, he led a patrol into No Man's Land where the *London Gazette* cited that he "handled his platoon with great courage and skill, reached his objective under the most trying conditions, and captured a prisoner. He set a splendid example throughout." Jack's reward for this action was to be awarded the Military Cross. Six weeks later, on the night of 2nd/3rd May, he went one better. Finding himself pinned down by machine gun fire in the German held area around the village of Oppy, well fortified by barbed wire, enemy machine guns and trench mortars and under a clear sky and full moon, Jack and his men faced a grave problem. Despite the darkness and smoke from the enemy barrage Jack addressed it by leading his men in an attack on the enemy trench. Under heavy rifle and machine gun fire they were forced to retreat. After regrouping in No Man's Land, Jack led his men in a counter attack under terrific fire but, on failing to silence the German guns, Jack single-handedly made a dash for the enemy machine gun hoping to knock it out and save the lives of his men. Using all his rugby skills of speed and sidestep, armed with just grenade and pistol, Jack finally silenced the machine gun. He was last seen throwing a grenade, silhouetted by flares. The Red Cross tried to establish if Jack had been captured and there was an anxious wait for Lillian as men were asked if they knew what had happened. In the meantime Lillian was told that Jack had been awarded the VC for "most conspicuous bravery and self sacrifice in attack." On the 13th December she was finally told by the War Council that his death must now be accepted, the end of a long, ultimately futile wait. She was not alone in her suffering. The 11th East Yorks War Diary records that on the day that Jack died eight officers went missing and four were wounded. Within the other ranks nine more were killed, ninety-eight missing and one hundred and fifty wounded.

Jack was not the only Rugby League VC from the Great War but he is the best remembered and the most tragic. Thomas Byron, a thirty-five year old Lance Corporal in the Northumberland Fusiliers, had also silenced a machine gun which was inflicting carnage, this time near Arras. Byron, who had played for Castleford, survived to receive his VC from King George V in front of a crowd of 40,000 at St James Park, Newcastle. He died in 1945. Thomas Steel was a Sergeant in the 1st Battalion of Seaforth Highlanders and won his VC in Mesopotamia when, reacting to a counter attack he and a comrade carried a machine gun into position and kept it in action to keep the line intact. Although wounded eleven times in the war, Steel returned to England and even continued his rugby career playing for Broughton Rangers, one of the founder members of the league and his local club, Healey Street. Jack's VC was presented to a very proud Lillian at Buckingham Palace in March 1918 and a fund was raised in Hull which served to pay for young Jackie's education. The tragedy of the Harrison family, however, was not yet over. Jackie, a captain in the West Riding Regiment, was killed on 1st June 1940 defending Dunkirk and is buried in Dunkirk Town Cemetery.

Hull has not forgotten the sacrifice made by Jack Harrison VC. In 2002 Hull fans set up the Jack Harrison Memorial Trust and a memorial was unveiled at the ground in May 2012. The Jack Harrison Memorial Medal has been introduced and awarded to youngsters who overcome adversity in order to play the game that Jack loved so much. An annual Inter Services Rugby League tournament has also been introduced with the winners receiving the Jack Harrison VC Memorial Trophy. Lillian meanwhile made arrangements that on her death Jack's medals, including the VC, would reside in the Regimental Museum at York. Perhaps nobody typifies so clearly the sacrifices made by families in the twentieth century better than Lillian Harrison. Losing the two most important men her life to two World Wars she paid the ultimate price in a century of turmoil and can stand as representative of the millions of losses suffered by families throughout Britain and its Empire. She died in 1977.

Boxers and Other Forgotten Heroes

Research into the deaths of sportsmen killed in the Great War will never be exhausted and there will always be stories left to discover. Boxing may be considered more a minor sport today but had a different status in 1914. Often brutal, yet hugely popular, in the early years of the twentieth century boxing was seen as a way out of the grim hardship of life in industrial Britain. The country was widely aware of the careers of Britain's boxers in a depth now rare. Although today's very top boxers, those that fight for world titles like Amir Kahn, Ricky Hatton and Joe Calzaghe are household names, very few members of the public could name regional champions or even those with national titles. This was not the case in 1914 when such men were local heroes, even more so when they went to war. Twenty-three members of the London Adelphi club joined up and by March 1915 seven were dead. It is thought that at this point thirty-three well known Welsh boxers had joined the conflict. Harris and Whippy tell us that no less than ten boxers, replicated their bravery in the ring on the battlefields of the Western Front, and were awarded the Victoria Cross. The vast majority of these hitherto acclaimed boxers have long become forgotten sporting heroes.

When Kitchener's army first saw action in 1916, the boxing fraternity was to the fore. One of the best known British boxers to lose his life was twenty-five year old British, Empire and World welterweight champion Tom McCormick. An Irishman based in Liverpool and a veteran of world title fights that lasted for up to twenty rounds, Tom was one of the first boxers to join up in 1914 but lost his life, like so many others, at Fricourt on the Somme battlefield on July 6th 1916. Five days earlier, on July 1st, in the same sector of the battlefield another boxer, Sergeant Harry Littlewood of the King's Own Yorkshire Light Infantry met his death. Harry from Wakefield was the nine stone 1913 'Pitman' champion, a tournament contested by boxers employed underground. The twenty-four year old, described by the *Sporting Chronicle* as "one of the most gentlemanly fellows who ever entered the ring", is buried at La Boisselle.

The loss of Tom McCormick who was from Dundalk, now part of the Republic of Ireland, reminds us of the sacrifices made by the Irish in the Great War. One was Allan Porter, who although born in Salford, fought for the Royal Irish Fusiliers due to his Irish extraction. A featherweight of some repute, although never a national champion, Allan fought approximately twenty bouts each year, some of which were the most brutal of fights. In his last fight against George Mackness he was hit twice while in a state of collapse. Mackness was charged with GBH and Allan, unconscious, spent over a week in hospital. On the 20th November 1917, Allan went over the top at Bullecourt in an attack that was a feint for the main push due to take place at Cambrai. In the resulting struggle Allan was killed, his body never found. His name took its place as one of the 34,715 names on the Arras Memorial for those Allied soldiers with no known grave. Not that Irish sacrifices were confined to the Western Front. The popular featherweight southpaw, Bob Darley was an exceptional Army champion. He died in Baghdad while taking part in an expedition to the Persian Gulf on 27th October 1916, three years to the day after his last fight. Boxers with an Ulster background also made the supreme sacrifice. English welterweight champion Charlie Allum was born in Notting Hill but became a Sergeant in the 13th Battalion of the Royal Inniskilling Fusiliers. A veteran of the Second Boer War where he was decorated numerous times, Charlie was awarded the Military Medal posthumously after being killed 21st July 1918 at Ploegsteert, Belgium. His body was never found and he was last seen fighting the enemy with his bare fists.

Away from the Irish theme, the ex-British flyweight world champion, Bill Ladbury was a boxer whose name is to be found on the Menin Gate following his death at Ypres on 27th June 1917. Only five foot two inches in height Bill, from the boxing breeding ground of New Cross, south London, had lost his World, European and British titles to the Welshman Percy Jones. Percy, the first Welshman to win a World boxing title and a forerunner to future early twentieth century Welsh heroes Freddie Welch, Jim O'Driscoll and Jimmy Wilde, also met an untimely death. A Sergeant in the Royal Welsh Fusiliers, he suffered serious leg injuries which, in the end, thirty operations could not save. Amputation was not his only misfortune. Percy had also been poisoned by gas and suffered from trench fever. He died, another victim of the Great War, on Christmas Day 1922, one day short of his 30th birthday.

The loss of these boxers reminds us of the range of sports affected by the Great War, that it wasn't just the headline-grabbing sports like cricket, rugby and football that paid the price. And there were many sportsmen who never fulfilled their potential, young men possibly on the cusp of greatness or at least on the way to a successful career. With so many dying young, before they were able to show the full extent of their talent, it is impossible to gauge accurately what was lost. In rugby and football this is particularly true as young men develop physically until their early twenties so it is not always possible to predict the future accurately. Many of us have seen the outstanding schoolboy who never made it into the local club's first XV or the much sought after football apprentice who in the end never played professional football. On the other hand, late developers are not uncommon and great rugby players and footballers can appear in their early twenties as if out of nowhere. Predicting the future in sport, like in anything else, is a hazardous occupation. However cricket, with its high profile school and university matches played in front of big crowds, on first class wickets and reported in the national press, can give us indicators as to the quality of the talent lost in the most costly of wars.

One schoolboy cricketer of note had already been lost to the sport well before the war that was to take his life began. Arthur Edward Jeune Collins was a short and stockily built pupil at Clifton College, Bristol when, in a House match, he made the highest score ever recorded. A rather messy, possibly inaccurate scorecard, records that in the summer of 1899 the fair haired, rather pale thirteen year old scored 628 undefeated runs in six hours twenty minutes spread over four afternoons out of a total of 836. His team, Clarke's House, won by an innings and 688 runs and the game gave young Arthur, who also took eleven wickets, a form of immortality. It did not, however, lead to a career on the cricket field. Tim Rice tells us, in an article written in the *Daily Telegraph* to celebrate the centenary of his history-making innings, that he was too reckless a batsman to make a successful career in the first class game so he turned to the army After training at the Royal Military Academy, Woolwich, Arthur joined the Royal Engineers and by 1907 he was a twenty-two year old Lieutenant. On 11th November 1914, with exactly four years of war still to fight, Arthur, by now a captain, was killed at the first Ypres. He left a wife, Ethel, who lived a further fifty years, and a younger brother, Herbert, who was killed near Boulogne in February 1917.

It is with those who would probably have made their way in cricket that that this chapter is concerned. In the introduction to this book mention was made of the outstanding Repton schoolboy, John Howell and there can be no argument that he be considered when discussing the loss of sporting potential on the Western Front. John was born in Esher, Surrey on 5th July 1895. By 1911 he was in the school XI and before he left in 1914 John had made two double hundreds for the school, a rare achievement indeed. With a future at Oxford University assured John had a trial for his home county and impressed with a confident century. Styled on the Surrey legendary opening batsman, Tom Hayward, John was, during the two summers before war broke out, the best schoolboy batsman in England. In his last two years at Repton he averaged 56 and 52 and also made his debut for the Surrey 2nd XI. *Wisden* reviewed his progress:

> As a batsman, and in cricket knowledge, he is as matured as was Knight in 1913, and his performances in the matches at Lord's, and in school matches show that he was as a whole very dependable, and not in the least perturbed by a crisis. Defence and back play are his strongest points, but though he is a little dull at times, he can score in a good many ways, and he is a very hard man indeed to get out... given the opportunity there is no doubt that as a sound and run-getting batsman he must surely take a high place in first class cricket.

Among his contemporaries John probably had the temperament best suited to becoming an outstanding success at Test level but, with the outbreak of war, Oxford and cricket were put aside and John joined the 9th Battalion of the King's Royal Rifle Corps as a Second Lieutenant. He was killed on 25th September 1915 at Ypres, his young body never found and his name inscribed amongst the thousands on the Menin Gate.

If John Howell had a rival among the many talented public schoolboys in 1914 then it was probably George Whitehead. George William Edendale Whitehead, born on 27th August 1895, just fifty-three days after John, possessed a potential for cricketing glory which was nearly as great. He was born in Bromley, the son of Sir George Hugh Whitehead and, like Arthur Collins before him, attended Clifton College in Bristol where he soon made his mark as an extremely talented cricketer. His four years in the school team resulted in a regular average of forty or more and he once scored an undefeated 259 against Liverpool. He was also a useful leg break bowler who captained the team in his last two years. George had trials for Kent and, unlike John, made his debut in the first class game, playing twice without success for Kent as part of a trial in the summer of 1914. He also played at Lord's on three occasions when he represented the Public Schools against the MCC. With the outbreak of war, George joined the RFA and saw action in the Battle of Loos and the Somme. He was twice invalided from active service but in 1917, by now a Lieutenant, George was able to transfer to the RAF. On 17th October 1918, nearly at the end of a war in which he had served more or less throughout, he and a colleague were shot down by German machine guns when flying over Lauwe. They had been repeatedly saluted by the town's inhabitants before being wounded by German bullets fired from just outside the town. The plane crashed and both men were killed. They were buried in Harlebeke New British Cemetery the following day. The reaction to George's death was understandably one of shock and the realisation of what had been lost. According to the 'Old Cliftonian', George himself did not know his full worth, such was his modesty. He supplied the following tribute to *Wisden*,

> George Whitehead was a perfect flower of the public schools. He was not limited to athletics only, great though he was in this respect. Intellectually he was far above the average, and was as happy with a good book as when he was scoring centuries. His ideals were singularly high and though gentle and broad minded, he always stood uncompromisingly for all that was clean. So modest was he that strangers sometimes failed to realise his worth. He insisted on being transferred to The Royal Air Force from the RFA, fully

> appreciating the risks, because he knew of his country's then urgent need of airmen and so he died, greatly patriotic. Clifton has lost more than 500 of her sons in the war. She is proud of every one of them, but none more than of this very perfect gentleman.

The family's suffering was not yet over. On 13th March 1919 George's older brother James, a Second Lieutenant in the 9th Battalion Queen's Own (Royal West Kent) Regiment died of his injuries. James, another useful cricketer who had represented Kent, was buried in the family vault at Wilmington, St Michael's Churchyard in Dartford.

Although there is less evidence of his potential to succeed in first class cricket, mention should be made of George Futvoye Marsden-Smedley, captain of the Harrow XI in 1915. The second son of John, a prominent knitwear manufacturer, and Gertrude Mary, George was born in Matlock, Derbyshire in 1897. Despite getting 'a pair' when batting for his school against rivals Eton in 1914, the following year he was made captain. George was also captain of the football team and Martin Middlebrook has described him as "probably the most outstanding sportsman of his generation". Although there are other contenders for this title it is clear that George was a rare talent and had the ability to make his mark in a variety of sports. However, with the war showing no sign of ending quickly, George joined the 3rd Battalion, Rifle Brigade at the first opportunity and was commissioned as a Second Lieutenant. By July 1916 the nineteen year old, who less than a year earlier had been leading a team of schoolboys on the playing field, was now commanding men in one of the most notorious battles in British military history, the Somme. George was to spend only twenty-five days on the front line.

The first, and last, action that George experienced was the Allied attack on Guillemont. On 17th August, on the eve of his first action, young George wrote thanking his parents for his new identity disc explaining that "it makes such a difference having a nice chain around one's neck instead of a dirty old bit of string…". The following day, seven weeks into the battle, dawn broke to reveal a wet, overcast day very different from the conditions of July 1st. Lyn MacDonald quotes the account of one of George's fellow officers in the Rifle Brigade describing the events of that day. Acting Lance Corporal Gale wrote,

> It was the waiting to go over that was the worst because we didn't go over until almost three o'clock in the afternoon.... During the morning the Sergeant came round with the old rum jar and gave us a dessert spoonful of rum just to put Dutch courage in us. It was strong that Army rum, and I think he had two or three spoonfuls to our one – or more!

One can only try to imagine how George must have been feeling at this point. It is unlikely that his experience of drinking rum was very extensive but perhaps it did help. Gale continued,

> We really needed that rum, waiting to go over the top.... you can't describe the feeling! You can't describe the noise! A couple of our own chaps were killed. One fellow had the top of his head took off with one of our own shells. His brains were all over the place.

The attack resulted in devastating losses and Gale goes on to describe what George must have seen.

> Five minutes after we went over the top we were finished! The German machine guns went through our lines just like a mow goes through a field of corn. I don't think we got two hundred yards before we were so mucked up that we just had to lay out in No Man's Land."

It appears that George did get further than most. He charged a machine gun which was holding up the attack near Guillemont Station, shooting one German and becoming involved in hand to hand fighting before being shot himself and falling on the parapet of the German trench. His new identity disc was of no help. George's body was never found.

Back home his family were devastated. At the end of the war memorials to his sacrifice appeared wherever George had a connection. A stained glass window was installed in his local church, Lea

Church, in 1919 and on his father's estate a new wood was planted to be known as 'Mr George's Wood'. Even today a memorial can still be found at the bus shelter at the bottom of the hill leading down from the village war memorial. At Harrow, scene of many of his cricketing triumphs, a memorial seat took its place on the school cricket ground with the appropriate inscription, "To love the game beyond the prize". But none of this could compensate his father for the lack of a body and named headstone. After much unsuccessful searching for his son's body, John Marsden-Smedley purchased the land where it was thought George died and fenced it off. He then arranged for a monument to be built on this land, the site of the German front line trench that George had so bravely attacked. This monument remains, protected by a brick wall and an iron gate. Inside the inscription, after giving details of his death, reads,

LIVELY AND PLEASANT IN LIFE
IN DEATH SERENE AND UNAFRAID
MOST BLESSED IN REMEMBRANCE

Both parents and George's five siblings survived into old age and the memorial was successfully maintained but by 1990 it was in need of repair. The family, supported by the Western Front Association, ensured this was carried out and on 19th July 1997, a century after George was born, a re-dedication service took place attended by thirty members of the family and numerous local dignitaries. The wish that George Marsden-Smedley never be forgotten remains intact.

Such losses were not confined to the cricket grounds of the English public schools. In February 1915, on the other side of the world in Australia, a young eighteen-year old cricketer was making his first class debut for New South Wales at Sydney Cricket Ground. Norman Callaway came into the match with rave reviews and high expectations following success in Sydney Grade Cricket. He came to the wicket after Queensland had reduced their opponents to a worrying 17-3 but on joining Charles Macartney, an established test batsman, the pair proceeded to rectify the situation. By the end of the day Norman had scored 125 in 130 minutes and the following day, after losing his partner for 103, went on to reach 207 before he was out. New South Wales won by an innings and 231 runs and the newspapers raved about Norman's debut. Although admitting that he was not yet a stylist, they wrote of his temperament, his stroke play on what was a slow outfield, his judgement and his crisp driving. The *Sydney Morning Herald* was very confident of a bright future and predicted that "he certainly should rise to great heights, all going well with him."

All did not go well with him. Remarkably, this was the only first class innings that Norman Callaway ever played. After joining the 19th Battalion of the Australian Imperial Force, Norman was posted as missing in action at the Second Battle of Bullecourt on 3rd May 1917. He was twenty-one. Norman remains the only cricketer to have scored a double century in his only innings in first class cricket and the records still show him as having a first class batting average of 207. How good a player Norman might have become remains one of the great 'what ifs' of sporting history.

CONCLUSION

The guns ceased firing at the eleventh hour on the eleventh day of the eleventh month 1918. During the first six months of 1919 world statesmen and politicians sat down in Paris to draw up the Peace Treaties and placed the blame for the war squarely on German shoulders. Empires were dismantled (and in some cases expanded), borders were redrawn and a new League of Nations was born. Europe saw the creation of new countries and the return of others not acknowledged for centuries, while the map of the Near and Middle East was redrawn in a way that reverberates in world politics to this day. The United States took its place as the world's most powerful nation only to retreat into isolationism, leaving a much weakened Britain and France to keep world order and a humiliated Germany in check. Dark economic clouds loomed on the horizon which would engulf the world in a financial crisis and, within a decade, result in the Great Depression. This had not been 'the war to end all wars' but the beginning of nearly a century of warfare which did not end until the coming down of the Berlin Wall and the demise of the Soviet Communist Block in 1989. The world, perhaps, has never really recovered. It certainly was never the same again.

But what of peace-time sport? How easy was it for players and supporters to return to the pre-war world in which sport was establishing itself as a central part of people's recreation and leisure time? There was certainly no time for people to indulge in a mass display of grief for the loss of so many sporting icons. Today we are constantly reminded, quite properly, of the dreadful tragedy of the Munich air crash of February 1958 in which eight Manchester United players, together with fifteen other passengers, were killed. Over twenty-five years after the Hillsborough disaster of April 1989 we remember the horrific scenes from our TV screens and the loss of ninety-six supporters who had set out to enjoy a football match that afternoon. Families, friends and supporters are still encouraged to grieve for those lost in these and other sporting tragedies. In 1919 there was no formal national recognition for what had been lost to sport. How could there be when families were grieving for husbands, fathers and brothers on a scale never seen before? The huge extent of the losses meant that the average supporter did not have either the time or the emotional capacity to grieve for the death of the local team's centre forward or promising opening batsman. To give context to the scale of loss it is helpful to remember that the number of British soldiers killed in the war in Afghanistan between 2001 and April 2014 stands at 453, each much loved and missed by their families. The average number of British soldiers, excluding those from the colonies, killed on each day of the four and a half years of fighting is 449. That scale of the loss is almost impossible to contemplate.

However, life had to return to something approaching normality and sport soon re-established itself as the most popular of pastimes. Cricket was first to find its feet and in May 1919, even before the signing of the Treaty of Versailles, Patrick Rucker of Oxford University bowled to Dick Twining of The Gentleman of England on his home ground, The Parks. Both had been affected by the war: Rucker, too young to fight himself, lost his brother at Amiens three weeks before the Armistice, and Twining suffered such horrendous leg injuries that it was a miracle that he was batting at all. With the irony reported from time to time in this book, it is sad to report that although Patrick Rucker escaped one war, he did not miss the next. He was killed at Amiens just as his brother had been over twenty years earlier. The seriously wounded, permanently lame Dick Twining became president of the MCC and lived until his ninetieth year.

For many it must have seemed like normal service had resumed but some things had definitely changed. Remarkably the counties had survived the financial difficulties that resulted from the loss of regular revenue over four summers. Worcestershire in particular had only survived as a result of the sixteen first class counties helping one another out during these difficult years. Nevertheless on the playing field things were different. The war had not destroyed the amateur player but their golden age was over. The days of patronage were numbered and the place of the amateur on the field of play grew more uncertain with each passing year although it was many years before Len Hutton became the first professional player to captain England. The era of country-house cricket was also ending. Patrons such as Sir Julian Cahn and H.M. Martineau still existed but they were typical of an earlier generation rather than their own. Their country-house gatherings were replaced by serious weekend club cricket and Sunday cricket, although this was not accorded first class status.

Some players, of course, did not return as they had left. One of the biggest losses was that of Frank Chester, the Worcestershire all-rounder described by *Wisden* as the best prospect since W.G. Grace after scoring three centuries in 1914. Frank Chester lost an arm in the war but went on to become one of, if not the, greatest cricket umpires. Frank Foster, bowling partner to S.G. Barnes before the war, went lame following a motor cycle accident at the Front and never played again although his ideas were inspirational to those responsible for cricket's biggest controversy: 'bodyline' bowling. When keen cricket followers think of the 'bodyline' tour of 1932/33 the image is often that of Harold Larwood felling the Australian wicketkeeper Bertie Oldfield at Adelaide with a ball that struck him on the side of the head, a delivery that might have killed his popular helmetless opponent. What is not well known is that inside Oldfield's head was a metal plate, his own particular souvenir of the Great War. Serving as a stretcher-bearer he was one of four men involved in the attempted recovery of an injured soldier at Polygon Wood in September 1917. Coming under enemy fire the soldier and the other stretcher bearers were all killed in the rescue attempt and Oldfield was lucky to survive, being half buried and semi-conscious when he was found.

Some players, five years older, remained intact. Hobbs, Woolley and Mead continued to be England's best batsmen while Barnes, although no longer picked at test level, was still England's best bowler. And there was always Rhodes who, after twenty years, still had another decade of cricket left in him. The Leicestershire cricketer A.T. Sharp survived. Sharp appeared in the Introduction to this book when on August 4th 1914 he returned to his regiment in the middle of a game. Now a solicitor, he played for Leicestershire as an amateur until 1934 becoming captain in 1921. Sharp even played in a few matches during the Second World War when he was over fifty years old. He died aged 83 in 1973 following a car accident.

The remarkable story of another survivor has been discovered by the ex-Prime Minister John Major. A.C.G. Luther of Sussex was wounded at the Battle of Le Cateau and lay motionless as German soldiers approached. Major Luther was only too well aware that many of the wounded were shot by the enemy as they lay. His watch and his wallet were removed before a voice spoke to Luther in perfect English. "You are a very lucky man. I see you are a member of MCC. You can go back to your lines." The Germans have never been renowned for their love or understanding of cricket but this particular German soldier had been a landowner in Derbyshire where he had played the game before the war. Luther did return to his lines, became Secretary of Berkshire C.C. and, later, assistant-secretary at the Oval. He lived until he was 80.

Crowds flocked back to the grounds to see their heroes in County Championship cricket, now played over two days but with play continuing until 7.30 in the evening. This wasn't popular with the players. Hobbs said that when play was finished it was too late to go anywhere while *Wisden* commented that by the evening the "craving for food was greater than the passion for cricket." Youngsters were still keen to play the game and in the public schools those lost, like Howell, Whitehead and Marsden-Smedley, although still very much remembered, were replaced as schoolboy cricketers. In 1919, the future England captain Douglas Jardine and the great cricket writer Raymond Robertson-Glasgow were dismissing one another in the match between Winchester and Charterhouse. At the same time, Walter Hammond was winning his place in the Cirencester Grammar School XI and Harold Larwood, fifteen years old, bowled for the Nuneaton 2nd XI in his sandshoes following completion of his nightshift down a Nottinghamshire coalmine. In the first class game, despite the loss of Major Booth and Alonzo Drake, Yorkshire dominated. The ten professionals, captained by the one obligatory amateur, won five titles between the years 1919-1929 and did not finish lower than fourth place in the other seasons. Lancashire (3) and Middlesex (2) won the other five titles. English test cricket, however, took longer to get back on its feet as defeats to Australia, 5-0 in 1920/21, and 3-0 at home the following summer indicate. Nevertheless, the fabric of cricket was gradually being rewoven.

Football took time to move forward after the war as many clubs needed to reorganise and restructure following the turmoil of the previous four years. It was suggested that a modified form of the FA Cup be introduced in 1918/19 but the clubs resisted and proper competition did not get underway until the following season. Two of the pre-war giants quickly re-established themselves with West Bromwich Albion winning the League and Midland rivals, Aston Villa, the FA Cup in 1919/20. But the post-war years belonged to one of the greatest ever football managers, Herbert Chapman. Walter Tull, Jimmy Speirs, Evelyn Lintott and Donald Bell had all benefitted from the great man's revolutionary methods before the war. Unfashionable Huddersfield, Chapman's first post-war club, became the first team to win three consecutive first division titles, although Chapman had already left for Arsenal by the time the third was won in 1926. He then went on to build an Arsenal team that would repeat the feat between 1932/3 and 1934/5, although he died after a heart attack on the eve of winning the second title. It is worth remembering that only Liverpool and Manchester United (twice) have managed to repeat the achievement of Chapman's teams. Some things didn't change, however, and the stench of illegal payments and financial irregularity remained. Leeds City, where ironically Chapman was manager, was expelled from the League for making illegal payments during the war to 'guest' players. Their squads were put up for auction and Chapman, rather fortunately, moved on to Huddersfield. Leeds City later re-emerged as Leeds United. In Scotland Rangers broke Celtic's dominance winning fifteen of the twenty championships between the wars, while Hearts, devastated by their war casualties, slipped down the table and were nearly relegated in 1922. Crowds, however, flocked to the games both in England and Scotland.

Indications that football was becoming the national sport had been present during the war. In 1914, Helen Franklin was the twenty-two year old daughter of a well known Anglo-Jewish banking family who quickly joined the Voluntary Aid Detachment, an organisation providing medical assistance in time of war. On becoming a VAD nurse, Helen discovered "a most interesting set of men at the hospital". On writing to a friend, Helen disclosed that the men took little interest in the war and that, when newspapers were brought to them, all they wanted to read was football. "Football," Helen wrote, "is the common bond among them, from whatever part of

Great Britain." By the end of the war there was no question as to which sport was number one with spectators.

Rugby Union stuttered back into life in the 1918/19 season with an Inter-Services tournament for the King George V Trophy between British and Dominion teams. However, old prejudices soon resurfaced. During the war the lines between the amateur and professional codes had become blurred but once normality returned the debate was revived. Professional Rugby League players had played with amateur clubs during the war and the Welsh Rugby Union was in favour of professional players being reinstated in the union code if they had served in the war. England, Scotland and Ireland were having none of it. The divisions between the amateur and professionals continued until very nearly the end of the century. Wales, in particular, lost many of its best players to Rugby League, particularly when unemployment in the heavy industrial towns and villages began to bite. In 1922/3 between forty and fifty of Wales best players were playing 'up north'. The result was a clear shift in the balance of power. England, strong before the war under the captaincy of Ronnie Poulton, now entered a golden era first under W.J.A. Davies and then Wavell Wakefield. Four Grand Slams were won in the 1920s while Wales had its worst decade until the 1990s. Rugby Union, though, never forgot the sacrifice made by those who had fought and died in the Great War. Wales in particular liked to remember their dead. Throughout the 1920s officials and players of the WRU visited the cenotaph in Whitehall on the Sunday morning following the England v Wales international at Twickenham. On the occasion of the first visit of the team to Paris since the war the WRU presented a wreath which was laid on the ground in front of the main stand before kick off. Before the game in 1926 supporters of both Wales and France sang together, with 'It's A Long Way to Tipperary' being particularly moving. Thomas Cook and Son regularly took supporters to the battlefields as part of the international trip to Paris.

Those players and supporters who remained after the great cataclysm had much to deal with as they struggled to adapt to the new peace. We are reminded of Major Booth's sister lighting a candle in his bedroom every night for forty years as she waited in vain for his return, of the widow of Jack Harrison VC struggling to bring up a son only to lose him in the next war, and of the efforts of

John Marsden-Smedley to find his son's body before commissioning a moving monument to his lost boy. And of the grief suffered by the mothers of Basil Maclear and Eddie Latheron, each of whom lost three sons in the war, as did the Gallaher family in New Zealand. Those left behind learned the meaning of suffering. Tragically, twenty years later the experience was to be repeated, although lessons had been learned. The FA announced the suspension of all football under its jurisdiction from the outbreak of war in September 1939 and Rugby Union and League followed suit. The cricket season remained unfinished and the West Indian tourists returned home with seven matches unplayed. Ironically the last game of cricket played before the outbreak of the Second World War was Sussex v Yorkshire at Hove, the very same fixture on the very same ground where cricket ground to a halt twenty-five years earlier. On this occasion, sport was not going to endure the criticisms of 1914. Besides, there was no expectation in September 1939 that the war would be over by Christmas. In the event the authorities used many of sport's biggest stars to work as physical training instructors charged with improving fitness and raising morale on a larger scale than in 1914. The contribution of Len Hutton, Denis Compton, Raich Carter, Stanley Matthews and Joe Mercer spring to mind. Not for them the sacrifice of Colin Blythe, David Bedell-Sivright and Tony Wilding, although some sports stars of the 1930s did make the ultimate sacrifice.

In conclusion what can we say about those players who gave their lives in the Great War? Were they, as is so often said, part of a remarkable generation? Would the sports stars of today, pampered and rich beyond fans wildest dreams, be prepared to make the same sacrifices? Possibly not but, if one had needed to endure the same experience of 'going over the top', I would have been comforted to have the likes of John Terry, Wayne Rooney and Steven Gerrard alongside me. I am confident that Alistair Cook and Tim Henman would have made fine young officers and that Brian O'Driscoll and Sam Warburton would have provided inspirational leadership. Perhaps we are too hard on today's youth. Fortunately today's young sportsmen and women are not faced with the situation that their predecessors confronted. There was nothing hypothetical about their choices. Some made their decision to fight quickly and without any hesitation. Others, often faced with family and professional pressures, took longer to commit to the cause, although the speed at which our sportsmen enlisted is an impressive feature of their stories. What cannot be in doubt is that the study of our lost sportsmen confirms that they were to a man brave, loyal and self-sacrificing. Without question they buckled down and did what was expected of them in a cause in which they believed and for a country they loved. Their service has earned our everlasting gratitude and respect. At the very least they deserve to be remembered.

Acknowledgements

That this book exists at all is due to the support and friendship of a number of people to whom I owe a debt of thanks. My first task is to thank Seren, Mick Felton in particular, for showing faith in this project and ensuring that it sees the light of day. With the arrival of the centenary commemorations and the predictable appearance of so many books addressing the many facets of The Great War, it would have been very easy for Seren to leave this competitive market to others rather than take a chance on a hitherto unpublished author. That they have supported me is something for which I will always be grateful.

Various libraries, museums and sports clubs have also been supportive. Unfortunately it has not always been possible to visit them in person but the wonder of modern technology has allowed me to overcome this problem. Particular thanks are due to Newport Library for access to back copies of the *South Wales Argus* and various secondary sources and to Cardiff City Library for allowing me access to *The Times* online. Libraries remain indispensable to historians – governments and local councils take note! The staff at Manchester United Museum did not disappoint this lifelong supporter, while thanks should also go to Celtic FC, Blackburn Rovers FC, Yorkshire CCC, Worcestershire CCC, Kent CCC and Newport RFC for the help and information that they provided. The websites of Bradford City FC and Heart of Midlothian FC have also proved vital to my research as has the site in memory of Jimmy Speirs set up by historian Andrew Pickles and the player's descendants.

Friends and colleagues, unbeknown to them, have also played a significant part in the writing of this book. Fellow members of the Gwent Branch of the Western Front Association have been inspirational in their enthusiasm for all things connected to The Great War while former colleagues at West Monmouth School have encouraged me through their posts via social media with promises to purchase copies. Now is the time to act! Particular thanks should go to one ex-colleague and friend, Beci Jennings, for proof reading sections of the book with typical thoroughness. A chance conversation in a Los Angeles airport led to Leon Vardon agreeing to carry out similar duties while my close friend of a mere fifty six years, Jeff Knock, offered suggestions and advice, in particular regarding the introductory chapters and those involving rugby players. I am grateful to all three for their efforts.

My greatest debt, however, is to my family. The biggest regret concerning the writing of this book is that my father, Len, did not live to see it. If he had then further marketing of the book would have been totally unnecessary, such was his enthusiasm and support for any task that I chose to undertake. Happily, my mother, Pam, has been able to give support and thanks are due to her for unstinting encouragement over many years. My children, Hannah and Tom, have lived with the idea of a 'retired' father and I am pleased that they can now see that my retirement has been productive. Their very existence is an inspiration and I hope that they, with their interest in sport and history, will enjoy reading this book. My greatest debt, however, is to my wife, Hilary. Not only was it Hilary who first took me to the Somme battlefields and subsequently encouraged my involvement in the WFA, but she has read the entire script twice, a task well above the call of duty. Her comments and suggestions are second only to the constant support that she has given me. This book is dedicated to her.

Bibliography

NEWSPAPERS

The Times 1900-1918

South Wales Argus 1900-1918

GENERAL SPORTSBOOKS

Mihir Bose: *The Spirit of the Game*, Constable 2011

Clive Harris & Julian Whippy: *The Greater Game,* Pen and Sword Books 2008

FOOTBALL

Patrick Barclay: *The Life and Times of Herbert Chapman*, Weidenfield and Nicholson 2014

Norman Barrett (ed): *Daily Telegraph Football Chronicle*, Carlton 1993;

Brian Belton: *Red Dawn: Manchester United In the Beginning*, Pennant Books 2009

Ian McCartney: *Old Trafford: 100 Years At The Theatre Of Dreams*, Empire Publications 2010

Chris Nawrat & Steve Hutchins: *Sunday Times Illustrated History of Football*, Hamlyn 1994

Peter Stead & Huw Richards: *For Club and Country: Welsh Football Greats*, University of Wales Press 2000

Phil Vasili: *Walter Tull, 1888-918 Officer, Footballer*, Raw Press 2010

Spencer Vignes: *Lost In France: The Remarkable Life and Death of Leigh Richmond Roose: Football's First Playboy*, Stadia 2007

RUGBY FOOTBALL

W.J. Collins: *Rugby Recollections*, RH Johns Publishers 1948

Stephen Cooper: *The Final Whistle: The Great War in Fifteen Players,* History Press 2012

J. Conner & M. Hannon: *Once Were Lions*, Harper Sport 2009

D. Fox, K .Bogler & M. Hoskins: *Century of All Blacks in Britain and Ireland* Tempus 2006

Philip J Grant: *Tommy Vile: A Giant of a Man*, Gomer Press 2010

John Griffiths: *Rugby's Strangest Matches* Robson Books 2000

Jenkins, Auty & Pierce: *Who's Who of Welsh International Rugby Players* Bridge Books 1991

Stephen Jones, Tom English, Nick Cain & David Barnes: *Behind the Lions*, Polaris Publishing Ltd. 2012

Steve Lewis: *Images of Sport, Newport Rugby Football Club 1874-1950*, Tempus 1999

Steve Lewis: *One Among Equals: England's Rugby Captains*, Vertical Edition 2008

Nigel McCrery: *Into Touch: Rugby Internationals Killed In the Great War* Pen and Sword 2014

David Parry Jones (ed): *Out of the Ruck: A Selection of Rugby Writing*, Pelham Books 1986

David Parry-Jones: *Prince Gwyn: Gwyn Nicholls and the First Golden Era of Welsh Rugby*, Seren Books 1999

Gwyn Prescott: *'Call Them to Remembrance': The Welsh rugby internationals who died in the Great War*, St David's Press 2014

Alan Roderick: *Newport Rugby Greats*, Handpost Books 1995

David Smith & Gareth Williams: *Fields of Praise: Official History of the Welsh Rugby Union 1881-1981*, University of Wales Press 1980

Clem Thomas & Greg Thomas: *125 Years of the British and Irish Lions*, Mainstream Publishing 2013

Gareth Williams: *1905 and All That*, Gomer Press 1991

CRICKET

Norman Barrett (ed): *Daily Telegraph Chronicle of Cricket*, Guinness Publishing 1994

Neville Cardus: *Cardus on Cricket*, Souvenir Press 1977

James P. Coldham: *FS Jackson: A Cricketing Biography*, Crowood Press 1989

Phil Edmunds: *100 Greatest Bowlers*, MacDonald, Queen Anne Press 1989

Bill Frindall: *English Test Cricketer*s, Willow Books 1989

Alan Gibson: *Jackson's Year*, Sportsman Book Club 1966

Benny Green (ed): *The Wisden Papers 1888-1946*, Guild Publishing 1989

Benny Green (ed): *Wisden Anthology*, Guild Publishing 1988

Benny Green (ed): *Wisden Book of Obituaries 1892-1985*, MacDonald Queen Anne Press 1986

Chris Harte: *A History of Australian Cricket*, Andre Deutsch 1993

Alan Hill: *Herbert Sutcliffe: Cricket Maestro*, Simon & Schuster1990

Harold Larwood: *The Larwood Story*, Sportsman Book Club 1965

John Major: *More Than a Game: The Story of Cricket's Early Years,* Harper Press 2007

Christopher Martin-Jenkins (ed): *A Cricketers Companion*, Leonard Books Ltd. 1990

Christopher Martin-Jenkins: *The Complete Who's Who of Test Cricketers*, Orbus Publishing 1980

George Plumptre: *The Golden Age of Cricket*, MacDonald, Queen Anne Press 1990
Clive W. Porter: *The Test Match Career of Sir Jack Hobbs*, Spellmount Ltd. 1988;
A.A. Thompson: Cricket: *The Great Captains*, Sportsman Book Club 1967
Anthony Woodhouse: *History of Yorkshire C.C.C.*, Christopher Helm 1989

WORLD WAR ONE
Max Arthur: *Forgotten Voices of the Great War*, Ebury Press 2002
Isobel Charman: *The Great War: The People's Story*, Random House Books 2014
Richard Van Emden: *Britain's Last Tommies*, Abacus 2006
A.H. Farrar-Hockley: *The Somme*, Pan Books Ltd. 1983
Gerald Glidden: *When the Barrage Lifts*,Glidden Books 1987
Peter Hart: *The Somme*, Cassell 2005
Philip Haythornthwaite: *Gallipoli 1915*, Osprey Publishing 1991
Richard Holmes: *The Western Front*, BBC Worldwide Ltd. 1999
Lyn MacDonald: *1914-1918 Voices and Images of the Great War*, Penguin Books 1988
Lyn MacDonald: *Somme*, Penguin Books 1983
Lyn MacDonald: *They Called It Passchendaele*, Penguin Books 1978
Martin Middlebrook: T*he First Day of the Somme*, Penguin Books 1971
Martin & Mary Middlebrook: *The Somme Battlefields*, Penguin Books 1991
Nigel Steel & Peter Hart: *Defeat at Gallipoli*, Pan Books 1994
Hew Strachan: *The First World War*, Simon & Schuster 2003
J.M. Winter: *The Experience of World War One*, Guild Publishing 1989

WEBSITES:
http://cwgc:Commonwealth War Graves Commission;
http://espnscrum.com: online rugby database;
http://www.footballersunited.co.uk
Forces War Records;
heartsfc.com.uk
Jimmy_speirs.co.uk
Bantamspast.co.uk
Blackandambers.co.uk

Index

Rugby Tours

WRITERS & HISTORIANS

War Historians

Sport Historians